When East Met West:

World History Through Travelers' Perspectives

by:

Robert E. Niebuhr

Trebarwyth Pr

Reading, Massachusetts

Publishing and Printing
Published 2010 by Trebarwyth Press
15 High Street, Reading, MA 01867
Typeset in Times New Roman
Printed in the United States of America by Acme Bookbinding
Acid-free paper
14 13 12 11 10   1 2 3 4 5
Library of Congress Control Number: 2010922169
ISBN-13: 978-0-9786597-2-1
ISBN-10: 0-9786597-2-4

Front Illustration: *A Tired Caravan*, Novi Sad, Serbia, by Robert E. Niebuhr (2007)
Rear Illustration: *Belgrade as a Borderland*, by Robert E. Niebuhr (2007)

When East Met West: World History Through Travelers' Perspectives

TABLE OF CONTENTS

ACKNOWLEDGEMENTS

During my studies in history since 1998, I have had the great privilege of working with superb instructors. As an undergraduate at Arizona State University I paid particular attention to teaching style and saw the great benefits of connecting with students. There, Roger Adelson took time to show me not only the importance of good style in writing but also emphasized the importance of a global outlook on education. Following my own travels in Eastern Europe, thanks in large part to a Fulbright award and a David Boren fellowship, both of which resulted from Stephen Batalden's encouragement, I grasped first-hand the benefits of a broad yet nuanced perspective. My doctoral advisor at Boston College, Larry Wolff, deserves credit for his highly intellectual yet seemingly laid-back demeanor that proved to me in practice what a former teacher and good friend of mine, Robert Friel, has said for a long time—when a student is a ready to learn, a teacher will emerge. Longtime Hapsburg historian Alan Reinerman chose me as his teaching assistant in 2005, and his direction of the European survey course proved illuminating. Alan did not forcefully push his students to learn; rather, he gave a diverse presentation with a focus on geography, historical film, lecture, frequent testing, and discussion. Of course, discussion was my job, and in my two years with him, I developed a style that favored the Socratic Method and engaged the entire class of seventeen students. While Alan moved towards retirement, I had the opportunity to work with Mike Chapman, a recent doctoral recipient and close friend, as an assistant for his year-long global history survey. Mike is a truly dedicated and limitless individual who challenges those around him to go ever forward. Mike's style gave me a better sense of how to lecture and combine my resources to give the students the best possible tools for learning. Mike's *Historian's Companion*—a collection of glossaries, chronologies, primary documents, and a condensed writing guide—organized into one place all of the resources to buttress the message that he had tried to convey throughout his classes. It is in that spirit that I hope this primary source reader functions for global history and western civilization courses—to that end, I am most grateful to Mike, though, I am indebted to all of the great instructors from whom I learned over the years. Despite all of this guidance, no one but me is responsible for any errors or abstentions contained herein.

ROBERT NIEBUHR

NOTE ON STYLE

While I am a conscientious writer and advocate of sound style, a collection of primary documents presents unique difficulties. I have chosen to maintain most of the text as it was and only inserted comments to clarify when appropriate. My text appears either in endnotes or in square brackets [ ]; I have chosen to replace British usage with American usage where such alteration makes no difference in the meaning of the text. This includes spelling—leaving out the "u" from words such as "colour"—and word meanings that have since expired or are archaic or incorrect (for instance, reckon). Otherwise, alterations are at an absolute minimum. Despite that, a major distraction for all readers of these texts will be the grammar, as semicolons, colons, and commas appear in a manner that today seems not only wrong but also irresponsible and random. Such was, though, how these authors wrote, and changing their style would drastically alter the text; therefore, I ask the reader to recognize that these texts span almost four centuries and will not conform necessarily to our norms of usage. At the beginning of each section and before each reading, I have provided background information and a short commentary. While I would otherwise never use block quotes, in this reader I have chosen to make an exception, because embedding these words into my own would disrupt the perception of voice and message.

LIST OF ILLUSTRATIONS AND MAPS

Illustrations

Maps

Image Credits

Pears' Soap, Carsten Niebuhr, map of Africa, conquistadors, and Nootka Sound, from Wiki Commons: http://commons.wikimedia.org/wiki/

Trieste and Queen of Romania from E. Alexander Powell, *The New Frontiers of Freedom: From the Alps to the Aegean* (New York: Charles Scribner's Sons, 1920).

Maps courtesy of University of Texas Library, Perry-Castañeda Collection, found online at http://lib.utexas.edu/maps/.

All other illustrations and maps from reading list or from author.

Keys to Illustrations by Jacob le Maire

Hoorn Island

A. Are the two kings meeting and welcoming each other with many strange ceremonies.
B. The two kings sitting on mats under the *belay*.
C. Our trumpeters and drummer playing before the kings, who took great pleasures therein.
D. Peasants of the country chewing a certain green herb, called by them kava, upon which, after it is chewed, they pour water, and so make a drink of it, greatly esteemed by them.
E. Is the shape of their huts, being round and pointed on top, and covered with leaves of trees.
F. The picture of the king, having a long plait of hair hanging down from the left side of his head to beyond his hips, bound up with a knot or two.
G. Are those of the king's nobles or council, having their hair tied up in two (or sometimes more) plaits; a few wore it ornamentally curled as under H, others standing straight up on end like pigs' bristles, but a quarter of an ell long, as under I.
K. A woman of that island, wearing her hair shaved short.
L. Are coker-nuts [coconut] trees, upon which the coker-nuts grow.
M. Eendracht Bay, where we lay with our ship at four anchors.
N. The rivulet near which we lay and where we got our water.
O. The king's belay, in the shade of which he say daily.

Cocos and Verraders Islands.

A. Is Cocos Island, so called on account of the quantities of coker-nuts that grow there.
B. Is Verraders Islands, so called because they mostly came form that island who tries to betray us [verrader is traitor in Dutch].

C. Is a skirmish with the savages, in which some were killed.
D. Is one of the ships of the savages, which they well know how to manage.
E. Is one shallop [shallow-water craft], capturing the vessel from the savages.
G. Is our ship, round about which the savages swarmed in numbers, in order to exchange their wares with us.
H. In this manner the savages sprang down into the sea after they had stolen something or other.

The Bay of Manilles [Manila]

A. Is the Bay of Manilles.
B. Is the harbor in which many of their vessels lay.
C. Is the town of Manilles, very populous.
D. Is a fort named the Cabitta.
E. Is the island of Maribella.
F. Is our fleet, consisting of six vessels.
G. Are our boats, with which we were very diligent to obtain some prisoners.
H. Are some of their vessels, which they call junks.
I. Are two of our vessels bringing two of their sampans to our fleet.
K. Is one of our boats making one of the Indian sampans haul down its sail, and bringing it to the fleet.

INTRODUCTION

Understanding global history is a daunting challenge for any student; teaching it can be even harder. This volume serves as a tool to help show how people from different cultures have interacted historically. Today, particularly in the United States, we find it appreciate and understand other cultures—we look back to a seeming golden age in American history when people assimilated and envisioned the American dream as the hope of all hopes. Partly because of this history, Americans typically find it difficult to master and retain languages other than English and frequently look with envy on Europeans, who apparently have a superb mastery of two or three tongues. Yet Europeans also find it difficult to maintain competancy in multiple languages, especially if they have no pressing need. Thus, perceptions of cross-cultural communications and dialogues often confuse the critical topic of how people see each other.

A critical piece of today's political dialogue includes how Americans view immigrants. How do those immigrants—let's say from Latin America—view America and the Americans who form the majority?[1] Do those diverse groups of Americans view Muslims the same way? Can we deny that a certain bias exists relating Islam with terrorism, most especially since 11 September 2001? But, more generally, what motivates people to travel to a new land in the first place, much less work and live in a strange place for an extended period? Today, people buy travel guides and have almost limitless access to electronic sources that facilitate a trip somewhere abroad—a visit to Google Maps, or online hotel booking, for instance. People may go to Germany for *Oktoberfest*, but Munich is much more than beer (really, it is). On a similar note, even a short trip to Sarajevo would be incomplete without a visit to Baščaršija, the old Turkish market that encompasses the heart of the downtown and resembles the legendary meeting point for Muslims, Jews, and Christians alike doing what people have always done best—conversing, gossiping over coffee or the water pipe, and engaging in trade. How can we take our perspectives on travel, immigration, or otherness and relate it to historical examples? What did the great adventurers of yesteryear think about the people and places they encountered?

Coffee in Sarajevo

Robert Heron noted in the preface to *Travels through Arabia and other Countries in the East* some of the advantages of travel:

> Hence is traveling so agreeable; and hence are the narratives of intelligent travelers so rich a fund of entertainment and instruction. To wander from city to city . . . affords perhaps the most delightful, at least the most improving amusement of which the human mind is susceptible. To see these things through the eyes of another, is indeed much less interesting than when we can view them ourselves. Yet, as a traveler cannot well help throwing into his work more of the vivid imagery and coloring of nature, than almost any different writer . . . therefore, one may enjoy no small share of that pleasure, and reap a considerable portion of the instruction, which an actual survey of the same scenes might afford.[2]

While reading travelogues can never substitute for actual experiences, I believe nonetheless that a careful analysis can yield a great deal of reflection about how people have behaved and developed over the last centuries. This collection of primary sources from European or European-American travelers to what they termed the Orient contributes greatly to any course of study on global history and Western civilization. Understanding the biases, generalizations, and perspectives of travelers helps us unravel some of the mysteries of how the past has unfolded. When we understand how these authors saw the so-called Orientals, we can make larger connections about political policies, economic treaties, and social interactions in both East and West. Such an exercise is difficult, though, because the Eurocentric viewpoint still holds sway within the humanities; as a result, instructors are trying feverishly to maneuver their scholarship to embrace a broader perspective. As this shift is still quite young, it seems many of the supporting educational materials are lacking, leaving instructors largely on their own in determining syllabi, mining resources (including images, film and audio clips, and reliable statistics), and finding suitable texts. Textbooks are in greater supply, but they have tremendous price tags and typically struggle to present the materials in a way that students can understand and enjoy. Primary source readers provide an accessible and satisfying way for students to see the history as it unfolded by actors from the time.

But simply presenting primary sources is not enough. By grouping these accounts by region, we can see similarities and differences between how Europeans viewed diverse peoples across the globe and relate that to today's American hegemony or the varying means of building identity in the modern world. Shaping identity still means comparisons with others, which mandates that some people suffer while others profit. We may not like to admit it, but we still profile based on things like race, religion, ethnicity, sexuality, and so on, and these necessarily determine how we view both individuals and groups. Bias often lurks under the surface and it takes something dramatic to wake us up and give us time to reflect and forge a new understanding (reflection and proper critical thinking in the spirit of philosophers like John Locke)—such a process, though, is simply part of how we learn as human beings.

Some of the most familiar books that we have grown up with were based on concepts of identity and human nature—Robert Louis Stevenson's *Robinson Crusoe* or Thomas More's *Utopia*, for instance. Go back even further in time to the Greek philosophers like Plato, Socrates, and Aristotle, and you will see a notion of an ideal society based upon uniformity or some other controlling aspect. All of those attempts to reach Shangri-la included an inherent mistrust of foreigners. Yet, wariness of outsiders was not limited to Europeans; Confucius, whose pronouncements did so much to shape Chinese history, declared ominously that there was nothing to be gained from contact with foreigners or strange things.[3] So, when the Yongle Emperor commissioned his loyal servant, the Muslim eunuch Zheng He, to embark on a whirlwind tour of the so-called Western Ocean in the early 1400s, he did so against prudent Chinese traditions. Merchants from China had traded with neighboring peoples for centuries and even set up diaspora communities abroad, but Zheng He's Treasure Fleets were unique in Chinese history. With more than sixty great ships—some estimated at 3–400 feet long, or more than three times the size of Christopher Columbus' flagship, the *Santa Maria*—the Chinese showed much of the known world their immense power and wealth. But with the death of Zheng He and the Yongle Emperor, these expeditions ceased and, less than a hundred years later, the Ming Dynasty's elites declared it illegal to embark on an ocean-going vessel.[4]

What is the West?

I have divided the readings into geographic regions that move further from the center of European power. Scholarship has recognized how Europeans forged their identities thanks to contact with other peoples different from themselves; moreover, it seems clear that such a process was dynamic and evolved over time. Larry Wolff has illustrated how Venetians who moved within Slavic circles developed a sense of self while verifying prejudices against Slavs.[5] Wolff elucidates his argument using the general period of intellectual stimulation known as the Enlightenment to illustrate how people not only constructed their identities in the face of others but also relegated the others to a generalized and often brutal description.[6] As a seminal work of the early Enlightenment, Montesquieu's *Persian Letters* unveiled an almost unending attack on traditional thinking; but by bringing to Europe his imagined accounts from the Orient, Montesquieu played on the most curious aspects of popular imagination and therefore not only reified European prejudices but also jump-started his career as a major literary figure and philosopher in eighteenth-century France. Voltaire followed up with his famous character of *Candide*, whose exploits in Europe and the New World mocked the ruling order and brought the exotic of the Mediterranean and the Americas home to Europe's readers.[7] Philosophes from the Enlightenment used stories to elaborate their points in an amusing and lively manner but much of the philosophy had a profound sense of seriousness. Immanuel Kant, the great Prussian thinker of the eighteenth century, also intertwined examinations of the other into his thinking:

> A third finds in himself a talent with which the help of some culture might make him a useful man in many respects. But he finds himself in comfortable circumstances and prefers to indulge in pleasure rather than to take pains in enlarging and improving his happy natural capacities. He asks, however, whether his maxim of neglect of his natural gifts, besides agreeing with his inclination to indulgence, agrees also with what is called duty. He sees then that a system of nature could indeed subsist with such a universal law, although men (like the South Seas Islanders) should let their talents rest and resolve to devote their lives merely to idleness, amusement, and propagation of their species—in a word, to enjoyment. . . . As a rational being, he necessarily wills that his faculties be developed, since they serve him, and have been given him, for all sorts of possible purposes.[8]

Kant's larger argument from which this paragraph came spoke of duty, morality, and how humans must adhere to the laws of nature. A practical example, let us say, is if I were a good automobile mechanic then it would go against nature for me to waste my automotive talent and instead sell cotton candy or perform on Muscle Beach in Los Angeles. I would, in that case, be going against my nature and failing in my duty as a rational being. Moreover, despite the opaque prose that Kant specialized in, we see much more in the above paragraph—namely, he explained to his readers how being idle and seeking merely pleasure was uncouth in part because that was how South Seas Islanders behaved. According to Kant, those unfortunate folks had not yet enjoyed the fruits of modern civilization and their behavior reflected the mind-set of children who needed only to be shown the correct way to live.[9] With education, the argument went, such lazy people could finally realize their situation and go about rectifying their purpose in life—or could they?

One cannot merely rely on such statements by prominent thinkers like Kant; rather, this issue becomes all the more pervasive once we see materials from the other side. Montenegro's ruler in the mid nineteenth century supposedly declared to a British visitor that "our neighbors have stigmatized the Montenegrins as robbers and assassins; but I am determined that they shall not be so, and will show that they are as capable of improvement, and civilization, as any other people."[10]

How can we account for such a statement, if presumed accurate, by the leader of Montenegro? Was he an Enlightened man who sought to bring his people out of darkness and into Europe as part of an earnest quest, or was he merely telling the traveler a tale? If in fact Montenegro's executive uttered such a statement, then we must inquire about his intentions and thoughts. Had he believed the other Western accounts that portrayed his people as barbarous wild men who needed taming and civilizing? If so, could education alone have fixed this dilemma and ultimately won the acceptance among Europeans in the West? Even today, we can easily find a bias against the corruption, criminality, and poverty that marks Montenegro (and other Balkan countries), including similar statements in the Montenegrin discourse about "joining Europe," as if it was not a part of that continent.[11] Such desires to connect with the West lend credence to the idea that civilization went hand-in-hand with soap or textbooks—naturally, it was not that easy.

Ideology and imperialism

German travelers made blanket assertions of where Europe (i.e. civilization) ended, and this, of course, transcended geography to include races of people deemed foreign. Prince Clemens von Metternich of Austria, master of the Habsburg lands from Napoleon's day until the great European revolutions of 1848, sought to Germanize the peoples of the realm to forge a more stable and prosperous union. In Austrian Galicia, the mixing of Germans, Poles, Ukrainians, and Jews brought

Metternich to explain during a carriage-ride across the countryside how they must not "make Poles into Germans all at once, but above all first to make true Galicians," since only through this course of stages can one hope to achieve the ultimate goal of creating Germans.[12] Regarding the differences in the people, Metternich exclaimed in a letter to his wife: "My dear, here I am in Moravia, that is, in a civilized country," but "I have never seen anything as striking as the passage from Galicia into Moravia." The land is the same, but the "first village on this side gives the impression of being finally inhabited by humans. No more rags; the houses are clean and the inhabitants well covered; no more Jews, no more mange, no more scurf, no more misery or death."[13] Having uttered such words, should we attribute an anti-Semitic disposition to Metternich and lay out a path that ended in 1945? Alternatively, did his assertions instead fall under the paradigm of a different epoch, whereby racial or ethnic discrimination fell in line with a civilizing mission and was not as brutal compared to what emerged a century later under Adolf Hitler's extremist dictatorship?

Identity politics

When did national identity become important? Perhaps it became a force during the earliest religious grievances that began the Reformation. England's King Henry VIII certainly pushed Europe forward when he declared his rule over the Church *in* England, but I would argue that Martin Luther foreshadowed the time when secular elites would break the power of the Roman Catholic Church. "If the pope only knew the poverty of the German people," Luther cried out in his first of 95 Theses. Furthermore, he argued, "Rome is the greatest thief and robber that has ever appeared on earth, or ever will." Luther appealed to his fellow "poor Germans" because "we were born to be masters, and have been compelled to bow beneath the yoke of our tyrants." Luther's plea to the "glorious Teutonic people" helped begin a new era in history that would focus on the realization of a nation-state and all of its accompanying attributes.

Literature on the topic of nationalism is enormous and continues to grow; the great political ideologies that dominated the last 150 years espoused either the triumph of the nation-state through economic and political means or the metamorphosis of nationalism into a global universalism that would diminish and ostensibly wither away. Part of why the latter ideology, based on the writings of Karl Marx and Friedrich Engels, and modified by the likes of V.I. Lenin, Joseph Stalin, Josip Tito, et al, failed by the end of the last century was that nationalism had not died and seemed unlikely to do so in the near future. In fact, identity politics grew in importance, with religion, nationalism, and linguistic/cultural factors all rising by the 1970s to dominate political discourse around the globe. I believe that you can understand the Iranian Revolution of 1979, the flood of moralists who refashioned the American Republican Party under Ronald Reagan, and the effective disappearance or failure of Marxism, by analyzing how individuals sought to identify themselves in a rapidly modernizing period (including altering views of morality) during the recent Cold War. This dynamic shift to religion and other aspects of nationalism definitively changed the body politic by the 1990s and continues today with the fight over resources and power.

Any scholarly work that examines the topic of identity necessarily butts up against the concept of borderlands and the construction of self. Trieste, the merchant city that supplied the heartland of Central Europe for decades as a multi-ethnic Habsburg possession, wrestled with the notion of national identity and belonging by the end of the nineteenth century. Despite Italian unification completed by 1871, thanks largely to non-Italians such as Napoleon III and, more specifically, Otto von Bismarck, regions with an Italian character that lay outside of Italy upset some folks who saw the nation-state for all Italians as a definite political goal. With a largely urban population that conversed in Italian thanks to shipping and business interests, nationalists argued that Trieste belonged to Rome. Such a view discarded the Slovene and Croat majorities throughout the hinterland of Trieste, including the Istrian Peninsula and parts of the Dalmatian coast. These people, Italians noted, could be absorbed into the Italian identity thanks to the supposed superior and civilized nature in Italy.

Trieste in the aftermath of annexation to Italy, 1920

By the end of World War II, Trieste again became a contested space, occupied in part by Yugoslav troops who flooded in to protect their fellow countrymen from what they saw as harassment by the domineering Italians, who had for the last 25 years ruled the greater Trieste region "by terror," complete with "concentration camps and murder," that had aroused nothing more "among the population" as "feelings of fear and hatred."[14] Arguments set forth to gain the territory for Yugoslavia used ethnicity but the various demographic records—most unreliable but nonetheless in general consensus—reinforced the reality of a dominance of Slovenes and Croats in the rural areas and Italians in the cities. Ethnic imbalance and persecution fueled Yugoslav claims, such as how "for 13 centuries the Slovenes and Croats" of the region had "toiled as slaves of foreign masters and shed sweat and blood upon their native soil."[15] Such language exaggerated the case for a national homeland (by Marxists, no less!), but, even so, it argued for what much of Europe had already achieved—namely, a nation-state that served its majority.[16]

Conclusion

It was no mistake that much of the literature that captivated Europeans with the Orient took place during the Enlightenment. With exploration and the discovery of new lands, and, most critically, new peoples, Europeans came face to face with the opposite of what they thought they had or could achieve—namely civilization. Scenes of the exotic enticed Europeans while the academic argument brought descriptions of the so-called state of nature and anarchic rule to life. If men were rational beings then why had some failed to develop the same way, or, as Kant expressed, why did they choose an idle life instead of one of virtue and duty? Europeans found entire races to study and generalize over and compare themselves with instead of the usual suspects in the Middle East—the Muslims, or Mohammedians, as Europeans fashioned them. A caregiver attitude frequently arose too, with some Europeans thinking that their mission was to save these souls for Jesus Christ and uplift them for their own good.

Mission San Jose, Texas

Accompanying the Mission San Jose outside of downtown San Antonio, Texas, is a small museum run by the U.S. Park Service. One of the placards that describes "the Indians," does so in what is a technically correct but misleading description of why the indigenous peoples sometimes inhabited such Spanish-run missions on the frontier:

> The Coahuiltecans usually came voluntarily to the missions. The choice was a matter of survival. At the missions they gave up a free-roaming life with abundant leisure for a regimented life of toil and obedience. In exchange they received protection and a consistent supply of food.

While weaker tribes would come to gain the protection of the Spanish against rivals, this placard takes for granted the same logic that Kant used to describe the South Seas Islanders—they were idle and led an adolescent existence without proper education and regimentation. Moreover, as uncivilized nomads, the indigenous peoples also suffered from a chaotic and brutal political atmosphere and had regular food shortages. Thankfully for them, if we are to believe the Park Service, these happy souls "voluntarily chose" to change their lives for the better and occupy the missions in the name of civilization and Christianity. If it were only that simple.

I have raised a number of issues already in this short introduction, but I think it worthwhile to elaborate a bit on some of them before the actual readings begin. One of the most important aspects of this literature stems from its reliability. Did these travelers really go to the places they wrote about so vividly? In some cases, that answer was no, while in other cases it is evident that they ventured somewhere, and may well have exaggerated their accounts. So, if some of this literature may not even represent first-hand account then what value does it have? My answer to that question is despite some of the authors having imagined their journeys from the comfort of some familiar place, the things they said represented and augmented the biases and assumptions that Europeans had for others around the world. Such repetition of prevailing knowledge of other places and peoples unveils important attributes about the author's society.

A second issue is the quality of the translation, if in fact the author did not originally write the work in English, which suggests the wisdom of continually questioning the value of words and the meaning of phrases. It is important, moreover, to think about the identity of the actors with whom the authors conversed. Most readings assured the authenticity of the information despite some authors having relied upon someone else for interpretation. So when authors claimed to have conversed with indigenous peoples, they typically did so through interpreters, whose fluency may well have been imperfect. But, such was not a hallmark of travel;

indeed, Zheng He's treasure fleets sailed with numerous Chinese scholars fluent in Arabic, thanks in part to the high-level of education among certain Chinese scholars and to a Muslim population in China whose knowledge of Arabic came directly from familiarity with the Qu'ran. In contrast, when Christopher Columbus ventured West across the Atlantic Ocean, he had with him one converted Jew who spoke Arabic, ostensibly to ease the communication gap between him and people in India and China. Likewise, when Columbus's predecessor Vasco da Gama set sail from Portugal some seven decades after Zheng He's last voyage, he also relied on an Arabic-speaking sailor but frequently suffered from miscommunication:

> On Tuesday [10 April], when weighing anchor to enter the port, the captain-major's vessel [Vasco da Gama's] would not pay off, and struck the vessel that followed astern. We therefore again cast anchor. When the Moors who were in our ship saw that we did not go on, they scrambled into a zavra [small craft] attached to our stern; whilst the two pilots whom we had brought from Mozambique jumped into the water, and were picked up by the men in the zavra. At night the captain-major questioned two Moors by dropping burning oil upon their skin, so that they might confess any treachery intended against us. They said that orders had been given to capture us as soon as we entered the port, and thus avenge what we had done at Mozambique [they had shelled the city]. And when this torture was being applied a second time, one of the Moors, although his hands were tied, threw himself into the sea, whilst the other did so during the morning watch.[17]

Clearly, poor da Gama suffered greatly at the hands of his help and avoided fate only with luck and cunning. Regardless of the accepted use of torture and violence to secure the mission's goals, da Gama was lucky to have seamen who spoke some Arabic, because that was the predominate language of Asian trade, or at least a common medium, as even the Swahili language along the East African coast developed partly with Arabic vocabulary. Arabic even allowed him to query Indians from the west coast [Calicut, for instance] when he arrived there; his description mentioned that, "Indians are tawny men" who "wear but little clothing and have long beards and long hair, which they braid." Most importantly, despite the fact that "their language differ[ed] from that of the Arabs," some Indians "know a little of it, as they hold much intercourse with them."[18] Trade not only moved goods from one place to another but also carried with it religion, culture, language, technology, and much more. While this volume seeks to illuminate just how people shape themselves and perceive others through difference, we must not forget just how much we share as humans.

PART I: TRAVEL TO EASTERN EUROPE

Eastern Europe was an integral part of the European continent long before people in the seventeenth century traveled there. As the seat of the Eastern Roman Empire, the city of Constantinople was the richest in Europe until at least the thirteenth century, as it stood at the crossroads of trade between Europe and Asia. Whether over the Silk Road or by ship from China to the Middle East, goods managed to converge on Constantinople (Istanbul) thanks to the Greek, Armenian, Jewish, and Italian merchants who called that city home. Even after the Ottoman conquest in 1453 and the continued lurch up the Balkan Peninsula, the city maintained a significant degree of control over traded goods between East and West. Indeed, when the great Kievan Rus and Muscovy states had emerged earlier east of Constantinople, merchants used the great Dnieper and Volga Rivers to intercept trade and integrate into Europe. Integration later became a prized goal, because the schism between the Orthodox and Roman Catholic faiths in AD 1054 effectively created Eastern Europe as an "other."

In addition to the bands of Teutonic Knights who campaigned to Christianize the East, the city-state of Venice served as an early colonizing force in the Adriatic region and Venetians supposedly brought civilization with their fight against piracy and barbarism. From the thirteenth century onwards, Venice competed to become the most powerful trading city in Southern Europe at the expense of Constantinople, but the rhetoric city leaders relied upon often went beyond actual contributions to their treasury. Bans on Jews, restrictions on Slavs in the public sphere, and the overall preoccupation with their own civilization prevented the Venetians from thoroughly instilling Italian culture into their Slav neighbors despite a dominant influence in the region more broadly. Hence, despite cultural impressions that took root among Croats and Serbs along the Adriatic, Yugoslavia's post-World War II government could physically expel most Italians from the Eastern Adriatic, as they numbered a mere few hundred thousand despite nearly 600 years of Italian colonization.

While not much different than Western Europe, the Balkan Peninsula had become exotic, partly because of the Ottoman conquest that began in the 1300s, but also because of the sense of difference that nearby Italians and Germans assigned to peoples in what would become the so-called powder keg of Europe.

Queen of Romania and an American officer

First Reading:

J. Gardner Wilkinson, *Dalmatia and Montenegro with a Journey to Mostar in Herzegovina, and the Remarks of the Slavonic Nations; The History of Dalmatia and Ragusa; the Uscocs* (London: John Murray, 1848).

From the middle of the nineteenth century, we can see in this reading how a British traveler envisioned the Adriatic littoral. Like many books of its genre, it sought to describe for its readers the lay of the land, the customs and mannerisms of the people (including the physical features), and the uncivilized nature of their existence. Happily, we can see that at the end, the author pointed out that the ruler of Montenegro desired greatly for civilization to come to his people—with little doubt, the author saw himself as a small piece of such a civilizing mission.

Regarding the people of Montenegro

I always imagined that the habit of using the name of God, on every trivial occasion, was most prevalent in the East; but the Montenegrins can compete with any Oriental in this respect; and every expression they use is accompanied by "Bogami," "Bogati," and that too, even by priests; which the Dalmatians [people in the Croatian region of Dalmatia] very justly consider both irreligious, and vulgar.

In *religion* the Montenegrins are all of the Greek Church [Orthodox], now that the Kutska department has detached itself from Montenegro; which adds to the influence exercised in the country by Russia, the Czar being the head of the Church, and the Vladika[19] being invested with the Episcopal office at St. Petersburg.

They have no knowledge of *medicine*, but prejudice does not prevent their applying to foreigners, who possess it; and not only the Vladika, but other persons of rank in the country, gladly avail themselves of medical advice at Cattaro [Kotor]. The climate, however, their frugal mode of living, and their active habits render illness very unusual; and few cripples are seen in the country. Their healthy condition also enables them to recover speedily from wounds, and other severe accidents; which in a more civilized state would often be fatal; and they have the usual skill of all wild people, in curing external injuries; like the Arabs, and others who lead an unartificial life. Much is, of course, left to nature, and the simplest remedies are sufficient.

Education is still in embryo, and many even of the priests know not how to read or write. The Vladika has lately established two schools; one at Tzetinie [Cetinje], for thirty boys, the other at Dobroskoselo, for twenty-four. There are several classes at each; and they learn writing, readings, and Slavonic grammar, arithmetic, Servian [Serbian] history, geography, and the catechism. Tzetinie also boasts a printing press; and it is a remarkable fact, that works in the Cyrillic character were printed in Montenegro, as early as the beginning of the sixteenth century.

The *language* of Montenegro is a dialect of the Slavonic, and is considered very pure; not being corrupted by the admission of foreign words. The Montenegrins themselves call it a Servian dialect; which is perhaps a proper distinction, as they were an offset of Servia, and once formed part of that kingdom; and Krasinski says "it is considered the nearest of all the Slavonian dialects to the original Slavonic tongue; i.e. that into which the Scriptures were translated by St. Cyril and Methodius, in the ninth century, and which continues still to be the sacred tongue, of all the Slavonian nations who follow the Eastern Church."

The Montenegrins are not deficient in intellect, which only requires to be properly cultivated; and the Cattarines even allow that they are capable of considerable mental acquirements. They have generally good foreheads; but the face is not well shaped, being rather square (which is particularly observable in the women), with rather high cheekbones, and the lower jaw projecting a little at the side. Many are, nevertheless, very handsome. Their eyes are rather near, than far apart, mostly hazel, and some few light blue. The hair is brown, sometimes dark, but rarely black.

The profile of the men has generally a decided outline, with a moderate aquiline, or a straight, nose; but neither of the extravagant dimensions found in the Turkish face, nor of the *retroussé* shape sometimes seen in Northern Europe. Their eyes are very animated, though without the fierce expression of the Turks, except when excited by anger. In stature they are much above middle height; some are very tall; and they are well proportioned. Their voices are powerful, and I have often heard them carrying on a conversation at a distance, not by shouts, but with a clear, distinct pronunciation; which can only be the result of experience, and the habit of communicating with each other from mountain to mountain. I observed the same among the Morlacchi, of the interior of Dalmatia.

The *dress* of the men bears some resemblance to the Albanian; but they have no *fostán*, and their white shirt falls over a pair of full blue trousers, which extends a little below the knee. They wear a white, or yellow, cloth frock, reaching almost to the knee, secured by a sash round the waist; under it is a red cloth vest, and over it a red, or green, jacket without sleeves, both richly embroidered; and the whole is covered with a jacket, bordered with fur.

On the head they wear a red Fez cap, and a turban, generally white, or red; below which projects, at the back of the neck, a long lock of hair. In this they also resemble the Albanians, as in the absence of beards. The fore part of the head is shaved, as far as the line of the ear, behind which the hair is allowed to grow to a great length; but they never have the long pigtail of the Morlacchi. Though all wear mustaches, none have beards, except the monks, and those priests who are intended for the offices of Bishop, and Archimandrite, and who properly belong to the monastic order. Besides the sash, they have a leather girdle, for holding pistols and yatagan, like the Albanians, Turks, and Morlacchi; and pouches, with various useful and ornamental bags, are fastened to a strap below the sash. Men and women carry the struccha over one shoulder. That of the women is varied in color; the other generally brown.

The female dress consists of a frock, or pelisse, of white cloth, without sleeves, and open in front, like that of the men, but much longer, reaching nearly to the ankles, and trimmed with various devices, in braiding, or colored cloth, and tassels; and in front are several gold ornaments. Around the neck are numerous chains, gold coins, and collars; they wear earrings, and pendants fastened to their plaited locks of hair: and the red cap of the girls is covered, in front, with a mass of small silver Turkish coins, mostly paras, arranged like scales; over which is an embroidered veil, falling upon the shoulders. The red cap of the married women, instead of paras, has a black silk border, and on gala days a bandeau of gold ornaments, generally half covered by a colored veil, fastened on the top of the head by a gold-headed pin. The shirt has its front, and its long loose open sleeves, worked with silk of various colors and patterns, or gold thread; it frequently reaches to the ankles, but sometimes only to the waist, and the apron then supplies the place of the lower part. This apron is of colored worsted, or cloth, with a deep fringe along the bottom; and the girdle is studded with three or four rows of real, or false, red cornelians. Short socks, worked in colored worsted, are drawn over the feet of their coarse white stockings; and men and women wear *opanche* (sandals), like those of the Morlacchi. With these *opanch*e they run over the most rugged, and slippery, rocks, with the greatest agility; and the comfort to the foot, when accustomed to them, is said to be greater than in any other sandal. The sole is made of untanned ox hide, with the hair taken off, and that side outwards.

Montenegrin man

About social relations

Blood was avenged by blood, and the *lex talionis* was carried out, much in the same way as among other people in a primitive state of society. If "the murderer had left the country, this vengeance fell on his nearest relation. He in turn found new avengers, and sometimes whole villages made war in this way, so that neither governor, nor Vladika, could stop the effusions of blood." Families were obliged to avenge the violent deaths, that happened in their villages; and villages, or even whole districts, to "take the part of their inhabitants, against those of another village, or district. Truces were sometimes established between the hostile parties, as, for instance, when they had common, or adjoining, fields to cultivate. In cases where one party stood more in need of the truces than the opposite one, it must pay for it; and the attack of a foreign enemy alone established a general truce for all private hostilities."

Montenegrin household

Like the Arabs, they frequently settle grave questions by arbitration, when not brought before a legal tribunal; though there is nothing corresponding to the tents of refuge among the Bedouina, or the cities of refuge among the Israelites of old. In Montenegro, when the case is to be amicably adjusted, each side chooses "an equal number of arbiters, amounting from ten to forty. These arbiters, called Kmeti, receive the complaints of both parties, minutely examine all the circumstances of the case, and estimate a gun-shot wound, or a yatagan cut, not according to the injury inflicted, but according to that which might have been done: and after mature deliberation, they give a verdict, from which there is no appeal. The guilty party is condemned to pay a fine, one wound being generally taxed at 10, two at 20, and a murder at 120, ducats." "In cases of homicide, the guilty person is obliged to beg pardon publicity, with the following ceremonies—The judges and spectators form a large circle, in the midst of which the culprit, having suspended from his neck a gun, or a poniard, must creep on his knees to the feet of the offended party, who, taking the weapon from his neck, raises him, and embraces him, saying 'God pardon you!' The spectators congratulate, with joyous acclamation, the reconciled enemies; who not only forgive their mutual injuries, but often become sincere friends. This ceremony, which is called the '*circle of blood*,' is concluded by a feast, given at the expense of the guilty party, of which all the spectators partake."

"Theft is mulcted [meted] by paying the sevenfold value of the stolen object;" which is a more severe law than with the Arabs, who, like the Israelites, "restore fourfold." The Montenegrins "have a curious manner of recovering this, without exposing the guilty person. The individual, who has been despoiled, publicly announces the thing stolen, together with the sum which he will give for its restoration. If anyone happens to know the author of the theft, he does not denounce him, but sends him word, by an intermediate person, that his crime is detected, and that he should not delay to reconcile himself to the injured party, by the restoration of the stolen object. When the thief perceived that he is known, he restores, by means of these goers-between, the stolen thing to its owner, who remains ignorant of his name."

These imperfect, and primitive, customs are now beginning to give place to the authority of established laws; and the Vladika, with great firmness and wisdom, has commenced a system of administration, likely to be highly beneficial to his country: the effects of which are already sensibly perceived.

Discussion Points for *Dalmatia and Montenegro*

1. Note the use of the passive voice. Where do you think he got his evidence? Who said such things in the first place and do you trust that the author made a correct judgment in reproducing such sayings?
2. Who were the Morlacci? Did these seem to be indigenous folks to the region and if not, why? Were they similar or different from the other inhabitants?
3. What sorts of generalizations did the author make about people in Montenegro? How were they like those in the East?
4. Why do you think women wore coins or other valuables as decorations on their clothing? Might it have been solely for appearances, or would there have been a practical value as well?
5. What of Montenegrin law—was it typically Eastern in origin and do you think it was unreasonably harsh? Or, in contrast, regarding its severity, do you think that we ought to be stricter today?

SECOND READING:

Arthur D. Howden Smith, *Fighting the Turk in the Balkans: An American's Adventures with the Macedonian Revolutionists* (New York: G.P. Putnam's Sons, 1908).

Adventures to the Balkans did not stop during the 1800s; in fact, as the twentieth century blossomed, more people took interest in the peninsula primarily because of the rich and dynamic political situation there. Serbs had governed themselves largely since the time of Napoleon, while Romania, Bulgaria, and Greece all had functioning states by the 1870s if not sooner. Pressing territorial claims on the Ottoman Empire became a regular item for the Russian and Austro-Hungarian Empires and the fight for allies among the newly independent states truly livened up matters. One such insurrection that caught the attention of outsiders was that of the Macedonian struggle for independence. Macedonians have long wrestled to find a unique identity for themselves, as linguistically and culturally they are so similar to Bulgarians that the latter claims them as their own. Serbs also historically had great influence in Macedonian lands, with Skopje having served as seat of a medieval Serbian kingdom.

After World War I, when Serbia expanded and created the new Yugoslav state (known before 1929 as the Kingdom of Serbs, Croats, and Slovenes), Macedonia simply became the southern reaches of Serbia. Only during World War II did the Yugoslav Partisan leader, Josip Broz Tito, recognize a unique Macedonian nationality and grant Macedonia the status of a republic within his postwar Marxist federation. Claims have withheld time, though, and even today, after the dissolution of Yugoslavia and the recognition of an independent Macedonia, the name itself stirs controversy, because within Greece and Bulgaria are constituent states called Macedonia and with people similar to those in Yugoslav Macedonia. While the United States under President George W. Bush recognized Macedonia's claim to call itself the Republic of Macedonia, Europe has not gone so far thanks to Greek objections and fears of a revisionist foreign policy. Moreover, with a large divide between Albanians and the various Slavicm speakers in Macedonia today, war seems ever-present, as had occurred briefly in 2001. But with foreign support Macedonia seems likely to progress in peace despite recent events there and the still-persistent notion that the Balkans are simply a "powder keg" waiting to explode.[20]

From the preface

This work is not a history of political events. It is simply an endeavor to present a phase of our twentieth-century life which is unknown to most of us. At rare intervals, echoes of Balkan conflicts have reached America, humming over the cables at a rate per word that precluded details. In Europe, the struggle of the Macedonian insurgents was noted more closely, but even there, within a few hundred miles of the theatre of operations, there was a surprising ignorance of the warfare and the issues at stake. People knew that somewhere in European Turkey, a guerrilla campaign was being waged by a race whom they vaguely imagined as half-brigands, half-outlaws. That was all.

Wholly aside from its bearing on contemporary history, the struggle of the Macedonian Bulgars, for liberty, was interesting, I think, because of its quaint setting, and its mingling of the barbaric color of the East with the more sober tones of the West. Macedonia is the shadow of the Orient. The passions, hatreds, loves, and shoutings of the East, and of the old-time West, can still be found within its borders.

Description of the land

To those who have not visited them, the Balkans are a shadow-land of mystery; to those who know them, they become even more mysterious, for, as one begins to fancy he has peered under the veil, he finds himself caught in its meshes, and the spell of the land has him in thrall. You become, in a sense, a part of the spell, and of the mystery and glamor of the whole. You contract the habit of crouching over your morning coffee in the café, and, when you meet a man of your acquaintance, at least half of what you say is whispered portentously. Intrigue, plotting, mystery, high courage, and daring deeds—the things that are the soul of true romance are to-day the soul of the Balkans.

The spirit and the battle-cries of the Crusades were resurrected by the combatants. Once more, the cry "For Christ! Down with the infidel!" sounded over the earth; and the sinister conflict of Cross and Crescent devastated as fair a country as there is in Europe. For centuries, the Bulgarians had been crushed beneath the Moslem's iron heel; they saw other lands, whose civilizations had once been inferior to their own, enjoying liberty and happiness. Is it strange that they revolted?

Their fight was not in itself for freedom; they knew they were not strong enough for that. It was a cry to Europe, to America: "For pity's sake, for Christ's sake, give us liberty, we, we are slaves!"

From his travels

Sofia [capital city of Bulgaria] has not been so entirely civilized as to lose its Old-World charm, its spicy aroma of the East. . . . quaintly garbed peasants, and at frequent intervals stand lean, dark-faced gendarmes [police], in blue-grey uniforms, armed with long swords and revolvers. Officers in fawn-colored great-coats, sparkling with gold-lace, shoulder their way through the throng, yelling orders. A Turk shepherds a group of veiled women out of the third-class waiting room, and you barely have time to realize that it is a harem in transit to one of the Macedonian towns to the south.

Short comparison with Serbia

Servia is in no sense as interesting a country as Bulgaria. It is miserably governed; its peasant classes are dirty, ignorant, and abused, and one notices in passing through the garrison towns that the barracks are the handsomest buildings. A hovel does for a school, and many of the peasants live in houses that are really caves, dug in hillsides.

These people of Bulgaria are striving to better themselves—striving with all the fierce energy of a young people, headstrong and proud. They want to be civilized. Thirty years ago [before independence in 1878] they were slaves, with no ideals, no distinct aspirations, no national sentiment. Sofia was then a village, with one presentable building, the church of Santa Sofia, eight hundred years old, that had been turned into a mosque by the Turkish conquerors. The inhabitants point out to-day the miserable mud-huts that constituted the place in those days. Now they are used as cow stables.

About his request to join the fight against the Turks

[War] is very difficult. You cannot rest. The ashkares [Turkish soldiers] follow you, always. You wear sandals which do not protect your feet. Often, you must go without food. When you are tired to weariness, it is your bread that you throw away, that you may not have to sacrifice any of your ammunition. . . . You do not understand the kind of warfare the Turks wage. It is not such as Western Europe knows. There is no mercy shown. It would do you no good to be a non-combatant. You would be slain, just the same, if they caught you. The ashkares never take prisoners. . . . There can be no middle course for the man who goes into Macedonia. He either goes with the Turks, or he goes with the chetniks [term for freedom fighters], and if he goes with the chetniks, he goes armed.

Fight in the pass

Looking back, now, through a perspective afforded by time, it is not easy, even so, to get a satisfactory view-point on those tempestuous nights of battle and death. The Macedonian struggle is over, they say. Turk, Bulgar, Serb, and Greek, all lie down, side by side, in peace and brotherhood. But it was not so a few short months ago. Like ravenous dogs, they went for each other's throats, and he was the most pleased who shed the greatest quantity of his rivals' blood.

On the night we left Yooddarroch, I had a particularly good opportunity to see the Bulgar peasant in his time of affliction. And I must say that there was a certain deadly, serious steadfastness of purpose, noticeable in the young man who acted as our guide, which went far to impress upon me a realization of the stubborn qualities of his race's courage—a courage which, having set for itself an object or attainment, knows no other goal.

At a notch in the side of a mountain, on a wide plateau covered with waving grass and cornstalks, we came to the violated homestead. A pool of blood smeared the doorstep, where a sheep had been killed to sate the first appetite of the marauders. To prove their ruthlessness, they had thrown the dead body aside as useless to them. A second man, young like the first, whose face, like his, seemed, in the light of Mileff's searchlight, overcast with a profound depth of gloom and agony, rose from a crouching position by this same pool of blood, and in monosyllables directed his brother which course to take, to catch up with the father, hanging onto the trail of the ashkares.

All through the night we marched, stopping every hour for a ten-minute rest. We made no sound, for we were edging into the enemy's country, and for the first time, I noted the use of an old trick of Indian warfare in America—that of covering the trail by making each man step in the footprints of the leader. Unless one has tried it, it is difficult to understand how tiresome it is, to be always under the necessity of stepping where another map has stepped, and of choosing the ground on which to plant every footstep.

[Later on they found the enemy camp]

With a curiosity I could not check, I glanced at the face of one of the sons beside me, and then along the line at his father and brother. There was the same dull look of agony in every face, but their eyes blazed like live coals. At first we did nothing, beyond assuring ourselves that our rifles were in order. Andrea made careful calculations of the range, and Mileff crept up and down the rear, making sure that the chetniks understood their orders. We were to fire two volleys at will and then charge. "How about the women?" someone asked. The old man interposed. "It does not matter," he said, grimly. "Do not think of them. They must take their chance. It might be as well should a bullet strike them."

I could understand his meaning; in fact, there was no mistaking the look in his eyes and the gesture he made toward the colored heaps on the ground [where the women were laying]. And I tried not to see where he aimed his rifle. The voivode [duke, or in this case, leader], from his position in the centre of the line, glanced inquiringly at his men. He saw a line of rifle-barrels leveled over the rocks. "Heidi," he exclaimed [more likely, the man yelled "hajde," which means "let's go"]. The mountain-walls echoed and re-echoed the crashing volleys. It seemed as though for miles and miles around the reports were caught up and hurled back again. There was no smoke-veil, and I could see the ashkares rolling on the ground, or running frantically toward the horses. One of the colored heaps leaped to her feet, staggered forward a pace or two, and fell to the ground, her hand clutching her side. It all happened very quickly, with the instantaneousness of vision of the moving-picture machine. For a minute, I pinched myself, to make sure I was not watching some lurid Bowery melodrama.

But no, it was real. The chetniks were charging down the hillside, stopping to fire at the men and horses beneath. Far in the lead, the old peasant plunged along, absolutely reckless, apparently only bent on getting to hand-grips with one of the Turks. A single ashkare was left standing, and he was tugging at the bridle of a horse. Bullets spat on the ground about him, and chipped the branches of the bush. I cannot be sure of it, but it looked to me very much as though it was a bullet that freed his mount, by clipping off part of the twig it was tied to.

At any rate, the man leaped on the horse's back, and regardless of the banging stirrups, galloped off down the ravine, out of the medley of dead men and screaming and wounded horses. When the first of the chetniks pulled himself from the water of the brook, it was to find a very slaughter pen, in which the old peasant was the central figure, kneeling beside a dead girl. The second girl and her mother knelt beside him, but there was no look of prayer in their faces; there was more of an expression of wonderment that Divine mercy could not have been showed to them.

We did not stay long—no longer than it took to loot the bodies of the dead ashkares, eat the meal they had been preparing (on the war-path one is not particular), and hold a short conference on ways and means.

Final words on Macedonia

Perhaps few Macedonians themselves know exactly what they want. They can frame their desires roughly, but they have always been so far from actual attainment that they have not devoted much thought to the future. The present has been with them, covering them like a huge red pall of unrest. They have had to think of their lives, of the lives of their families and friends. Property has never been safe; the visits of the tax collectors have invariably meant extortion and graft. Poor people, they have not known which way to turn. Badgered, down-trodden, shut out from the world's mercies, abused for their religion [Eastern Orthodox in Muslim Ottoman Empire], they revolted. They turned on their oppressors, snarling.

What a pity it was that after this the spark of national ambition could not have been nursed into a flame of patriotism, rising supreme above the differences of race and creed. Had that been accomplished, one might picture a Macedonia ultimately free and independent, a sovereign, autonomous state. As it is, I fear that that can never be.

Macedonia is not likely, however, to remain for long a part of the Turkish Empire. Sooner or later the blow will fall, and she will be separated—but how? Could the small Balkan states, for once, settle their petty differences, their trivial squabbles and jealousies, and join forces, there is little doubt that they could accomplish the desired end. But that is a castle in Spain which would not look real, even in a dream.

> "East is East and West is West,
> And never the twain shall meet."

says Kipling [Rudyard Kipling, author of the famous poem "The White Man's Burden"]. Also, it is written in the Book of Things that no two men of different races in the Balkans shall agree.

Discussion Points for *Fighting the Turk in the Balkans*

1. What does this account say about warfare in the Balkans? How did the Turks and various Balkan militias treat each other?
2. As an American, do you think this author brought any noticeable biases to this story? If yes, name something that seemed typical.
3. How melodramatic could the author have made this account? It seems that emotion drove his writing to the point of excess. How might that have fit within the mood in pre-World War I Europe? How might it instead have been simply the musings of an unrealistic and immature boy who seemingly lacked a sense of manliness?
4. During the Greek War of Independence in the 1820s, Americans rallied to the support of the so-called noble Greeks against the Turkish oppressors. But, when wealthy merchants in Boston, for instance, realized the amount of trade with the Ottomans, they promptly sought a stable balance. Does such an attitude—one of coolness—typically prevail over uninformed calls for intervention? What examples of diplomacy by emotion can you cite from recent American history?
5. What sort of fighting skills did the Macedonians/Bulgarians seem to have, according to the author? Were they professionals or rugged militiamen?

Third Reading:

M. Edith Durham, *Twenty Years of Balkan Tangle* (London: G. Allen & Unwin Ltd. 1920).

Thanks to the brutality of the Balkan Wars (1912–13) and especially World War I, writers sought to explain why the region was prone to such violence. M. Edith Durham authored several books outlying the situation there for an English-speaking audience. With almost 300 pages of text, this book analyzed Montenegro, Bosnia, Albania, Serbia, and Macedonia—including various conflicts, as in 1908 when Austria-Hungary formally annexed Bosnia and created a crisis because Serbs had held out hope of incorporating Bosnia into a larger Serbia. Austro-Hungarian control meant a termination of that dream, as the Vienna government could win in war against Serbia and would have the support of the German Emperor. Serbia thus looked for a solid commitment from Russia after 1908, and the alliance network that functioned in 1914 thoroughly destroyed the old order in Europe.

From the introduction

Along with a friend I boarded an Austrian Lloyd steamer at Trieste, and with high hopes but weakened health, started for the ports of the Eastern Adriatic.

Threading the maze of mauve islets set in that incomparably blue and dazzling sea; touching every day at ancient towns where strange tongues were spoken and yet stranger garments worn, I began to feel that life after all might be worth living and the fascination of the Near East took hold of me.

A British Consul, bound to Asia Minor, leaned over the bulwark and drew a long breath of satisfaction. "We are in the East!" he said. "Can't you smell it? I feel I am going home. You are in the East as soon as you cross Adria." He added tentatively: "People don't understand. When you go back to England they say: 'How glad you must be to get home!' They made me spend most of my leave on a house-boat on the Thames, and of all the infernal things . . ." I laughed. I did not care if I never I saw England again.

Description of Centinje, capital of Montenegro

Cetinje was then extraordinarily picturesque. The Prince did all he could to emphasize nationality. National dress was worn by all. So fine was the Court dress of Montenegro that oddly enough Prince Nikola was about the only ruling Sovereign in Europe who really looked like one. The inroads of Cook's tourists had stopped his former custom of hobnobbing with visitors, and he dodged with dignity and skill the attempts of American snap-shooters to corner him and say: "How do, Prince!"

A vivid picture remains in my mind of the Royal Family as it filed out of church on the feast of the Assumption of the Virgin. The Prince, heavy-built, imposing, gorgeous; his hair iron grey, ruddy-faced, hook-nosed, keen-eyed. Danilo, his heir, crimpled, oiled and self-conscious, in no respect a chip off the old block, who had married the previous year, Jutta, daughter of the Grand Duke of Mecklenburg Strelitz, who, on her reception into the Orthodox Church, took the name of Militza. Montenegro was still excited about the wedding. She looked dazzlingly fair among her dark "in-laws."

From Cetinje we went to Podgoritza where for the first time I saw Albanians. Podgoritza was full of them, all in national dress, for Montenegro had as yet done little towards suppressing this. Nor in this first visit did I go further inland.

But I had found "the land where I could have a complete change"; had learnt too, of the Great Serbian Idea; had had the meaning of the Montenegrin cap explained to me; and been told how the reconstruction of the Great Serb Empire of the Middle Ages was what Montenegro lived for. Also that the first step in that direction must be the taking of the Sanjak of Novibazar, which had been formed as a barrier between the two branches of the Serb race by the Powers at the Berlin Congress [1878].

The one pre-eminently Italian town of Dalmatia is Zara. From Zara south, the language becomes more and more Slav. But the Slav speaking peasants that flock to market are by no means the same in the physical type as the South Slavs of the Bosnian Hinterland. It is obvious that they are of other blood. They are known as Morlachs, that is Sea Vlachs, and historically are in all probability descendants of the pre-Slav native populations which, together with the Roman colonists, fled coastward before the inrush of the Slav invaders of the seventh century. Latin culture clung along the coast and was reinforced later by the Venetians. And a Latin dialect was spoken until recent times, dying out on the island of Veglio at the end of the nineteenth century. The Slavizing process which has steadily gone on is due, partly to natural pressure coastward of the Slav masses of the Hinterland and partly to artificial means.

On Montenegro

Ivan Tsrnoievitch, chief of the tribes of the Zeta, was so hard pressed by the oncoming Turks that he burnt his capital of Zhablyak and withdrew to the mountains, where he founded Cetinje in 1484. Tradition thus corresponds closely with historic fact. The strength of Turkish influence is shown by the fact that even to-day the peasant speaks of Ivan as Ivan Beg [Beg was a term used by Ottomans to denote aristocracy or status].

Ivan and his refugee tribes successfully resisted the Turkish attacks on their stronghold and were helped by Venice. But conversions to Islam became frequent. One of Ivan's own sons turned Turk and fought against Montenegro. Finally, the last of the Trsnoievitch line, Ivan II, who had married a Venetian wife, decided that the leadership of a band of outlaws in the poverty-stricken mountains was not good enough. He retired to the fleshpots of Venice, trusting the defense of the district to a civil, hereditary leader and charging the Vladika [Bishop] with the duty of preventing more of his flock going over to Islam, as the Serbs of Bosnia were now doing in great numbers.

Of Albanians

Study of the Macedonian question had shown me that one of the most important factors of the Near Eastern questions was the Albanian, and that the fact that he was always left out of consideration was a constant source of difficulty.

Throughout the relief work in Macedonia, we had employed Albanians in every post of trust—as interpreters, guides, kavasses and clerks.

The depot of the British and Foreign Bible Society at Monastir was entirely in Albanian hands. The Albanian was invaluable to the Bible Society, and the Bible Society was invaluable to the Albanians.

Albania was suffering very heavily. Every other of the Sultan's subject races had its own schools—schools that were, moreover, heavily subsidized from abroad. The Bulgarian schools in particular were surprisingly well equipped. Each school was an active centre of Nationalist propaganda. All the schoolmasters were revolutionary leaders. All were protected by various consulates which insisted on opening new schools and protested when any were interfered with.

Only when it was too late to stop the schools did the Turks perceive their danger. First came the school, then the revolution, then foreign intervention—and another piece of the Turkish Empire was carved off. This had happened with Serbia, Greece and Bulgaria. The Turks resolved it should not happen in the case of Albania.

Albania was faced by two enemies. Not only the Turk dreaded the uprising of Albania, but Russia had already determined that the Balkan Peninsula was to be Slav and Orthodox.

The Turkish government prohibited the printing and teaching of the Albanian language under most severe penalties. Turkish schools were established for the Moslem Albanians, and every effort made to bring up the children to believe they were Turks. In South Albania, where the Christians belong to the Orthodox Church, the

Greeks were encouraged [by the Ottoman government] to found schools and work a Greek propaganda. The Turks hoped thus to prevent the rise of a strong national Albanian party. The Greek Patriarch went so far as to threaten with excommunication an Orthodox Albanian who should use the "accursed language" [Albanian] in church or school. In North Albania, where the whole of the Christians are Catholics, the Austrians, who had been charged by Europe with the duty of protecting the Catholics, established religious schools in which the teaching was in Albanian, and with which the Turkish Government was unable to interfere. The Jesuits, under Austrian protection, established a printing press in Scutari for the printing in Albanian of religious books. But this movement, being strictly Catholic, was confined to the North. It was, moreover, initiated with the intent of winning over the Northern Christians to Austria, and was directed rather to dividing the Christians from the Moslems and to weakening rather than strengthening the sense of Albanian nationality.

Not only among the Christians, but among the Moslems too, there was a marked sense of nationality. A very large proportion of the Moslems of the south were by no means orthodox Moslems, but were members of one of the Dervish sects, the Bektashi, and as such suspect by the powers at Constantinople.

Albania had suffered woefully from the Turk. But Albania was not dead. Far from it. There was another, and a far worse foe—one that grew ever stronger, and that was the Slav: Russia with her fanatical Church and her savage Serb and Bulgar cohorts ready to destroy Albania and wipe our Catholic and Moslem alike . . . "Over yonder," he [Abbot Premi Dochi of Albania] said, "is the land of Serbs called Old Serbia. But it is a much older Albania. Now it is peopled with Albanians, many of whom are the victims, or the children of victims, of the Berlin Treaty: Albanians, who had lived for generations on lands that that Treaty handed over to the Serbs and Montenegrins, who drove them out to starve. Hundreds perished in the mountains. Look at Dulcigno—a purely Albanian town, threatened by the warships of the Great Powers, torn from us by force. How could we resist all Europe? Our people were treated by the invading Serb and Montenegrin with every kind of brutality. . . . The spirit of the nation is awake in both Christian and Moslem. The Turk is now our only bulwark against the Slav invader. When the Turkish Empire breaks up, as break it must, we must not fall either into the hands of Austria nor of the Slavs."

Of Bosnia

The Summer of 1906 saw me no longer restricted to two months' travel, but free to go where I pleased for as long as I liked. I planned a great scheme for the study and comparison of the traditions and customs of all the Balkan races, and in August started for Bosnia.

In ancient days all Bosnia and the Herzegovina formed part of Illyria, and was inhabited by the ancestors of the modern Albanian. Thousands of prehistoric graves, similar to those found also in Serbia and Albania, are scattered over the land. A huge cemetery exists at Glasinatz above Sarajevo. The multitude of objects found in these graves reveal a very early Iron Age. Bosnia was one of Europe's earliest "Sheffields."

A sect known as the Paulicians arose in Samosata in Asia Minor, which combined Manicheism with a peculiar reverence for the teaching of St. Paul. Fiercely persecuted by the Christians, they revolted, joined with the Mahommedans, and wasted much of Asia Minor. The new faith was known as Bogumil (dear to God) from its reputed Slav leader.

The rapidity with which it spread shows the very slight hold Christianity had as yet taken. The sun and the moon, which figured prominently in it, probably appealed to the old pre-Christian nature-worship of the Slavs. Alexius Commenus vainly tried to extirpate the heresy by savage persecution. Basil, its high priest, was burnt alive. The sect fled westward and Bosnia became its stronghold. Religion in the Middle Ages was a far greater force than race. Nationality was hardly developed. Bosnia, into which the Orthodox faith seems to have penetrated but little, if at all, was thus cut off from the Serb Empire, for the bulk of the Bosniaks were either Bogumil or Roman Catholic.

We find a great many monuments of the Bogumils scattered through Bosnia and the Herzegovina. Huge monolithic gravestones often curiously carved. The sun, the moon and the cross appear as symbols, and portraits of warriors kilted and armed with bows and arrows and a cuirass, which give a good idea of the chieftain of the Middle Ages. The kilt is still worn by the Albanians.

Of the Bogumil creed not much is known, and that chiefly from its enemies. Catholic and Orthodox alike regarded the heresy with horror. But even its enemies allowed the Bogumils to have been an ascetic and temperate people. They abhorred the use of icons and images, and unless the subterranean chapel at Jaitza [Jajce] be one, have left no church. Their doctrines spread into west Europe, and by the end of the twelfth century had developed in France into the sect of Albigenses which was suppressed by the Roman Church with terrible ferocity. It is of interest that the rayed sun and the moon are still found in the armorial bearing of South of France families.

In Bosnia Bogumilism almost superseded all other faiths. In the twelfth century the Catholic Dalmatians and Hungarians in vain tried to suppress it by force. In 1189 Kulin Ban, the ruler of Bosnia, himself turned Bogomil. He recanted under pressure from Rome, but soon relapsed again, and in spite of an Hungarian crusade which ravaged the land, Bogumilism triumphed, the palace of the Catholic Bishop of Kreshevo was burnt and the Catholic episcopacy banished. The Bishop of Bosnia had to reside in Slavonia [Eastern Croatia], and Bogumilism spread into Dalmatia and Croatia.

Nationality is the craze of to-day. Religion, in the Middle Ages, played a similar part. Catholic, Orthodox, and Bogumil, hated each other more than they hated the less known Turk. Each was willing to use him against the other. People of the same race and language then fought each other because they differed about religion. To-day, even when holding the same religious views, they fight in the sacred name of nationality. But then, as now, there were a few people who recognized the folly of the fashionable differences.

Discussion Points for *Twenty Years of Balkan tangle*

1. What sorts of ideas of nationalism do we see from this author's perspective—was nationalism a long-standing, deep-seated element in the lives of folks? Or something more recent?
2. What can we infer about Bogumils? Do you have any sense that the author really presented her knowledge on the topic well?
3. What larger role did religion play for this author, and other people for that matter? How did this Bible Society seemingly influence affairs in Balkan politics?
4. Would you say that the author's reliance on Albanians for information on other peoples was responsible or irresponsible given the ethnic heterogeneity of the region?
5. How important is education in society? Countless governments, religions, and ideologies found their most ardent the exercise the education of children—from the Hitler Youth to the Khmer Rouge's ruthless indoctrination. What do you see here in how people manipulated the role of learning?

Montenegrin men in mixed dress

Peasant women in Croatia

Fourth Reading:

F. Kinsley Hutchinson, *Motoring in the Balkans* (London: Hodder & Stoughton, 1910).

While hundreds of thousands of tourists from Western Europe and America annually flock to the Dalmatian coast, more are increasingly taking advantage of the proximity of great Bosnian cities like Mostar and Sarajevo. Although Bosnia suffered greatly during the wars in the early 1990s, tourists are rediscovering the region for its wealth of outdoor pastimes. Driving a car along the winding mountain roads is a truly grand experience; yet in 1910, we only can imagine the difficulties that the author and her party had. Her description of the people and the land of the lower Dalmatian region and the drive through Bosnia exposed a lot about important topics like Bogomils and the influence of Islam in Bosnia—note how the author described these latter folks generically as "Turks" and denied them their Bosniak/n identity.

Women at the market in Zadar

In Dalmatia

For nearly fifteen kilometers after leaving Metković, the rough road follows the contours of the hillsides above the flooded delta of the Narenta [Neretva], crossing narrow inlets on dykes. Wherever the water ends, the fresh, green growth begins; young walnut-trees are busting into red-bronze leaf; many vineyards are under water; and the highway from lack of use is covered with a weak, thin grass. On the stone walls, near the village of Vidouje, large round nets are dying.

Below us, suddenly, a blue estuary appears in the landscape; a mountain point; a tiny town. "What is it?" we ask in chorus of the map-holder. "It is the Canale di Stagno piccolo." Oh, the musical Italian syllables! "And the village is Hodilje, on the peninsula of Sabioncello?" The fishermen's boats look like flies on the water. We pass under a ruined watch-tower on the hilltop.

"Probably that marks the frontier, a relic of Turkish domination; now we are out of the Herzegovina and in Dalmatia again," remarks the Leader.

But the landscape does not change, nor the appearance of the people. Two women pass us, bent double under immense bundles of firewood; the two men accompanying them carry between them—one umbrella! This attitude of course, is a survival of the ancient barbarian customs, when the man was the warrior, the hunter, the food provider; and the woman did the rest. It is said that the man loses the respect of his kind if he condescends to assist his wife; and that the wife would be the first one to object, with horror, at his taking a share in so-called woman's work.

More olive groves and the first carob-trees; a chapel and a cemetery; a wayside cross, cut from the mountain stone—and suddenly two magnificent planes or sycamores, monarchs of all the countryside! At this time we did not know that these trees—forty feet in diameter—are one of the sights in the environs of Ragusa [Dubrovnik]. We experience all the joy of discoverers. Their fresh spring foliage is exquisite in color, contrasting with the dark branches and mottled bark—and their enormous size dwarfs all comparison!

Ragusa [Dubrovnik]

Ragusa was the crowning point of our Dalmatian experiences. Never did I appreciate the beauty of the open sea until I came to this stronghold of the Adriatic, this proud and ancient city, this wonderful survival of mediaeval times. Zara, Sebenico, Spalato, Ragusa [Zadar, Šibenik, Split, and Dubrovnik], each has its own peculiar charm, the interest increasing as we go southward. Zara, complete in itself, a tiny walled city on a narrow peninsula shut in by islands; Sebenico and Spalato built on large bays with more extended outlooks; but of them only Ragusa alone basks in the freedom of the open sea. Great waves dash against her worn rock fortress, and no islands shelter her from the Adriatic's storms. To be sure, there are the "Pettini," sharp teeth-like rocks, projecting just enough to warn the sailor where hidden danger lurks; and Lacroma [Lokrum], a dome-like wooded islet, crowned by an old fort, but on every side the sea stretches away to meet the sky in limitless horizon.

I really need not go outside for amusement, for under my window passes a constant procession from the fascinating old city gate to the surrounding country. Occasionally one sees an open landau, with red-fezzed gentlemen gazing about, as strangers are wont to do.

There is great variety in the costumes and they are prettier than those of the north. The skirts are dark wool and finely plaited. The aprons vary, and the fluted and fringed white kerchiefs are worn either tied under the chin or looped up on top of the head. Neither are the gold filigree beads allowed to hide their elegance; but, strung on a plain cord, which is supposed to lie snugly in the folds of the fichu at the back, they begin juts at the collarbone in front and fall low on the bosom.

An officer in the pale blue uniform of the Austrian cavalry goes slowly by on his well-groomed horse. A young woman in a dark stuff gown, red and white checked apron, green kerchief, and carrying one of the flat embroidered bags of the country, accompanies a child of six, perhaps to school, for there is a fine new school-house on the hill. A Dominican friar, his white frock floating about him; a flock of small school-children with an old servant in their midst; a man bent double under a load of firewood; three more officers gravely walking their horses down the long hill; a pretty kerchiefed Ragusan; an unmistakably English tourist in knickers, with his red guide-book; three women, each carrying a brilliant-hued bundle on her head, like walking poppies; a squad of cavalry;—

Woman in Dubrovnik *note the writing behind her

"Did you notice that big Oriental-looking fountain just inside the gate?" the Leader asks. "No, the sun was so hot I was hunting for a shady spot." "There should be a cloister near here," he answers—following the new lead—and we turn aside where a sign reads "Ljecarnica, Farmacia, Apotheka," [pharmacy] with an index hand.

A charming spot, indeed, is this old cloister of the Franciscans, with its double columns supporting narrow arches, its fifteenth century fountain between long stone benches, and the roses!—only the orange-tree in the corner opposite vies with them for fragrance, while the palms' sharp fingers cast black shadows on the friars' walk.

On one side of the cloister is the famous Franciscan Farmacia [pharmacy], where the shelves are still filled with rare blue jars and vases—an inheritance from the Middle Ages, for this apothecary shop, founded in 1307, is one of the three oldest in Europe.

At the farther end of the Stradone [pedestrian zone crossing the old city in Dubrovnik] is the fifteenth century clock tower; and beside it stands La Sponza, the ancient mint and custom house, a wonderfully charming building, a Venetian *façade* with a Renaissance loggia, and a double cloister about its small *cortile*, where still the *contadini* gather to dispute the weights and taxes. This constant presence of the gaily dressed country folk adds so much to the charm of Ragusa, that sometimes architectural details are overlooked.

But for the loveliness of the Rector's Palace, a short distance beyond the Custom House, no adjectives are adequate. The massive columns, the richly carved capital, supporting graceful arches, are but an introduction to the splendid entrance—the Porta della Carita, flanked by long, arcaded benches of marble; and the dignified double cloister, with its comparatively modern stairway; and the details—it is not enough to revel in the sensuous beauty of the whole, the perfect proportions, the creamy color, the lights and shadows in its deep reveals. Surely those curious pictured scenes upon Onofrio's capitals, the exquisite finish of those leaves and flowers, veritable gems of Gothic sculpture, must not be overlooked.

Mostar

At Mostar we are surprised to find a comfortable modern hotel on the banks of the Narenta River whose eastern windows face a shady park and all our meals are served on the open terrace. . . . The lemonade vendor, with gorgeous shining brasses, no sooner appears than small be-fezzed boys swarm about him. It must be recess at the Turkish school-house, for a flock of trousered mites run gaily to the fountain. A white hooded being approaches and turns toward the bridge, her hands discreetly folded; only a narrow slit in the spotless muslin enables her to see her way. A Servian [Serbian] peasant in coarse white linen knickers and tucked-up skirt, a bag over her shoulder, stalks by with a free and splendid swing, her veil blowing back from her braided hair. With all her toiling she is more to be envied than her Turkish sister in the harem.

"Do you see that curiously dressed woman coming down the street by the mosque. What is that pointed thing she has on her head?" cries the Gentle Lady, breaking the long silence. "That is a costume peculiar to Mostar," answers a voice in English from below. . . . Mounting the incline to the centre of the bridge [the famous bridge in Mostar, commissioned by the Ottoman authorities] we look down at the green water rushing between its rocky shores, then raise our eyes to the city on either side. "Eleven, twelve, thirteen," a voice beside me counts, and I turn to question. "Yes, we can see thirteen minarets from here, I have counted them."

Group of men in Mostar

How symbolic they are—those slender, balconied towers pointing skyward! . . . we hurry across the bridge and dive down into the narrow street of the bazaar in eager search of a way to them. Before a sunlit archway we linger aside his long pipe, rises and without a word leads the way down the stone-paved path and within the stuccoed wall. Behold, a fountain of running water under a protecting roof, great spreading green branches, and a broad, covered patio of a mosque. Here we being women and therefore forbidden entrance, he halts, removes his shoes and recites his formula of explanation in the few words of German which he knows—

"The mosque of Mahomet Pasha, the first on in Mostar, four hundred years old, and that is the Mecca—the name Mahommed—there the preacher stands, and this leads to the minaret," pointing to a tiny, winding stair. "I am the muezzin," he proudly adds. The rich rugs, the dim light, a cross-legged figure conning [examining] the Koran by a low window, the age-mellowed walls and the Moorish lattices make a most effective picture.

From the tourist's standpoint there are not many "sights" in Mostar; but there are pictures, living ones at all times, and the costumes are even more varied and attractive than in Dalmatia—which, is saying much. The Oriental character of the buildings, too, forms a fitting background and the brilliant white light reminds one of Cairo and the East. In the bazaar, through high-walled streets, beside the mosque, on the curving bridge, men, women, and children gather in gaudy groups daily; but on Sunday the service in the Franciscan church is a sight long to be remembered. The soldiers in their khaki and red fezes forming one solid mass of color; the peasants in their gay-embroidered sleeveless jackets over clean white shirts, full baggy trousers, white gaiters and *opanka* and scarlet fezes; the white-gowned women with veils over their coin-bedecked head-dresses; all rising, bowing, or kneeling in unison, produce an effect as striking as it is picturesque.

From Mostar to Sarajevo

A caravan of horses laded with firewood descends from the mountains led by women. Later we meet an industrious peasant woman twirling a carved spindle of wool as she walks rapidly along, driving her pack-mule. European mountain ash are in blossom and flocks of birds rise overhead—yellow, black, white, and brown, in tantalizing variety.

Just without the gorge lies a group of Bogomile stones in a field about three hundred feet from the road, and we go over to look at them. They are most extraordinary in their huge bulk and barbaric markings. As we return to the car we beg the Leader to enlighten us. . . . The Bogomiles are a religious sect among the Southern Slavs, who, in the thirteenth century, rebelled against the Roman Catholic Church and founded this kind of Protestantism. At first they were protected both from Servia and Bosnia, and the faith made rapid strides, even reaching Cattaro, Spalato, and Zara. Strenuous persecution began and continued for centuries; but they have never been entirely extirpated and even as late of 1876 it is recorded that over 2,000 Bogomiles took refuge in Ragusa from the one district of Popovo in the Herzegovina. Little is really known of their habits or opinions, as their annals have been written by their enemies, and their faith is held in secret to this day. In various parts of the country their strangely shaped gravestones have been found, some with rude carvings and in the museum at Sarajevo are reproductions of the most important examples. One of these is a block between nine and ten feet long, four and a half feet broad, and five feet high, with elaborately sculptured sides. It is supposed to have belonged to a Djett or Bogomile bishop.

Muslim girls in Sarajevo

In Sarajevo

"There are over two hundred mosques in Sarajevo, but by a regulation recently passed no Christian is allowed in any of them," so we content ourselves with the outside, glancing at the shady courtyards with the inevitable fountain and the groups of picturesque men.

Our guide takes us, however, to see an ancient Servian or Greek church, shut away from the business street within a shady court, where beneath a loggia there are arrangements for out-of-door services. It looks odd to see the name of Christ outlined in colored lights upon the wall. The small dark interior of the church, with its gilded *iconostas*, its many pillars and few windows reminds us forcibly of Russia.

We visit the new town hall, from the upper windows of which one gets a good view of the city. But to the Occidental visitor the real interest of Sarajevo is in the bazaar and the endlessly queer street scenes. One merchant is selling cherries from a large round tray, but fond as I am of fruit, these look too young and hard to taste. A group of trousered maidens lost in curious contemplation of us, half drop their protecting drapery from before their faces. One bazaar is underground and delightfully cool and comfortable. An open market-place is faced with tiny, box-like booths in two stories, each so low that the owner sitting cross-legged on the floor almost touches the roof with his turban.

On our return from Sarajevo, in the afternoon, I rub my eyes to see whether I am dreaming. What a wonderful climate Bosnia possesses! Banana plants have appeared and grown to three feet high, geraniums, heliotrope, salvia, pansies, even roses and fuchsias have come out of the ground and brought forth blossoms—it is Aladdin's magical lamp again! I don't know at what time the gardeners begin their work, but at 6:30 they are in the midst of it—between 8 and 8:30 they all disappear, possibly for coffee. In their spotless turbans, red vests and broad sashes, dark full trousers, embroidered leggings, and pointed *opanka*, they are very decorative among the flowers.

Muslim women in Jajce

In Jajce

Turkish women comb their hair but once a week, it being considered bad for the hair to do it oftener! The young girl had a dreadful carbuncle on her cheek, but before she would permit a man to look at it she would die—and she nearly did. It is difficult to believe that there are still thousands of poor women living in this dreadful atmosphere of ignorance. We shiver, as we come away, at the hopelessness, the misery, of these forlorn creatures. For man, the Moslem religion may be all very well, certainly there are phases of it which are extremely beautiful! But for women! Following the crowd through the shady streets, we came out on the market-place, and here I grew bolder and bolder. Evidently these good people had no objection to the camera, for they posed with childlike eagerness. Someone nearby would translate for me, and I was so busy turning my spool, I scarcely had time to look up and thank him before another subject still more beguiling appeared.

Women working in a quarry in Crkvenica

The scene was most diverting; the people themselves enjoyed the opportunity for a pleasant chat, the women seemed to be more on an equality with the men, and certainly they were openly admired by them in many cases. A boy selling doughnuts strung on a stick called his wares in sweet, minor tones. Some girls were buying shoes, others were laden with cotton cloth. There were Spanish Jewesses, wearing the unbecoming cap which distinguishes them; and many gypsies at their traditional craft of begging. The women were lavishly bedecked with jewelry, necklaces, belt buckles, rings, and head bands; often they wore an oval silver box on a chain around their necks. In Cyprus this would contain a prayer, in India the betelnut. Both men and women had drawn-work and embroidery on their shirt sleeves, and beaded *opanka* on their feet. Girls of the Greek Church let their hair hang in long braids, while those of the Roman wound their braided tresses about their heads. A lady in black satin Turkish trousers, short, fitted jacket, and a close black cap was evidently of the higher classes.

Journey near Plitvice Lakes

We know that the Croatians are intensely patriotic and cling tenaciously to their mother-tongue—but we are hardly prepared for the extent to which they carry it here. All the room notifications, the announcements, the time tables, the bill-of-fare, even, are printed in that Slavic language. The only bottled water obtainable is tagged with the, to us, formidable cognomen "Jamnička Kiselica"; but it tastes like our Poland water and so thoroughly satisfies us. The steward is the only person on the premises who even understands German; the boatman, who ferries us across the Lake Kosjak, knows no language but Croatian, and when we wish to make excursions along the beach into pools where water lilies grow, all explanations have to be by gestures.

Near Karlovac

Through the Oriental-looking shoe market, over the broad Kulpa River, across the railroad, we take the first road to the right. In the maze of animals, wagons, and people we are obliged to go very slowly and often to stop; but the way is broad, if somewhat rough, and the surrounding country is charming.

Discussion Points for *Motoring in the Balkans*

1. What did the relationship between the various peoples in Bosnia seem like—natural in variety or hostile?
2. How did the author see religion in Bosnia and what sorts of things differentiated people?
3. Why was the author so surprised that people in Croatia knew only Croatian language, with merely a few folks versed in some basic German? How often do people in rural areas know much about the larger world?
4. What kinds of attributes did the author note of the so-called Turkish women? Do you really think they were of Turkish ethnicity or could they have been Bosnian Muslims (i.e., indigenous converts to Islam)?
5. How prevalent did the Italian influence along the Adriatic seem? The author noted Italian culture and language, but might those things merely have coexisted as a minority identity alongside an otherwise Slavic-dominated countryside? How might the multiple cultures have interacted?

PART II: TRAVEL TO ARABIA AND THE ISLAMIC WORLD

Arabia—or the Middle or Near East, more broadly—was not only one of the major cradles of civilization but also served as the most direct point of contact for Europeans. Trade between Europe and North Africa indeed also flourished since the days of Ancient Greece, Carthage, and Rome; but, after the fall of the Rome in 476 AD, the European lands stagnated and in fact retreated in most cultural, economic, political, and social arenas. As home to two great world religions, the modern-day area of Israel and Lebanon far surpassed the culture present in Western parts of Europe. Yet, when Muhammad left Mecca and recited his vision of conversations with the Angel Gabriel, a third powerful religion soon emerged that redefined the Middle East, Africa, Eastern Europe, and Asia. Islam spread quickly thanks to its easy portability and simple tenets (the five important pillars: *shahada*, declaration of faith; *salat*, mandatory daily prayers; *zakat*, almsgiving; the *sawm*, fasting during Ramadan; and the *hajj*, the pilgrimage to Mecca). Moreover, in the political vacuum that followed Rome's fall, Muslims easily moved about the Middle East and eagerly preached their new faith. As the center of the known world at the time, the many urban centers that dotted the Middle East were home to merchants and centers for Arabic language—the language of Muhammad and a unifying force among the various tribes throughout the region. By the 700s AD, Islam had not only moved East into Asia but also quickly overtaken Judaism and Christianity in the Holy Land, Egypt, and westward to Morocco. From their most western point, Muslim armies crossed the Straits of Gibraltar into Iberia. Christian forces on the Iberian Peninsula succumbed quickly to powerful and advanced armies. Meanwhile, Christians began to see their battle with these Moorish and Berber tribes from Africa as a sort of civilizational struggle between the faiths.

Soon after Moorish armies had secured much of Iberia, Christians—including warlords like Charlemagne—charged themselves with the *Reconquista* (reconquest) of the peninsula. A religious battle ensued that lasted until 1492, when Catholic armies finally drove the Moors out of Europe with victory at Grenada. But the political and religious ideas that permeated the reconquest created a new spirit that increased the zeal of the Spanish Inquisition (with trials against Jews, heretics, and Muslims as early as the 1480s), and charged a new era of exploration. Battles to liberate Iberia solidified the exotic "other" in the European mind-set and rallied Europe to the cause of Christianity versus Islam. Not only was an Islamic presence identifiable in western Europe but also during the 1300s nomadic Turkic horseman from Central Asia overran much of Southeastern Europe for the glory of the Ottoman Empire.

Having roamed Central Asia for generations, the Turkic-speaking tribes under Osman the Great finally abandoned their nomadic lifestyle with the conquest of Bursa in 1326. Much of present-day Turkey quickly fell to Osman's armies thanks to their superb techniques as horseback warriors, and Ottoman armies soon threatened Byzantium, or the Eastern Roman Empire. In decline since the 700s AD, the Eastern Roman Empire nonetheless held an important role in guarding holy cities like Antioch and facilitating the trade to Europe that came through the Middle East. As the wealthiest city in Europe, Constantinople had a metropolitan lifestyle with multitudes of different peoples—Jews, Armenians, Greeks, Venetians, Genoese and more—naturally, it made a desirable target. While Ottoman armies bypassed the city's stronghold and went directly to the Balkan Peninsula in the fourteenth century, by 1453 the final siege of Constantinople succeeded. Not only did the Ottoman Turks obtain immense wealth thanks to their control of the city but they also gained an immensely important strategic city from which to further their advance into Europe. With such a substantial base of operations, the Christian forces in the Balkans stood at a clear disadvantage, as they had ever since the Battle of Kosovo in 1389, when the combined armies under Serbia's Prince Lazar failed to defeat the Turks. While the various Christian armies had a difficult time unifying in the face of the Turkish onslaught, the defeat at Kosovo spelled doom as the Christians had few reserves to constitute another army. Turkish forces, in contrast, had large reserves in Anatolia with eager leaders ready to advance further. Christian nobles as far north as Hungary fell to the Turks and only luck saved the Viennese from succumbing too in 1529. The largely unchecked Turkish advance thus came to a halt at the gates of Vienna, but Ottoman control lasted in the Balkans until the beginning of the twentieth century with cultural, social, and political legacies clearly visible today.

Even as contact with Islam occurred with regularity from the southern reaches of the Hapsburg lands, the Muslim lands still seemed exotic for Europeans. Artists such as Eugene Delacroix painted provocative pieces ostensibly showing the intimate side of Muslim life. Meanwhile, actual knowledge of Arabic and Islam waned in comparison to studies of ancient Greek, Latin, and even Hebrew at European universities. As a result, reliance upon middle-men—often Jewish or Greek merchants—painted the larger picture of the East for most Europeans. Moreover, as civilization in Europe increasingly progressed, Muslims became ever more different. Palestinian-born literary critic Edward Said noted this history in his seminal study, *Orientalism* (1978), but while his argument no doubt suffered from a postcolonial or post-modern syndrome, it nonetheless made a compelling case for how people in Europe and the Middle East have grown to know, or at least, identify each other—unfortunately, much of that has persisted in a negative fashion.

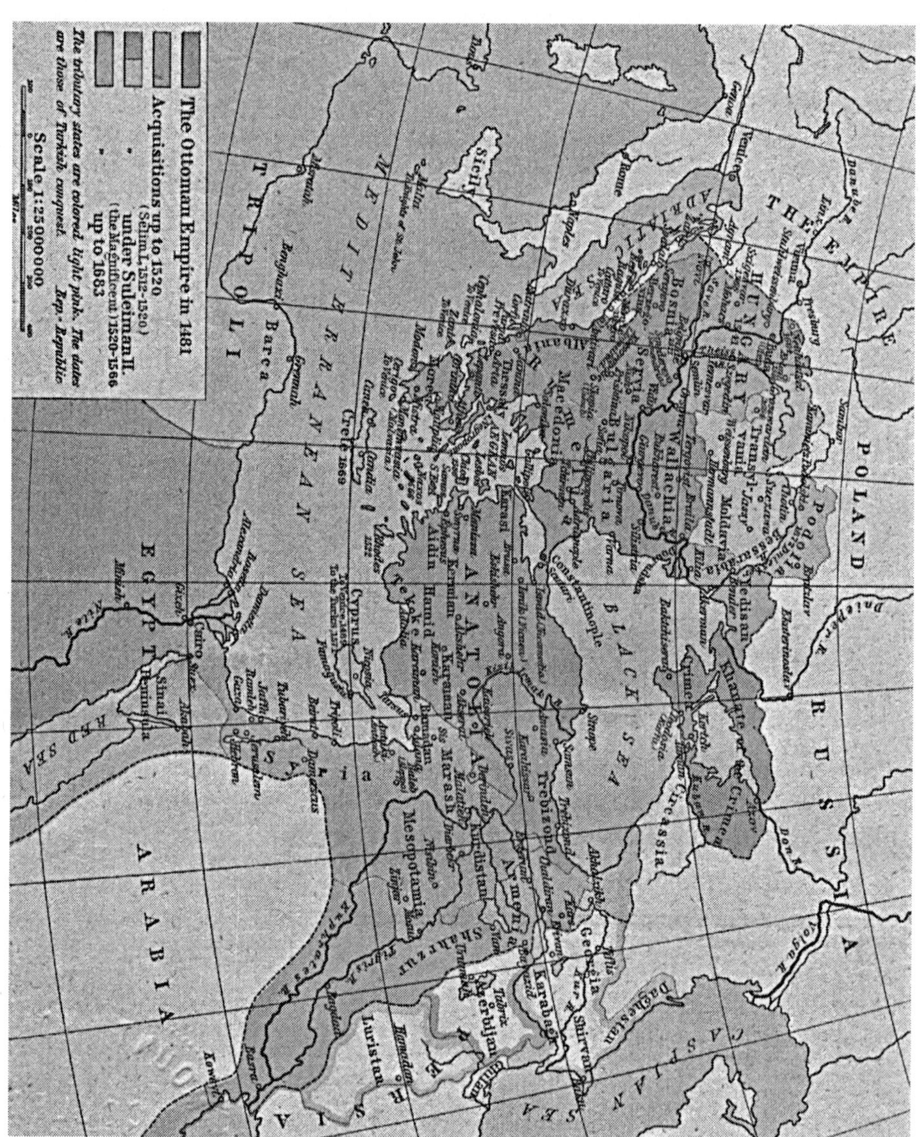

Map of the Middle East in the fifteenth century

First Reading:

Carsten Niebuhr, *Travels through Arabia and other Countries in the East*, Robert Heron, trans. (Perth: R. Morison Junior, 1799).

When the Danish king selected qualified men in the 1760s to set out and explore the Middle East, he chose a group familiar with the Arabic language who could "explore" and, presumably, speak with authority on the "various curiosities of Egypt, but especially of Arabia." In the end, Carsten Niebuhr (of Lower Saxony, in Germany) was the sole survivor of the expedition and he had set off for Bombay on an English ship before returning home to report on his travels in Arabia for the Danish king.

Denmark in no way had a powerful commitment to overseas empire, but the government did attempt to enhance its economy through various trading posts in both the East and West Indies. Several small settlements in India began in earnest with the colony at Tranquebar in 1620, but the British either captured or bought most of what Denmark had acquired. Similarly, the United States purchased Caribbean Islands from Denmark in 1917 to form the U.S. Virgin Islands. Niebuhr's adventures, though, represented a serious attempt to understand the Middle East and better allow Danish merchants to do business there. This is an already edited account of his large writings on this subject, which by the Enlightenment had truly enamored Europe's literate population.

Portrait of Carsten Niebuhr

From Copenhagen to Egypt [during a war between the French and English]

After viewing the curiosities of Marseilles, we set sail on the third of June, in company with the other three Danish ships. Although at peace with the English, yet we did not think ourselves safe from being insulted by the fleets of that nation; as they insist upon going on board, and examining even neutral vessels. Our Captain had determined not to yield to such an infraction of the rights of nations; and accordingly prepared for making a vigorous defense, if any insult of this nature should be offered him. As we had expected, we fell in with English ships three different times; and they attempted to come on board of us: But our Captain strenuously refusing to submit to any such indignity, they made off with a bad grace, and suffered us to continue our route unmolested.

On the fourteenth of June, we arrived at Malta and cast anchor in the grand harbor . . . this city has a fine appearance when viewed from the harbor: The houses, with terraces on their roofs, and built against steep, pointed rocks, have quite an oriental aspect.

Of the public buildings, the most superb is St. John's church. . . . It has thus been enriched with a great number of valuable curiosities, and, among others, a luster, with a chain of pure gold, 500,000 crowns in value. The riches of this church are said to exceed those of the *Kaaba* at Mecca, and of the tomb of Mahomet at Medina.

We were shown a Turkish ship of war, of 84 guns, which had been seized and brought into Malta by Christian slaves.

Constantinople

Constantinople appears larger than it really is: for, as the houses rise upon the sides of hills, they present themselves in the form of an ampitheatre, and thus appear to spread over a wide extent of ground. Towards the sea, however, the city consists of new houses, and is receiving continued additions. Of late, they have even encroached upon the harbor and filled up some part of it, in order to gain ground for new buildings.

It would be hard to fix the number of the inhabitants: It is always stated too high, from a mistake common to travelers, in estimating the population of the cities of the East. They regard those cities as equally populous, in proportion to their extent, with those of Europe. But the houses in the East are low. Persons in easy circumstances, chose to have a large area behind their houses. The palaces of the great, with their gardens and seraglios, occupy much ground. . . . The streets are full of joiners, ironmongers, goldsmiths, jewelers, etc. busy in the exercise of several trades.

Whatever be its population, Constantinople exhibits a delightful prospect. Its harbor, one of the finest in the world, is always full of vessels. The medley of superb mosques and palaces, gardens and trees of all sorts, which the city displays, appears remarkably striking to a stranger. But within, the arrangement and appearance of the city, correspond not to its splendor when seen from a distance. The streets are almost all narrow, dirty, and irregular; the houses are of wood, slight and ill built, and appear more like coops for birds than dwellings for men. Of palaces built of stone, nothing is to be seen but the high walls that surround them. In this city, it is equally dangerous to live in stone and in wooden houses. In the former, one is liable to be buried in ruins by earthquakes; in the latter, to be burnt, by the breaking out of a fire—These two species of awful events being equally frequent in Constantinople.

The Sultan has many houses of pleasure, both in the neighborhood of the capital, and on the shores on the channel of the Black Sea. But the reigning Sultan goes nowhere but to Kara Adadfeh, the gloomy, solitary, situation of which suits the melancholy complexion of his mind. He is suffering the others to fall into ruins: He has caused several of them [houses] to be pulled down, and the materials to be employed in building public baths and mosques.

The Greeks have three and twenty churches in Constantinople, and the Armenians three; exclusive of those which the two nations have in the suburbs. A catholic clergyman resides at Pera, on whom the Pope confers the pompous title of Archbishop, placing him at the head of a great many imaginary bishops.

Journeying from Constantinople to Alexandria

There are a great many Greeks in the isle of Rhodes, but they are not suffered to live in the city. Misters Von Haven and Cramer witnessed an instance of the ill treatment which that people suffer from their conquerors. My companions had gone with some Greeks to visit their bishop, in a village near the city. While they were with him, some Turkish musicians made their appearance and insisted upon entertaining the good prelate with music, which he had no desire to hear. Although he refused their concert, the musicians would be paid; and did not retire without insulting him and his company.

Our [Turkish] Captain, his secretary, and two pilots spoke Italian tolerably well. The secretary had been at Venice, in different other Italian cities, and even at Vienna, where he received the following information. When we asked him if there any Pagans in the Turkish Empire, he replied; "No; but in Germany and Hungary there are; they are called Lutherans, and have no notions of God and his prophets." This zealous secretary was at the same time Imam, or almoner of the vessel. The Imam's business is to direct the crew in their evening prayers, which the Mahometans perform regularly after washing. The Imam then spreads his carpet, kneels with his face towards Mecca, and mutters his prayers, prostrating himself from time to time, and crying Allah Akbar, God is Great. The assembly repeat his words, and regularly imitate his motions and gestures. One thing essential, is, to put the thumbs behind the ears, to mark the perfect abstraction of the mind from all worldly cares, and the elevation of the soul towards heaven . . . In our ship, which was too full, the Musulman passengers were seated on the decks. . . . In a cabin above us were lodged some slaves intended for the market, girls who had received a good education in the Turkish mode, and were destined for the Haram [Harem] of some grandee.

In Alexandria

The Mahometans in general, and especially the inhabitants of Alexandria, break down the finest monuments of antiquity, to employ the fragments in the most wretched structures imaginable. Whenever they are at any loss for materials for building, they scruple not to dig up the foundation-stones of the ancient walls and palaces. If one happens to find a beautiful column in his garden, he will rather make mill-stones of it, than preserve it.

This city [Alexandria] might be in a more flourishing condition; did not disadvantages of all sorts concur to depress it. Its inhabitants appear to have a natural genius for commerce; were it not checked by the malignant influence of the Government. I have nowhere met with so many people who could speak the European languages, and even those of the North of Europe, correctly. The inhabitants of Alexandria are in use to enter as sailors on board Christian ships; and when they have seen the world, and learned some languages, they return home and become couriers, or interpreters to the nations they have served. The Mahometans have commonly a great aversion at living among Christians, because they cannot join in the ceremonies of their religion. The modern Egyptians, being less attached than other Musulmans to the peculiarities of their religion and manners, are fitter for commercial intercourse with the Europeans.

Down the Nile to Cairo

We left Rosetta on the sixth of November, and two days after passed *Fue*, once a considerable city, and the staple of the trade between Alexandria and Cairo. The canal between Alexandria and Fue is no longer navigable; and Fue entirely deserted. The Nile carries so much of the soil from the lands, that it gradually fills up the canal; although they are cleaned from time to time; but in a superficial enough manner. The earth taken out of the canals forms those mounts which are observed in the Delta and which appear strange in so flat a country as Egypt.

The navigation of the Nile would be still more agreeable, were it not infested with pirates. But, when a great number of people on board of a vessel, they keep on their guard; they discharge a few shots from time to time . . . There is much more danger in trusting to a Reis, or master of a vessel, with whom you are unacquainted, who may favor the robbers, and share their plunder. Whole villages are said to follow this trade: and for this reason the boats never stop in their neighborhood.

Sifta, at which we arrived on the third of May 9 [1762], is a pretty considerable village, between Cairo and Damietta. It is the property of an old Kiflar-Aga, from Constantinople, living at present at Cairo; who keeps here a Kaimacan, or bailiff. It has three mosques, and a church belonging to the Copts [Coptic Christians], the congregation of which consists of three hundred families. Those good people asked me to see their church: it is ill-built, dirty, and hung with cobwebs. During the public worship, they stand, leaning on their staves. Their churches are adorned with bad paintings. I saw one in which Jesus Christ, and the Blessed Virgin, with several of the saints, appeared mounted proudly on horseback.

In Cairo

In this city are a great many *kans* or *oquals*, as they are called in Egypt. These are large and strong buildings, consisting of ware-rooms and small chambers for the use of foreign merchants. Here, as well as at Constantinople, are several elegant houses, where fresh water is distributed gratis [free] to passengers.

The public baths are very numerous. Although externally very plain buildings, they have handsome apartments within, paved with marble, and ornamented in the fashion of the country. Several servants attend; each of whom has his particular task, in waiting upon and assisting those who come to bathe. Strangers are surprised when those bathers begin to handle them, and afraid of having their limbs dislocated. But after being a little accustomed to the ceremony, they find it sufficiently agreeable.

No water fit for drinking is to be had at Cairo, unless out of the Nile; from which it is brought every day into the city, in skins, upon asses and camels. Under several mosques, are large reservoirs, in which water is preserved for the use of the public, during the swell of the Nile; for the river is then muddy, and its water thought unwholesome. Indeed the water of the Nile is always something muddy; but, by rubbing with bitter almonds, prepared in a particular manner, the earthen jars in which it is kept, this water is rendered clear, light, and salutary. The use of this water is generally thought to be the occasion of a cutaneous eruption to which the inhabitants of Cairo are subject, at a certain season of the year. It is troublesome, but does not injure the health.

Description of government

Like the Mammelukes, who, having been all slaves, chose their chiefs only from among those who had risen to honor through the path of servitude, the present Beys [Ottoman equivalent of aristocratic status, prior noted as *Beg* for the Balkans] have been almost all slaves, bought for fifty or not more than a hundred sequins. They are often Christian children, from Georgia or Mingrelia. But these places have, for some time, been conferred likewise on free and high-born Mahametans. Of the eighteen Beys who were in office when I was in Egypt, only five were of this latter character; the other thirteen were descended from Christian parents, and had been slaves in their youth.

Our surprise at the elevation of so many slaves will cease, when we attend more particularly to the manners of the people of the East. The Mahometans, in general, and especially the Egyptians, treat their slaves with great kindness. The Beys, and the principal inhabitants of Cairo, buy many Christian children, whom they educate with the same care as their own children, in everything necessary to accomplish the character of the Mahometan lord. When their education is finished, they procure them employments in the army. Those emancipated slaves retain the most lively affection to the generous masters to whom they owe their fortune, and even their moral existence. By this means it often happens, that a master, when he finds any of his slaves to possess extraordinary talents, and tried fidelity, spares no pains or expense to raise him to a more considerable employment than that which he occupies himself. Thus the master raises his credit and influence in the administration, by introducing into it his own creatures.

The members of this aristocracy are extremely haughty and insolent. In Cairo no Christian or Jew may appear on horseback. They ride only asses, and must dismount, upon meeting even the most inconsiderable Egyptian lord. Those lords appear always on horseback, with an insolent servant before them, who, with a great staff in his hand, warns the riders on assess to show the due marks of respect to his master, crying out *enfil* [infidel], get down. If the infidel fails to give instant obedience, he is beaten till he dismounts. . . . At first, when I went about in Cairo, I made my janissary go before, and my servant follow, both mounted on asses as well as myself. But, after having the mortification to see these two Musselmans remain upon their beasts, while I was obliged to dismount, I determined to walk on foot.

It is true, that in Egypt, these distinctions between the Mahometans and persons of other religions, are carried a greater length, than anywhere else in the East. . . . They [Christians and Jews] are not even suffered to walk by several mosques in high veneration for their sanctity . . . even the ground on which they stand, is so sacred in the eyes of the people, that they will not suffer it to be profaned by the feet of infidels.

Regarding the police in Cairo

The great officers of the police and of justice outfit the different parts of the city, both by night and day, attended by a numerous train, and at season when they cannot be expected, in order to inspect the markets, and to take up suspected persons. Those officers give instant sentence upon offenders, and condemn them to the bastinadoe, without any form of process; they will even hang them up if they take them in the act. The fear of being every moment surprised by these officers, restrains the people from mutiny or pillage. I have often witnessed the terror which those awful inspectors inspire. At sight of them, my Egyptian servant, was so struck with fear, that he ran hastily homewards, and I was obliged to use force before I could make him turn and proceed.

Regarding the life and economy

As Egypt is without wood, its inhabitants are obliged to burn the dung of their domestic animals. The dung of asses, and camels is chiefly used for fuel, because these two species are the most numerous, and the most common. Little girls go about, gathering the dung in the streets, and upon the highways; they mix it with cut straw; and of this mixture make cakes, which they place along the walls, or upon the declivity of some neighboring eminence, to dry them in the sun.

The lower class live usually in chambers vaulted with unburnt bricks. In these chambers, those cakes are burnt, with a little straw intermixed, or instead of it, stalks of certain plants; and this both for warming the apartments in winter, and for dressing the victual [cooking]. A soot, very rich in salts, is thus produced, which fastens to the roofs of the chambers. It is sold to the merchants, who judge its quality by its taste, and employ it in the manufacture of fal-ammoniac [fertilizer].

Coffee is an article that is both consumed in the country, and conveyed through it. As this is the favorite beverage of the Turks, they are desirous of having it in the most genuine purity. The importation of American, and exportation of Arabian coffee, are equally forbidden. But these prohibitions are eluded, by means of presents to the great, and to the officers of the customs; so that the Europeans procure, every year a considerable quantity of their Levant coffee out of Egypt.

Gum-arabic is one of the most considerable articles of commerce that pass through Egypt. Every year, in the month of October, two or three small caravans of the Arabs, from the neighborhood of Par and Mount Sinai, arrive with about 70,000 pound weight of the gum. Those Arabs are very much in the way of debasing their goods with an intermixture of extraneous matters; and yet oblige the Mahometan merchants to take them without any examination of their quality. Out of an aversion to cities, or probably to avoid corporal punishment for their frauds and robberies, the Arabians never enter Cairo. They encamp at half a league's distance from the walls. The merchants are obliged to go out to them, in order to transact for the purchase of the gum. The Arabs don't take money, but clothes, and such other things as they stand in need of in the desert.

Those African caravans bring at the same time, several other commodities; slaves, ivory, ostrich-feathers, tamarinds, and gold dust. They take in exchange, Egyptian cloth, false pearls, coral, arms, and even full suits of clothes, which the inhabitants of Cairo make up, according to their taste. This is what has, of late, increased the demand for broad-cloth in Egypt.

Regarding the people of Cairo

Arabs and Turks from all the provinces in the Ottoman Empire, form the most numerous part of the inhabitants of Cairo. There are also Magrebbins, or Arabs from Barbary, other Africans, Persians, and Tartars: All these are Mahometans, and most of them are attached to the sect of Schafei.

After the Mahometans, the Copts are the next in numbers. They occupy whole quarters of the city, and very large streets. They have a great many churches, both in the capital, and at Masr-el-atik in its vicinity. Their patriarch also resides at Cairo.

The Jews are the most numerous class, next after the Mahometans and the Copts. Some Phrarisees of Talmudists, reside here, as well as Karaites, who, though not numerous, have a synagogue of their own. The Talmudists are numerous and powerful. . . . One proof of the consequence which the Jews enjoy under the aristocracy of Cairo, is, that the offices of the customs are shut upon their Sabbath, and no goods can pass on that day, although belonging to Christians or Mussulmans.

The Greeks have only two churches in Cairo, in one of which the service is performed by the patriarch of Alexandria and in the other by the bishop of Mount Sinai. The Armenians, who are not numerous, have only one church, but that a handsome one. From Europe here are several French and Italian merchants, but no Dutchmen; yet the Dutch have a Consul here, as well as France and Venice.

If Cairo come ever to want European merchants, yet it is not probable, that it will be without ecclesiastics of the Roman Communion. Here are Jesuits, Capuchins, Cordeliers, and Fathers of the Society for the propagation of the Christian Faith.

These monks are all eager to make proselytes, and sometimes succeed so far as to convert schismatic Christians of the East.

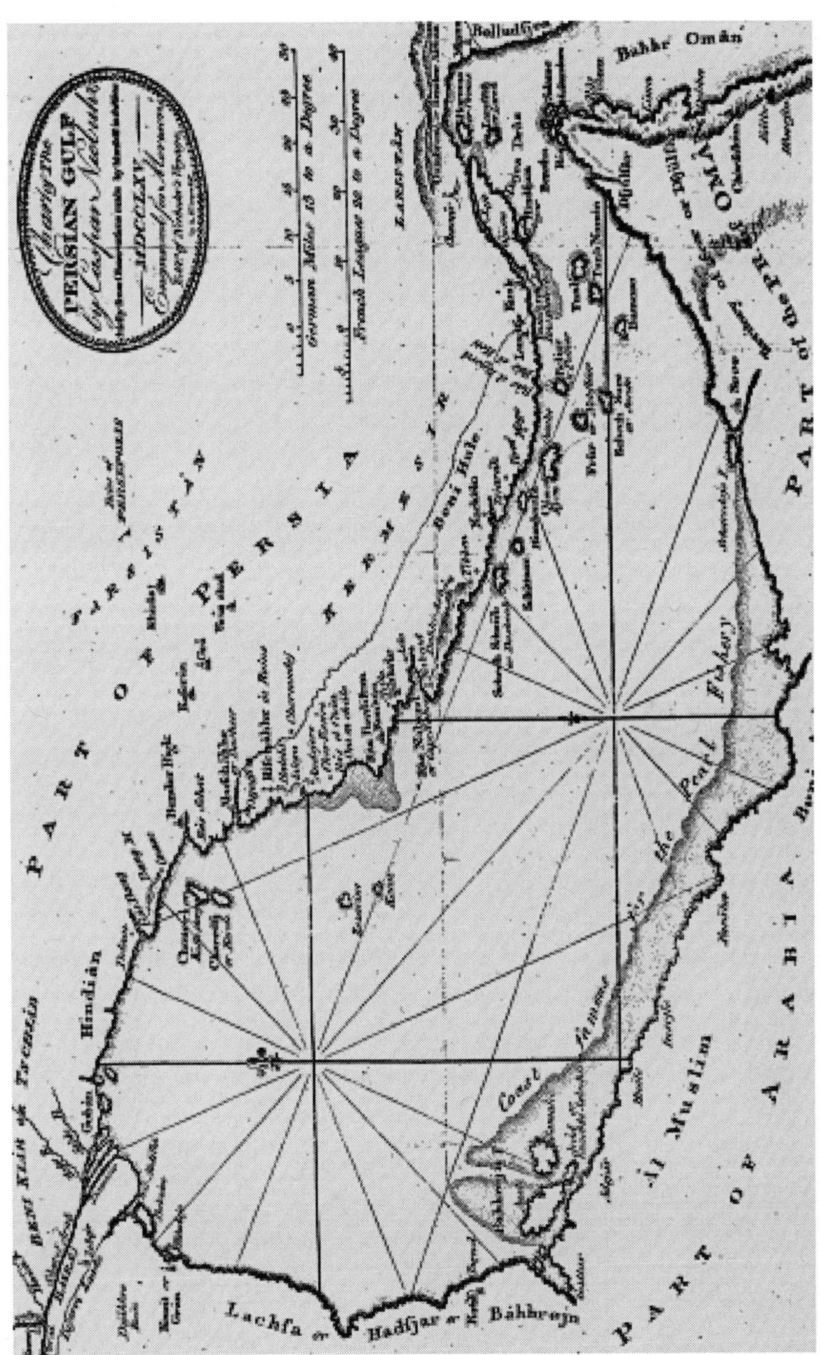

Map of the Persian Gulf by Niebuhr

The Arabic language has, from the circumstances here enumerated [conquest by Arabs], become the language of Egypt: But, in the mouths of the Egyptians, and those vagabond Bedouins, it displays little of its genuine purity. Mr. Forkal left a long list of words used at Cairo, which differ entirely from the words expressive of the same ideas in the dialect of Yemen. The last, being the dialect of a province shut up in a manner from strangers, and therefore not liable to be debated by any infusion of foreign idioms, is to be regarded as the test of the other dialects. That of Egypt is contaminated with forms of expression from all the diversity of languages which the vicissitudes of its fortune and the diversity of its inhabitants have occasionally introduced into that country.

Regarding the dress of women

All the women in the East wear drawers, even where the men do not wear breeches. The poorer sort wear nothing but those drawers, and a long blue shirt. But, although in this manner half-naked, they all, without exception, wear veils.

The veil seems to be the most important piece of their dress: their chief care is always to hide their face. There have been many instances of women, who, upon being surprised naked, eagerly covered their faces, without showing any concern about their other charms. The Egyptian peasants never give their daughters shirts till they are eight years of age. We often saw little girls running about quite naked, and gazing at us as we passed: None, however, had her face uncovered; but all wore veils. The veil, so indispensable a piece of dress with the female sex, is a long, triangular piece of linen cloth, fixed to the head, and falling down before, so as to cover the whole face, except the eyes.

Of the so-called diversions of the Orientals

The climate, customs, and government, conspire to give the manners of the Orientals a melancholy cast. Their seriousness is increased by the want of social intercourse, from which they are secluded by means of that jealousy which hinders them from admitting one another into their houses. They are silent, because, when shut up with their women, where they have few topics of conversation, they unavoidably acquire habits of taciturnity. As power is confined to a few hands, and industry oppressed by Government, the subjects of the Eastern despots naturally become gloomy and languid for want of employment; and the more so, for their being unacquainted with letters, or with the fine arts, which afford the best relief from the *tedium* of such a life.

In the evening, the great generally shut themselves up in their harem. We know not what passes in these solitary retreats: But, as the women of the East are excessively ignorant, and merely great children, it is very probable that the amusements of the harem are extremely childish. Some hints which have occasionally escaped from husbands of my acquaintance confirm me in this opinion.

Over great parts of Asia, the Persian pipe is used, which by passing the smoke through water, renders it [tobacco] milder, and more agreeable to those who swallow it. In Egypt, the Persian pipe is nothing but a cocoa nutshell, half filled with water, with two stalks, one communicating with the bole, the other entering the mouth of the person who smokes. *Kerim-Kan*, the present *Schah* in the south of Persia, seems to distinguish himself at his amusement; for the pipe that is most in fashion, is called, after him, a *Kerim-Kan*.

Suez region

Ship-building is the chief employment of the inhabitants of Suez: Although wood, and iron, and all the other materials, are to be brought from Cairo upon camels, and are, of consequence, very dear. I know not the precise number of vessels annually employed in the navigation between this port and Jidda [in Yemen]: I was informed that four or five are freighted by the Sultan with corn for Mecca and Medina, which they convey to Jidda and Jambo; and that fourteen others serve to carry passengers between Jidda and Suez. The ships built at Suez have a very awkward rudder, made of a large beam, the use of which is dangerous and inconvenient. I saw a vessel in this harbor of a different construction, which had been built at Surat. So durable was the wood of which it was formed, that, although it had been in constant use for twenty years, it was still in a perfectly sound state.

From a trip to Mount Sinai

During their [Arab guides] absence, we met with a young Arab, riding on a dromedary [single-humped camel], who had made himself drunk in one of those gardens. Understanding that we were Europeans and Christians, he began to pour out abusive language against us much in the same strain in which an insolent and ill-bred young man in Europe might perhaps wantonly abuse a Jew. From this incident, we judged that the Bedouins use wine. We could not help remarking, at the same time, that the law of Mahomet, with great wisdom, forbids the use of strong liquors, as they have such tendency to warm the passions, which, with the inhabitants of hot climates, have naturally but too much violence. In the cities, indeed, many of the Mahometans are in the habit of getting drunk. But, either for shame, or for fear of punishment, they never appear drunk in public; and take this vicious indulgence only in private, in their own houses. Except that young man, I never saw another Mahometan brutally drunk, in all my travels.

Niebuhr traveling in the desert

Travels in Yemen

The preparation for our journey were easily made. We hired two asses, and the owner attended us on foot, as our guide, our servant, and occasionally our interpreter. We had already large beards in the Arab fashion; and these, with our long robes, gave us a very oriental appearance. To disguise ourselves still more, each of us assumed an Arabic name; and, under these pretensions, our real condition was so perfectly concealed, that even the owner of the asses thought us Christians of the East; and had no suspicion that we were Europeans. In this garb, and attended by the ass-hirer, we set out on the twenty-sixth of March, from Beit el Fakih.

Except the immediate neighborhood of Udden, the whole tract of country through which we traveled in this excursion is thinly peopled. But the territory of the town is so much the more populous, on account of the abundant produce of its coffee-trees, which is esteemed as the very best coffee in all Arabia.

The Arabs of Yemen, and especially the Highlanders, often stop strangers, to ask whence they come, and whither they are going. These questions are suggested merely by curiosity; and it would be indiscreet therefore to refuse an answer. We told them commonly, that we came from Fschau, the north; which led them to imagine, that we were Turks from Syria. When asked whether we were Turks, we replied that we were Massara; and they then supposed us Greeks or Armenians. We concealed our country, lest we should have exposed ourselves still more to the impertinence of their curiosity. The mistress of the coffeehouse supposed us to be Turkish clergymen, and recommended herself to our prayers. At Dsjobla a man saluted me by the name of Hadji Achmed; taking me for an old acquaintance.

Through the whole of this journey, we were not once seized for passports, or required to pay duties of any sort, nor subjected to any of those difficulties, which, even in Europe, are so generally troublesome to travelers. Although it was in Ramadan, we still found our ordinary food, even in the most solitary coffee-houses; and, in the towns, gave no offense, when we purchased those articles which we preferred, in open day.

In court in Yemen

In Turkey no person is admitted to an audience of the Sultan, till after he has visited the Vizier. The custom in Yemen is directly contrary. . . . We were at the same time desired to bring with us those curiosities which we had shown to Emir Farhan at Loheia, and to several Arabs of distinction in other cities. Those rarities were only microscopes, telescopes, prospect glasses, thermometers, maps, and other such things. I did not choose to produce my mathematical instruments, lest perhaps some Schech [Sheik] might persuade the Vizier to ask them for his use.

The Vizier received us with great politeness, and expressed himself highly pleased with what we showed him. He put various questions to us, from which he appeared to possess considerable knowledge, and to have studied the sciences with a degree of care far more common among his countrymen. By means of Turkish, Persian, and Indian merchants, he had acquired tolerably correct notions of geography. The Arabians imagine that Europe lies south from them, because the Franks whom they see, come from India. But the *Fakih* knew very well the situation of the different states of Europe, with their respective powers and force both by sea and land.

Of the countryside around Sana

Jews are not permitted to live in the city of Sana. They live by themselves in a village named Kao el Ibud, situated near Bir el Assah. Their number amounts to two thousand. But, in Yemen, they are treated even more contemptuously than in Turkey. Yes, the best artisans in Arabia are Jews; especially potters and goldsmiths, who come to the city, to work in their little shops by day, and in the evening retire to their village.

Those Jews carry on a considerable trade. . . . The disgrace of Orceki [a prominent Jew from Sana] had drawn a degree of persecution upon the rest of the Jews. At that period, the government ordered fourteen synagogues, which the Jews had at Sana, to be demolished.

Words on social life

We imagine in Europe, that the inhabitants of the East keep Eunuchs for the guardians of their harems: yet Eunuchs are not common through the East, and in Arabia there are none. The Turkish Monarch keeps more Eunuchs in his seraglio at Constantinople than are in all the rest of his dominions. The Pasha of Aleppo had two, and he of Mosul one, whom he kept, because he had belonged to his father. It is wrong, therefore to regard Arabia as the seat of Eunuchism. They are brought from Upper Egypt, but are mostly natives of the interior and little known provinces of Africa. The Arabians abhor the cruel operation which is requisite to render a man a fit guardian of the chastity of a harem.

Manners of the Hindoos [Hindus]

[Niebuhr made it from Arabia to India on an English ship]

The Hindoos are the primary inhabitants of the vast empire of Indostan [India]. Having lived among these people at Bombay and Surat, I shall here bring together some observations which I made upon the Hindoos in those two cities, and also upon the Persees, a stranger colony settled in this part of India.

This people, perhaps the earliest civilized nation in the world, are mild, laborious, and naturally virtuous in their dispositions. All who have opportunities of observing the lives of Hindoos, admire their patience, probity, and benevolence; but they are at the same time the most unsocial people in the world. By their manners and religious principles, the Hindoos detach themselves not only from other nations, whom they consider as impure races; but even the different casts or tribes of themselves have little mutual intercourse. No Hindoo will eat with a stranger; nor any Hindoo of a superior cast with another of a cast that is inferior. A poor servant, if a *Bramin*, would think himself dishonored by sitting down at able with a *Rajaput* or *Banian*, although his master.

It is generally known, that the Indians are distributed into a number of tribes or casts. As far as I could learn, there are four principal casts; the *Bramins*, or priests; the *Rajapats*, or men of the sword; the *Banians*, or merchants; and that of the artisans and laborers. These four general casts are subdivided into more than 80 others, each of which has its own ceremonies, and patron deities, as I have been assured by several persons.

Those permanent divisions have led some travelers into the mistake that the son was always obliged to embrace his father's profession. The son may not quit his native cast, but may choose among the employments which are practiced by that cast. . . . This custom hinders strangers from being naturalized among the Hindoos, or embracing their religion; and there is no people less inclined to make proselytes. But it is their rigorous observation of their ancient laws of separation which has reduced these people to their present humiliated state. If, at the time of the conquest, the Hindoos had suffered the Tartars to incorporate with the vanquished nation; the conquerors must have adopted the manners and the religion of their new subjects. Their conduct in China give probability to this idea [Mongol conquest and the acculturation of the Yuan Empire under Kublai Khan in China]. But the Hindoos expressing so great an aversion for their new masters, made them prefer Mahometism, and forced them to bring in from time to time foreign Mahometans, to govern the conquered people. Since that period, the Hindoos have been an abject herd of slaves, subject to the vexatious oppression of a despot who returns the contempt which they have expressed for him.

The power of the Mahometans indeed becomes daily less; and there are at present some Hindoo princes who may restore the nation to its ancient splendor. The Mahrattas have successfully begun a project which has this aspect. It is the exorbitant power of the English that at present retards the progressive improvement of the Hindoos. But, when this colossal statue, whose feet are of clay, and which has been raised by conquering merchants, shall be broken in pieces, an event which may fall out sooner than is supposed, then shall Indostan become again a flourishing country.

In almost all the circumstances of their mode of life, the Hindoos distinguish themselves from the rest of mankind. Their usual diet consists of rice, milk, and fruits. The law, however, which forbids them to eat animal food, seems to have been rather suggested by the climate, than by religious consideration. The Rajaputs eat mutton [flesh of sheep], as well as the flesh of some other animals; but all the casts alike respect the cow, and abstain from eating beef.

The Hindoos still retain the practice of burning their dead. But the European and Mahometan governments prohibit, and the Mahrattas seldom allow the living wife to burn herself on the funeral pile of her deceased husband. A Bramin told me, that his family had been highly distinguished, by his grandmother having, in honor of her virtue, obtained permission to burn herself with her husband.

Discussion Points for *Travels Through Arabia*

1. What sorts of differences do you see between the peoples of Constantinople, Cairo, Yemen, and Bombay?
2. How did Niebuhr describe the treatment of Jews in Arabia? How was that in comparison with how Jews in Europe fared (according to Niebuhr and your own knowledge of anti-Semitism and the Holocaust)?
3. Do you think his view of Hindus was more negative or positive than his view of Muslims?
4. How do you think he was able to pretend to be from the Middle East despite being from northern Europe? Do you believe that his dress, accent, and mannerisms were good enough for him to blend in or do you attribute his success more to ignorance of outsiders by those in Yemen?
5. Describe how Niebuhr interacted with the peoples of the Middle East. Do you think he exaggerated his descriptions?

SECOND READING:

Charles M. Doughty, *Travels in Arabia Deserta* (New York: Random House, 1921).

In his introduction to this volume, the famous Arabian traveler and agent, T.E Lawrence, praised Charles Doughty as the "classic," whose "insight, judgment and artistry" enamors respect. Doughty was, for Lawrence, "a great member of the second, cleaner class," because he claimed never to be "oriental, though the sun made him an Arab." Moreover, his "seeing" was "altogether English" but at the same time, "his externals, his manners, his dress, and his speech were Arabic, and nomad Arab, of the desert."[21] Such men who longed not only to travel but also to attempt assimilation indeed conjures an image of a sympathetic and thoroughly detailed account.

From Damascus on the hajj

I thought the stars were so disposed that I should not go to Arabia; but, said my Moslem friends, "the Pasha himself could not forbid any taking this journey with the caravan; and though I were a Nasrany, what hindered! When I went not down to the Harameyn (two sacred cities), but to Medain Salih; how! I an honest person might not go, when there went down every year with the Haj [pilgrimage to Mecca] all the desperate cutters of the town." . . . There is every year a new stirring of this goodly Oriental city in the days before the Haj; so many strangers are passing in the bazaars, of outlandish speech and clothing from far provinces. The more part are of Asia Minor, many of them bearing over-great white turbans that might weigh more than their heads; the most are poor folk of a solemn countenance, which wander in the streets seeking the bakers' stalls, and I saw that many of the Damascenes could answer them in their own language.

Not distance from hence are proud Greekish ruins of Philadelphia, now *Amman* [currently, the capital city of Jordan], anciently *Rabbath* (the metropolis of) Amman; the place, in a small open valley ground, I found to be less than the site of some very inconsiderable English town. A Roman bridge, of one great span, rides the river, which flows from a mighty spring head, little above, of lukewarm water. "Why gloriest thou (says Jeremy) in thy valleys, thy flowing valley?" The kingdom on Ammon was as one of our countries; hardly threescore small townships and villages. A few miles southward I found in some cornfields, which are tilled from the near-lying *es-Salt*, a sumptuous mausoleum (el-Kasr) of white crystalline limestone blocks; within are ranged sarcophagi of the same marble and little less than that great bed of Og which lay at the next town. Such monuments of old civil glory are now an astonishment to our eyes in a land of desolation and of these squalid Arabs.

We were to depart betimes by the morrow, some enquiring of the hour; "At cannon's word," answered a laughing Damascene of the Haj service. That shot is eloquent in the desert night, the great caravan rising at the instant, with sudden untimely hubbub of the pilgrim thousands; there is a short struggle of making ready, a calling and running with lanterns, confused roaring and ruckling of camels, and the tents are taken up over our heads. In this haste aught left behind will be lost, all is but a short moment and the pilgrim army is remounted. . . . Hot tea, ready in glasses, is served with much sugar, in the Persian lodgings, also the slave will put fire in their nargilies (water-pipes) which they "drink," holding them in their hands, as they ride forward. Hajjies on horseback may linger yet a moment, and overtake the slow-footed train of camels. There are public coffee sellers which, a little advanced on the road, cry from their fires to the passengers, *Yellah! Yellah! Yellah! Yesully aly Mohammad, Allah karim*, which is "Come on, the Lord bless Mohammed, the Lord is bountiful." So in all things the Semites will proffer God's name whether for good or for evil.

And there is a third lesser camp of Greek Christians which, of late times, are suffered to dwell here in Beduin country, at the gate of Arabia; but they are less worthy and hospitable than the Moslems, their formal religion is most in pattering and dumb superstition. They have a church building of St. George: a lickdish peasant priest and another Syrian his deacon are their clergy. It is strange here to see the Christian religion administered in the tents of Kedar! I could not find that these gospellers had any conscience of the sanctity of Christ's lore: to the stronger Moslems I would sooner resort, who are of frank mind and, more than the other, fortified with the Arabian virtues. Nevertheless Mohammadens esteem of the Christians and their priests' faith, in the matter of a deposit; this is ever their fantasy of the Nasara. . . . Mohammed has made every follower of his, with his many spending and vanishing wives, a walker upon quicksands; but Christ's religion contains a man in all, which binds him in single marriage. The Moslem town-sheykh deals tolerantly with them, they are part of his "many," but the Christians complain of vexations; they are all rude men together.

The Mountain of Edom

Here the 19–20 November our tents were stiffened by the night's frost. Mount Seir or J. Sherra before us (*sherra* is interpreted high), is high and cold, and the Arabs' summer clothing is as nakedness in the winter season. The land is open, not a rock or tree or any bush to bear off the icy wind; it is reported, as a thing of late memory, that wayfaring companies and their cattle have starved, coming this way over in the winter months. In the night they perished together, and the men were found lying by the cold ashpits of their burnt-out watch-fires. Not far from this wady [valley or dry riverbed], in front, begins that flint beach, which lies strewn over great part of the mountain of Esau; a stony nakedness blackened by the weather: it is a head of gravel, whose earth was wasted by the winds and secular rains.

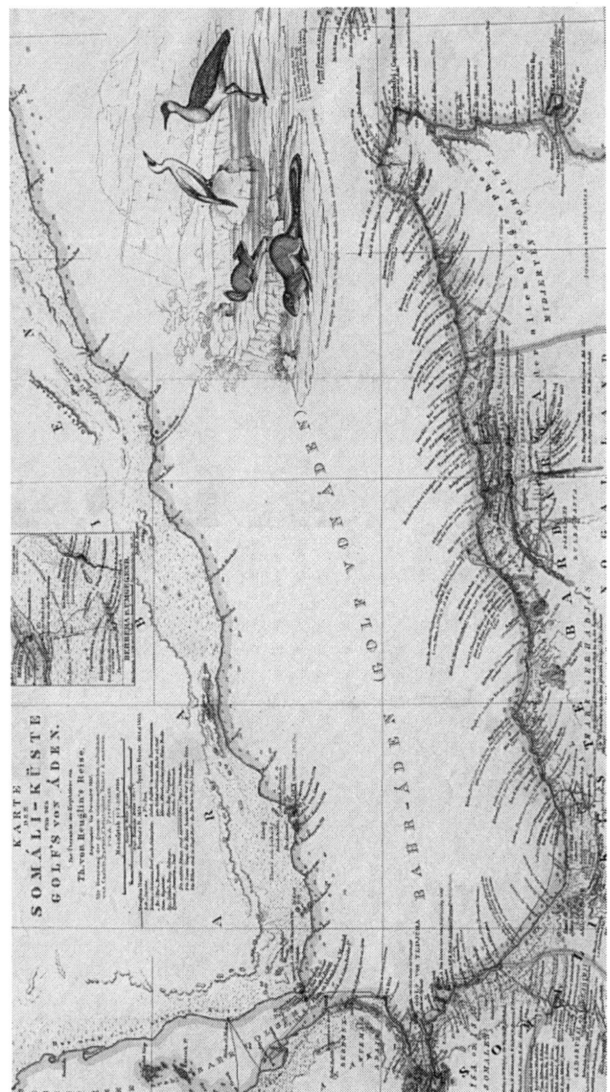

Gulf of Aden

Of the Bedouins

[T]hey all day take God's name in vain (as it was perhaps in ancient Israel). . . . To speak of the Arabs at the worst, in one word, the mouth of the Arabs is full of cursing and lies and prayers; their heart is a deceitful labyrinth. We have seen their urbanity; gall and venom is in their least ill-humor; disdainful, cruel, outrageous is their malediction. "Curse Allah, thy father (that is better than thou), the father of the likes of thee! burn thy father! this is a man fuel for hell-burning! bless thee not God! make thee no partaker of His good! thy house fall upon thee!" I have heard one, in other things a very worthy man, in such form chide his unruly young son: "Allah rip up that belly in thee! Curse the father (thy body) of that head and belly! Punish that hateful face!" And I have heard one burden another thus: "Curse thee all the angles, curse thee all the Moslems, let all the heathen curse thee!" The raging of the tongue is natural to the half-feminine Semitic race.

Driven from town

Driven thus from Aneyza, I was in great weariness; and being here without money in the midst of Arabia, I mused of the Kenneyny, and the Bessam, so lately my good friends!—Could they have forsaken me? Would Kenneyny not send me money? and how long would this people suffer me to continue amongst them? Which of them would carry me any whither, but for payment? and that I must begin to require for my remedies, from all who were not poor: it might suffice me to purchase bread—lodging I could obtain freely. I perceived by the grave looking of the better sort, and the side glances of the rest, when I told my name, that they all knew me. "To-morrow will be time for these enquiries." I heard the emir himself say under his breath, 'they would send me to the Helalieh, or the Bukerieh.—Their coffee was of the worst: my Khubbera hosts seemed to be poor householders. When the coffee-server had poured out a second time the company rose to depart.

Only old Aly remained. He crept over where I was, and let himself down on his hands beside the hakim; and gazing with his squalid eyeballs enquired, if with some medicine I could not help his sight? I saw that the eyes were not perished. "Ay, help my father! said the emir, coming in again; and though it were but a little yet that would be dear to me."

Ibrahim was one of the many East Nejders that, some years before, went down to dig for wages in the work of the Suez Canal: he thought there were two hundred men from el-Kasim. And he had seen, in that enterprise, "the peoples of the Nasara."—French, Italians, Greeks, whom he supposed to speak one language! Some parcels of the Canal had been assigned to petty undertakers: Ibrahim wrought in the service of a Frankish woman; and the wife-man, he said, with pistols in her belt, was a stern overseer of her work-folk. There was a Babel of nations, a concourse of men of every hard and doubtful fortune:—and turbid the tide-rips of such an host of adventuring spirits on the shoals! Moslem and Christians—especially the fanatical Oriental Greeks (*er-Rum*) were mingled together; and peaceable men were afraid to stray from their fellowships. He saw in these natural enmities only a war of religions: "It was the Rum, he pretended—they had the most arms—that set upon the Moslem." The Greeks are execrated by el-Islam in those parts; so that even among nomads of the Sinai coast I have heard a man say to his adversary—using the Frenjy word, "Thou are worse than a *Greco*!" These disorders were repressed, Ibrahim said, with impartiality, by the Egyptian soldiery.

Of the Wahabis

"Three hundred" were fallen of Saud's men; his few tents and the stuff were in the power of Ateyba: and the shorn Wahaby wolf returned as he might over the deserts, to er-Riath. By the loss of the horses the Wahaby rule, which has lasted an hundred years, was weakened to death; never—such is the opinion in Nejd—to rise again! Founder of the Wahaby reform was one Mohammad ibn Abdel-Wahab, a studied religious elder, sojourning in the oasis *eth-Ther'eyyeh*, in East Nejd; and by blood a Temimy or, as some report, of Annezy: he won over to his puritan doctrine the Emir of the town, a warlike man, *Saud ibn Abd-el-Aziz*. The new Wahaby power grew apace and prevailed in Nejd: in the first years of this age they victoriously occupied the Hejaz! Then Mohammad Aly, the Albanian ruler of Egypt, came with a fleet and an army as "the Sultan's deputy, to deliver the Harameyn."—We have seen Ibrahim Pasha, his son, marching through the midst of Arabia. After leaving Aneyza, he took and destroyed eht-Ther'eyyeh which was not afterward rebuilt: but the Wahabies founded their new clay metropolis at "the Rauthas" (er-Riath). When they had rest from the Egyptian expeditions, they ruled again in all Nejd and desert Arabia, as far as el-Yemen; and the Gulf coast towns yielded tribute: but the Wahaby came no more into the Hejaz.—We heard an unlikely rumor, that the Gulf Province el-Hasa, occupied by the Turks, had been ceded by them to the Wahaby (under tribute).

The Wahaby rulers taught the Beduin to pray; they pacified the wilderness: the villages were delivered from factions; and the people instructed in letters. I found it a reproach in Aneyza to be named Wahaby.

On social relations

He [an old merchant] answered, "There are adulteries and fornication among them, secretly."

We should think their harem less modest than precious. The Arabs are jealous and dissolute: and every Moslem woman, since she may be divorced with a word, fears to raise even a wondering cogitation in such matter. Many poor harem could not be persuaded by their nearest friends, who had called the hakim, to fold down so much of the face-cloth from their temples as to show me their blear eyes. A poor young creature of the people was disobedient to her mother, sooner than discover a painful swelling below the knee. Even aged negro women [here they too go veiled], that were wall-eyed with opthalmia, would not discover their black foreheads in hope of some relief. And they have pitifully answered for themselves, "It is be not the Lord's will here, yet should they receive their sight—where miserable mankind hope to inherit that good which they have lacked in this world!"

Intense desert heat

About nine o'clock we came to the oasis-village *ed-Doeh*; and alighted a little without the place, at a new 'usha; which had been built by a rich man, for the entertainment of passengers.—The good Sherif, careful for my health by the way, had charged Nasir to bring me to the houses of worthy and substantial persons; to journey always slowly, and if at any time they saw me fainting in the saddle, they were to alight there. The cabin was of studs and fascine-work a foot in thickness, firmly bound and compacted together; and the walls, four-square below, were drawn together, in a lofty hollow overhead. My companions thought that our pleasant 'usha, which was a sure defense from the sun and not small, might have cost the owner a dozen crowns (less than 3 British Pounds). By the village is a spring, where the long-veiled women of the country, bearing pitchers of an antique form set sidewise on their heads, come to draw water.

The altitude was now only 1100 feet. We felt cool as we sat in our shirts in the doorless 'usha, with a breathing wind, yet I found 102 ° F. A field-servant of the household—a thick-set, great-bearded husband-man from Tayif—who had brought us out the mat and cushions, wiping his forehead each moment exclaimed, "Oh! this Tehama heat!" The valley is here dammed by three basaltic bergs (*Mokesser, Th'af, Sidr*) from the north wind; and quoth the host, who entered, "The heat is now such in W. Fatima, that the people cannot eat: wellah there is no traveling, after the sun is up." I asked What were the heat at Jiddha? "*Ouf*! he Answered, insufferable." *Nasir*: "Khalil, hast thou not heard what said Saud ibn Saud when—having occupied Mecca—he laid siege to Jidda [1803]; and could not take the place: 'I give it up them, I cannot fight against such a hot town: surely if this people be not friends, they are nigh neighbors to the devil.'"

Traveling to Jidda

We remounted . . . and rode half an hour in a plain: and fell then into the *derb es-sultany*, or highway betwixt Mecca and the port town of Jidda.—Long trains of camels went by us, faring slowly upward; and on all their backs sat half-naked pilgrims, girded only in the *ihram*. They were poor hajjies of India and from el-Yemen, that had arrived yesterday at Jidda: and they went up thus early in the year to keep the fasting month, with good devotion, in the Holy City.—I saw, in the morning twilight, that the W. Fatima mountains lay now behind us [they may be seen from Jidda], and before us an open waste country (*khobt*), of gravel and sand,—which lasts to the Red Sea. . . . Not much beyond is a coffee-house: there is a Kahwa at every few miles' end, in this short pilgrim road.

Then I saw by the highway-side a great bank of stones; which now encroaches upon the road. "Every hajjy, said my companions, who casts a stone thereon has left a witness for himself; for his stone shall testify in the resurrection, that he fulfilled the pilgrimage."—The wilderness beside the way is grown up with certain bushes, *reym*; and Nasir said, 'Thee berries, with the beans of the sammar (acacia) are meat of the apes whose covert is the thicket of yonder mountain!" We saw a lizard, a yard in length, which carries his tail bent upwards like the neck of a bird. The road now rises from the Wady ground: and we soon after descended to a Kahwa and dismounted; and leaving our thelûls [camels] knee bound, we went-in to pass the hot hours under the public roof.—Whilst the landlord, a pleasant man, was busy to serve us, I drew back my hot kerchief. But the good soul, seeing the side-shed hair of a Frenjy! caught his breath, supposing I that I arrived thus foothot from Mecca. Then smiling, he said friendly, "Be no more afraid! for here all peril is past."

Discussion Points for *Travels Through Arabia Deserta*

1. What sort of observer do you think the author was? Did his travels through Arabia seem to compare well with Niebuhr's story?
2. What does his description of the natural environment tell you about the way people in the Middle East dressed and lived? How did he seem to adapt?
3. Coffeehouses seemed rather common; what sorts of things might have happened there and why do you think there were no taverns or restaurants for travelers?
4. What seems significant from his short description of Muslim women? Do you think things have changed much since the late 1800s? In Yemen? In Turkey? In Jordan, or Egypt? Explain.
5. What influence in the Arab world do the Wahhabis have today? How did the author see the Wahhabis and how do people today understand this view of Islam?

Third Reading:

John Windus, *A Journey to Mequinez; The Residence of the Present Emperor of Fez and Morocco* (Dublin: George Ewing, 1725).

Arabia for the European of the eighteenth century accounted for a large swath of the world. Almost any Muslim—Turk, Moor, Arab, or Persian—fitted into a generalized European description of blind followers of Mohammad's strange faith. Contact between North Africa and Europe was long-standing and peoples well versed in each others' customs. Yet, because the people of Morocco were predominately Muslims, they were part of another world, a place inhabited by different customs, pirates and eunuchs, veiled women, and ruthless despots. Members of the British delegation to Morocco in 1721 should not therefore have been surprised by their cultural contacts, but again we see the generalities of the exotic as a sort of lazy exercise in self-justification. In fact, the author noted in his preface that the "Country I write of is very little known to us, whatever intercourse we seem to have had with it; and tho' we have been pretty well accustomed to see its Natives in our Streets." To prove the value of his book, John Windus noted how much it was in their "Interest to be better acquainted with it."[22]

Memoirs from a former diplomat to the court in Morocco named Corbiere, buttressed Windus's account by adding observations of the land and its peoples. The Barbary Coast was important, of course, because of the piracy that had flourished in its ports. With irregular allegiance to the Ottoman Sultan, this area was truly a frontier on the fringes of the Muslim world. As the original spearhead of Islam into Europe through Spain, the North African coast controlled trade in the Western Mediterranean and had a thriving exchange with the peoples of the Sahel, just south of the Saharan Desert. Salt, gold, and other African goods such as ivory came overland across Africa, even after the Portuguese explored the western African coastline in the 1400s. Morocco was in an enviable position but the issue of piracy—a lucrative trade winning prizes worth millions in today's dollars—redirected the attention of European powers in the 1700s. As we see here in this account, the British signed a treaty to avoid more losses from sea-borne raids. Interesting to note, too, was the prevalence of European sailors who served as slaves after capture. Voltaire's famous *Candide* mocked such occurrences and noted the European attitude towards the "barbarous" pirates who murdered, raped, and conducted violence.[23] Not all the trading powers in the Mediterranean paid off or signed treaties with the Moroccan leadership. During his early years as president, Thomas Jefferson ordered the United States Navy to sail to the North African coast and force the Barbary pirates into submission. Not without losses, the Navy eventually proved victorious; the USS *Constitution*, one of the participating ships, remains today in the Charleston Navy Yard, in Boston, Massachusetts. War against the pirates of Tripoli showed an early instance of American foreign policy that would ostensibly serve the greater good and usher a new era in global politics.

From the preface

The People of this Country are of two sorts; one consists of *Berebbers* [Berbers], (as they call themselves) or Barbarians properly so named, who chiefly dwell in Huts upon *Atlas*, and other Mountains, are the old Natives; and by not being entirely subdued to this Day, have kept their own Customs both Civil and Domestic; and their Language called *Shilha*, supposed to be the ancient *Punick* or *Carthaginian*, which, I think, would greatly deserve being particularly inquired into.

The other sort of Inhabitants are the Arabians, who cultivate the Plains, move (as they ever did) from Place to Place, dwell in Tents, and make what was formerly called Pecunia, (or Cattle) and Corn, their principal Wealth. These also are particularly tenacious of their ancient ways, and of their Language, both which, as far as we can learn from History, they have preserved with very little Alteration near two thousand Years.

They are the Race of Men who after having over-run a large Tract of *Asia*, and all the Northern Parts of *Africa* from East to West, did, in the Space of three Years, subdue the whole Kingdom of Spain, which they were forced to quit after a Possession of seven hundred Years, and retire into those Parts that are now under the Emperor of *Morocco's* Subjection, and then belonged to Men of their own Race and Religion. They are the People who stood the fairest, of any since the *Romans*, for universal Monarchy, who pushed their Conquests with incredible Rapidity, during those Ages when Christendom was involved in Dissensions, Bigotry and Ignorance; and then it was they who taught the World all Arts and Sciences, by reviving the Mathematics and translating into their own Language, the best *Greek* and *Roman* Books. But now they are the very People whom, since their Expulsion out of *Spain*, we have justly called Barbarous, from their Cruelty, Pride, and Inveteracy against the Christian Name, and are as famous for their Craft and Insincerity, as the old *Africans* were reckoned by the *Romans*; and being no less idle than ignorant, they have little troubled themselves for many Years pass, but to exert their hatred to the Christians, and to enrich themselves by the Number of Slaves they made amongst them; 'till the Emperor, within these thirty Years, assumed to himself the Property in all Slaves whatever, and even attempted to make every one of his Subjects such in Name, which they are in Reality.

First days on the Barbary Coast

[T]he Emperor [of Morocco] had sent from his Court one *Moses Ben Hattar*, a *Jewish* Merchant, who had been often employed in the former Treaties, and was a Person more artful and interested than any other in the Country . . . to make the Negotiation successful. . . .

Sunday the 7th. the Ambassador went to visit the Basha in his Tent, who renewed his kind Expressions towards the *English* and his Desire that the Ambassador should find every Thing agreeable to him. After that, as we were walking about to see the Camp, we had an Instance of *Ben Hattar's* unlimited Power of the *Jews*; for he having employed one *Ben Saphat* as his Agent or Factor in *Gibraltar*, round, upon going thither himself, that he had wronged him considerably, reported Things falsely, and dealt unfaithfully in his Commission; wherefore as *Ben Saphat* was not coming down to meet him, before he could get within hearing, *Ben Hattar* ordered him to be strangled, upon which the *Jews* and some *Blacks* belonging to the Emperor immediately ran to him, pulled him off his Mule, and in an Instant stripped off his Clothes, and whipt a Rope about his Neck, which they began to draw, and in that manner bringing him nearer to us, pale and gasping, he cried out to the Ambassador to intercede for him: The Surprise of the Thing kept every Body silent and in suspense what would be the Event; but after *Ben Hattar* had reviled and threatened him, he ordered that he should be carried to Prison, where (as we afterwards heard) he was daily bastonaded, as well for the Fault he had committed, as to make him discover all his Effects, which *Ben Hattar* seized on for his own Use.

Music of Morocco

The Governor had his Music with him, which consisted of four Persons, two of them played upon small Violins; one had a piece of Parchment drawn tight over a little broad Hoop, with pieces of loose Tin on the Sides, which he shook with one Hand, and drummed on it with the other; another beat Time to their Music, by striking the Palm of his Hands together, very loud and well. This part of the Country abounds with fine Oranges, Lemons, Citrons, Olives, Grapes, Figs, Melons, Pomegranets, and Apricocks [apricots].

Drinking habits

The 24th. the Governor and some of the principal *Moors* of the Town, supped with the Ambassador; They not observing the Custom of drinking regularly as we do, but taking all that was given, replenished so much, that some of them could not go down Stairs without Help. The Governor continued his usual good Temper before the Ambassador, but when he got out of Doors, being more overcome by the Liquor, he drew his Cimeter [saber with curved blade] and lay'd about him among his own People, which was certainly owing to the great quantity he had drank; for, when sober, he's of a very mild and sweet Disposition, of which we had several Instances.

The Houses of *Tetuan* [Tetuan, ancient Roman city of Tetuanum, and seat of the Basha, also called Teteguin] are very good, but the Streets exceeding narrow, and hardly any Windows to be seen, but little Holes to look out at, the Light coming in at the inside of the Houses, where there's a Square Court-yard, open at top, with Pillars supporting Galleries, and painted wooden Balustrades round the inside of the House almost like some of our Inns. In the middle of the Court-yard there's a Fountain, if the House belongs to a Person of any Consideration: The Rooms are built long and narrow, and are generally four on a Floor, answering to the Galleries, from whence opens into each Room a large folding Door, by which all the Light that they have is let in. The Houses are but two Stories high, except the Basha's and some few other belonging to particular Men: They are flat at top, so that in many Places they can walk a great way upon them; but those belonging to Christian Merchants have a Battlements, to keep them within the Bounds of their own Houses; for the *Moorish* Women live in the upper Apartments, and often visit one another from the tops of their Houses: They are white-washed on the out-side, as well as within, which casts the Reflection of the Sun so bright, that it hurt our Eyes to continue upon them in the Day-time. They raise not their Walls as most Nations do, by laying Brick or Stone even upon one another, but their way is first to make a strong wooden Café, into which they cast the Mortar, and beating it down hard, take the Café away when it is dry.

The Town is populous and healthful, enjoying a very good Air, but the People poor and next-kin to Slaves, no Man possessing anything but at the Pleasure of the Basha, who is Absolute in his Province, as any Monarch whatsoever, commanding over the Lives and Fortunes of his People, giving or taking away Houses, Land, Horses, or anything just as he pleases; for which Reason, when a Man has acquired Wealth by Trade or Industry, he endeavors to conceal it and seem poor; for if it should come to the Knowledge of the Basha, he would throw him into Prison, and cause him to be bastonaded and tortured, to make him discover all that he has in the World.

The Inhabitants are of a swarthy Complexion, intermixed with a Race of well-looking Men, somewhat fairer than the rest; they generally are lusty, strong-limbed, and, I think, a little out-size the Europeans. They are very good Horsemen, active, hardy, laborious, and needy, so that a Messenger will go from *Tetuan* to *Mequinez* (which is 150 Miles) for a Barbary Ducat, and perform his Journey with great Expedition [speed]: For they are wonderfully patient of Labor, enduring the Heat of Summer, and cold Rains of Winter to Admiration: And when the Ground is all covered with Rain, and a Storm, over-head besides, they'll only look for a Bush, or a great Stone, sit down on their Hams with their Back towards it, and remain in that posture the whole Night, or else wrap themselves up in their Albornooce, and pass the Night upon the Grass. Some of the most famous Footmen of the Country (it is said) will go sixty Leagues [207 miles] in three Days. They swim the Rivers in the depth of Winter, in the Rapidity of the Current doth not deter them: These Men are generally thin, eat but very little, and for seven or eight Days Journey carry only a little Meal, and a few Raisins or Figs in a small Goat's skin.

Women's dress

The Women, when they go abroad [in public], are attired almost like the Men, their outward Garment being an Alhague, with which they cover their Heads, bringing it down over their Foreheads close to their Eyes, and underneath tie a Piece of white Cloth, to hid the lower part of their Face; the Alhagues cover all Parts but their Legs, which generally are naked, when they are at home, or visit from the tops of their Houses; only some of the better sort have their Drawers so long, that the reach to their Feet, hanging in great loose Folds about their Legs; the Shoes are the same as the Mens; within Doors they appear in their Hair, having only a single Binder about their Foreheads; their Hair is pleated in two large Pleats, that hand down behind at full length: They wear a Vest which is open from the Bosom to the Waist, to show their Smocks that are embroidered; they fasten large pieces of Muslin to the Sleeves of their Vests, which hang down very low in the nature of Ruffels; their Drawers are longer than the Men's, reaching to the Calf of their Legs; over their Drawers they wear a short Petticoat; they put Bracelets upon their Legs and Arms, and large Ear-rings in their Ears.

They have very fine Eyes, and some of them beautiful Skins, which we sometimes had an Opportunity of seeing; for tho' a Man many live a Year in *Tetuan*, and not see the Face of a *Moorish* Woman in the Streets, yet when we met them in the Fields, or saw them on the House-tops, if none of the *Moors* were in sight, they would unveil, laugh, and give themselves a little loose, 'till the Appearance of one obliged them to their Faces again.

Adultery is punished with Death; and if a Christian or Jew is found to have to do with a *Moorish* Woman, they must either turn to the Mahometan Religion or be burnt.

Any Man may divorce his Wife (if she was not given him by the Emperor) when he pleases, giving what he agreed (before the Cady) to lay out upon her, and keeping the Children he has by her: The Form is only delivering her a Letter that he has done with her, and she may seek a new Husband. Those who desire to indulge in having many Wives, marry the handsome Daughters of poor Men, by which they avoid the Inconveniency of drawing on themselves the Ill-will of powerful Relations, in case of Divorce, and get rid of them at a small Expense.

Hatred of Christianity

They have a great Hatred for the Name of the Christian; and I have been told by a Gentleman, (who heard them dispute whether a Christian or *Jew* should be most esteemed,) That in their Discourse they urged against the Christians, their eating of Pork, and Meat strangled in Blood, and their not washing as the *Jews* do. . . . And that they may be sure to grow up in Hatred against them, they celebrate a Feast every Year about *St. John's* Day, in memory of some Victory gained over the Christians; at which time the gravest People will be passing thro' the Streets with wooden Horses, Swords, Lances, and Drums, with which they equip the Children that can scarce go and meet in Troops in the Street, and engaging, say, *Thus we destroy the Christians*. They also firmly believe, that those who are killed fighting against them go straight to Heaven, and they deserve no less than an infinite Reward for destroying those Enemies of their Law.

Journey from Tetuan to Mequinez

The 15th. at three in the Afternoon we left Darzerboh, traveling through a mountainous Country, the Road leading us over the Tops of such rocky Hills, that it was difficult to get along: We came to our Tents between six and seven, which were pitched eighteen Miles from our former Camp.

[On the journey they encountered] the flying Villages of the *Arabs*, of which we had this Day past by several: The inhabitants of them seem to live miserably, having but very indifferent Lodgings, their Houses consisting of nothing but Sticks, with a Rosh or Cloth Covering in Imitation of a Tent, moving from place to place for a conveniency of Pasture, and Water. These Towns are generally built in the shape of a Ring, by placing one row of Houses close together, and going round with them 'till they meet, leaving a large vacant space in the inside; in the middle of which there stands a House by itself, which we supposed belonged to their Sheick or Chief, whom they have the Liberty of choosing out of their own Tribes; the Emperor gathering the Tribute from them by a Person whom he lends from Court, and makes an Alcayde [local leader or administrator] for that purpose. These *Arabs* are for the most part very tawny, live nastily with their Cattle and Poultry, and their young Children run about naked; they have abundance of fine black Cattle, which I take to be the Chief of their Substance.

Monday the 3rd. we set forward at four of the Clock in the Morning, the Moon being up, and a little before Sun-rise entered the City, to avoid the prodigious Crowd we should have met with, had the Day been farther advanced, by which means we got to our House with very little Interruption. The Basha of *Tetuan* not having been at Court for three Years, this Morning appeared before the Emperor, to whom he had been accused of being careless of his Government, in letting the *Spaniards* drive him out of his Camp before *Centa*, and was in great danger of his Life; the Emperor severely threatening him, and telling him he was not fit to command; but after he had been sufficiently frightened, he bid him go into the Palace to see a Sister of his, who was one of the Emperor's Women; which he did to send him out of the way, while he vented some part of his Anger on his Followers; for somebody had given him a List of those about the Basha who were most in his Esteem. . . . The next was one of the Basha's Secretaries, whom the Emperor ordered to be tossed, which being a Punishment different from any used in *Europe*, it will not be amiss to give some Account of it.

The Person whom the Emperor orders to be thus punished, is seized upon by three or four strong Negroes, who taking hold of his Hams throw him up with all their Strength, and at the same time turning him around, pitch him down head foremost; at which they are so dexterous by long use, that they can either break his Neck the first Toss, dislocate a Shoulder, or let him fall with less Hurt: They continue doing this as often as the Emperor has ordered it, so that many times they are killed upon the Spot, sometimes they come off with only being severely bruised; and the Person that is tossed must not stir a Limb, if he is able, while the Emperor is in sight, under penalty of being tossed again, but is forced to lie as if he was dead, which if he should really be, nobody dares bury the body 'till the Emperor has given Orders for it.

Religion

He likewise explains the Law to them himself, which they follow according to the Opinion of their Doctor *Melish*, who taught that there is but one God, and *Mahomet* was his chief Prophet, born of a Virgin, whose Name was *Mary*; that he was very holy, and wrought Miracles, but did not die as we believe, for when *Judds* [Judas] betrayed him, God caused one of his Disciples to appear in his likeness, who was crucified in his stead: That there is a Heaven and a Hell, and the eternal Blessings will consist in a fight of the Sovereign Being, of his Angels, and *Mahomet*, in the enjoyment of beautiful Virgins, whose Virginity will daily be renewed, indulging their Appetites with all sorts of delicious Food, which they shall have at a Wish, bathing in Rivers of Milk and Rose-water; and that their Lodgings will be in glorious Palaces, built with Diamonds, Pearls and precious Stones. That Hell will conflict in the extremities of Heat and Cold, and the damned will be created and destroyed every Day.

The *Moors* observe a *Lent* of one Moon, (called *Ramdam* [Ramadan]) abstaining from all manner of Food, 'till the appearance of the Stars; neither are they allowed to smoke, wash their Mouths, take Snuff, smell Perfumes, or converse with their Women.

Those who are obliged to travel, may drink a little Water; and such as are sick may borrow a few Days of their Prophet, but they must and to repay punctually when they recover Strength. In the Towns they run about the Streets, and wake all those People they think are asleep, that they may eat, and so be the better able to support themselves in the Day; they rise three or four times in the Night, and sleep again. Such as are Libertine, and used to drink Wine, abstain from it in this time.

Of slaves

At our coming to Mequinez, there were reckoned to be above 1,000 Christians, about three hundred of which were *English*, not including nineteen who had turned *Moors*; four hundred *Spaniards*, one hundred sixty five *Portuguese*, one hundred fifty two *French*, sixty nine *Dutch*, twenty five *Genoese*, and three *Greeks* of the *Morea*; some of all these different Nations had turned Moors, thereby forever losing hopes of Redemption.

Nor are the Expectation of the rest much better, it being very unlikely that there ever will be a Peace between the *Moors*, and any of the afore-mentioned Nations; tho' there are now and then Treaties of Redemption for them, particularly for the *French* and *Spaniards*, the former of which have Consuls in the Chief Ports, notwithstanding the state of War they are in; and the latter very often a couple of Friars residing at *Tetuan*, besides those I have mentioned belonging to the Convent at *Mequinez*.

And this inhuman Custom of giving Money for the Destruction of another, and also buying a Man to have him entirely at his Disposal, is practiced all over this Empire, both among the *Moors* and *Jews*; whereby the Enjoyment of Life or Fortune is not only precarious, but a Man is liable, in an Instant, to fall into the extremest [*sic.*] degree of Misery, at the pleasure of any one who will be at the expense of buying another, and run the Risk of being reimbursed out of the effects of the person he buys; in which case they go to the Basha, Alcayde or governor of a Province, and bargain with him (for so much Money) to have the Person they have a mind to; upon Receipt of which, the Basha will deliver the Wretch into the Hands of the Buyer, to do what he pleases with him. So that the bought Man is frequently tortured in the cruelest manner, to make him discover what Money he has. For an Instance of which barbarous Custom I have inserted part of a Letter from Mr. Hatfield, an *English* Merchant residing at *Tetuan*.

Trade with Africa

They trade into Guinea with Salt, Cowreys, wrought Silk, about five hundred pieces of British Cloth, and the Woolen Manufactures of Barbary. The Salt, I have been informed, is the chief Commodity, which they keep to rub their Lips with, being apt to corrupt and rot for want of it; and they covet to be rich in having great quantities by them. Cowreys are little Shells brought from the East Indies, and pass for Money of the most value, as bitter Almonds do for the least: Silk and Woolen of Barbary they wear, and tie a small stripe of British Cloth about their Heads, and have no other Consumption for it, tho' five-hundred Pieces go thither yearly. From thence they return richly laden with Gold-dust, Ostrich Feathers, Elephant Teeth, and Negroes, who are the Emperor's Property: This journey is performed in six or seven Months.

The Method of trading in some of those Parts is very extraordinary; for they do not see the Persons they trade with; but passing over a little River, leave their Salt, (at the accustomed Place) in a Pot or Jarr, and retire; then the People take the Salt, and put into the same Pot as much Gold as they judge it worth, which if the *Moor* approve of, they take it away; otherwise, they set the Pot on Edge, and retire again, and afterwards find either more Gold or their Salt returned.

Concerning the treaty between the British and the Emperor of Fez and Morocco

It is agreed, that all Ships and Vessels whatsoever, belonging to the Subjects of the said King of Great-Britain, as also all Ships and Vessels whatsoever, belonging to the King of Fez and Morocco, or to his Subjects, shall freely navigate and pass the Seas, without any Search, Hindrance or Molestation from each other, and that all Persons, or Passengers of what Country or nation soever, as also all Monies, Goods, Merchandizes or Moveables to what People or Nation forever belonging, to either Party, shall be wholly free, and shall not be stopped, taken away, embezzled, or plundered, nor receive any Harm or Damage whatsoever from either Party.

Discussion Points for *A Journey to Mequinez*

1. How do you suppose this treaty affected politics and trade between Great Britain and the Barbary Coast?
2. How did his mission and description fit within other perceptions of Muslims in general? What was different about the people in N. Africa?

3. What affect do you think contact with Europeans had on Morocco? How did the wars in Iberia influence relations?
4. How was trade across the Sahara (with Guinea) conducted and how did it differ from other customs? Do you suppose that Islam traveled to sub-Saharan Africa thanks to the established trade networks?
5. What sorts of relations did the various peoples of the Barbary Coast have (between Jews, Christians, and Muslims)?

City of Fez

Fourth Reading:

William Lithgow, *The Totall Discourse of The Raree Adventures & Painful Peregriniations of the long Nineteene Yeares Travayles from Scotland to the most famous Kingdomes in Europe, Asia and Affrica* (Glasgow: James MacLehose and Sons, 1906).

*Because of the archaic English usage of this text, I have made small updates.

In the early 1600s when William Lithgow ventured forth from Scotland to discover what he termed the Orient, he set out to discuss the situation in the borderlands between Christianity and Islam. With analysis of the Mediterranean region and Turkey, Lithgow's words here show a sort of rejection of Islam's success over the Christian states in Europe. While the Crusades effectively ended centuries earlier, Lithgow here seems to have harkened back to that Crusading spirit whereby nobles, inspired by the pope and commanding armies of commoners, sought to conquer, and, of course, plunder the Holy Land.

Warfare and the Turks

For true it is, the natural Turks were never skillful in managing of sea battles, neither are they expert mariners, nor experienced gunners, if it were not for our Christian renegades, French, English, and Flemings, and they too sublime, accurate, and desperate fellows; who have taught the Turks the art of navigation, and especially the use of munitions; which they both cast to them and then become their chief Cannoniers; the Turks would be as weak and ignorant at sea, as the silly Ethiopian, is unexpert in handling of arms on the Land. For the private humor of discontented castaways is always an enemy to public good, who from the society of true believers, are driven to the servitude of Infidels, and refusing the bridle of Christian correction, they receive the double yoke of despair and condemnation. Whose terror of a guilty conscience, or rather blazing brand of their vexed souls, in forsaking their faith, and denying Christ to be their savior, condemns most of them, either over in a torment of melancholy, otherwise in the ecstasy of madness: which indeed is a torturing horror, that is sooner felt than known; and cannot be avoided by the rudeness of nature, but by saving grace of true felicity.

Island of Cyprus

Twelve days was I between Rhodes and Limisse in Cyprus; where arrived, I received more gracious demonstrations from the islanders, then I could hope for, or wish, being far beyond my merit or expectation; only contenting my curiosity with a quiet mind, I redounded thanks to my embraced courtesies.

The people are generally strong and nimble, of great civility, hospitality to their neighbors, and exceedingly affectionate to strangers. The second day after my arrival, I took with me an interpreter, and went to see Nicosia, which is placed in the midst of the kingdom. But in my journey there, extreme was the heat and thirst I endured; both in respect of the season, and also want of water: And although I had with me sufficiency of Wine, yet durst I drink none thereof, being so strong, and with all had a taste of pitch; and that is, because they have no barrels, but great jars made of earth, wherein their wine is put. And these jars are all enclosed within the ground save only their mouths, which stand always open like to a source or cistern; whose insides are all interlarded with pitch to preserve the earthen vessels unbroken a sunder, in regard of the forcible wine; yet marking the taste thereof unpleasant to liquorous lips; and turneth the Wine, too strong for the brain in digestion, which for health groweth difficult to strangers; and to themselves a swallowing up of disease. Nicosia is the principal city of Cyprus, and is environed with mountains, like until Florence in Etruria; wherein the Beglerebeg remains: The second is Famegusta, the chief strength and sea-port in it: Seilina, Lemisso, Paphos, and Fontant Morosa, are the other four special towns in the land.

This island of Cyprus was of old called Achametide, Amatusa, and by some Marchara, that is happy: It is of length extending from East to West, 210 large 60 and of circuit 600 miles. It yields infinite canes of sugar, cotton-wool, oil, honey, corn, turpentine, aluminum, verdegreece, grogranes, store of metals and salt; beside all other sorts of fruit and commodities in abundance. It was also named Cerastis, because it butted toward the East with one horn: and lastly Cyprus, from the abundance of Cypresse trees there growing. This island was consecrated to Venus, where in Paphos she was greatly honored, termed hence, Dea Cypri.

Cyprus lays in the gulf between Sicily and Syria, having Egypt to the West: Syria to the South: Sicily to the East: and the Pamphilian Sea to the North [these directions, are, of course, incorrect]. . . . The chief and highest mountain on this island, is by the Cypriots called Trohodos, it is of height eight, and of compasse [footprint] forty eight miles, whereon there are a number of religious monasteries, the people whereof are called Colieros, and live under the order of Saint Basile. There is abundance here of Coriander seed, with medicinal rhubarb, and turpentine. Here are also mines of gold in it. . . . The greatest imperfection of this island, is scarcity of water, and too much plenty of scorching heat, and fabulous grounds. The inhabitants are very civil, courteous, and affable; and notwithstanding of their delicious and delicate fare, they are much subject to melancholy, of a robust nature, and good warriors, if they might carry arms. It is recorded, that in the time of Constantine the Great, this island was all utterly abandoned of the inhabitants, and that because it did not rain for the space of six and thirty years. After which time, and to replant this region again, the chief colonies came from Egypt, Judea, Syria, Sicily, Pamphilia, Thrace, and certain territories of Greece: And it is though, in the years 1163 after that Guy of Lusingham, the last Christian King of Jerusalem had lost the Holy Land, a number of Frenchmen, stayed and inhabited there; of whom sprung the greatest race of the Cyprian gentility; and so from them are descended the greatest families of the Phoenician Sydonians, modernly Drusians: though ill divided, and worse declined; yet they are sprung both from one original: the distraction arising from conscience of religion, the one a Christian and other a Turk.

Turkish control of Cyprus

It was under their [Venetian] jurisdiction 120 years and more; till that the Turks, who ever oppose themselves against Christians took it in with a great Armada.

About 1570 and so till this day by them is detained. Oh great pity! that the usurpers of God's word, and the world's great enemy, should maintain (without fear) that famous kingdom, being but one thousand and fifty Turks in all, who are the keepers of it: unspeaking is the calamity of that poor afflicted Christian people under the terror of these infidels; who would, if they had arms, or assistance of any Christian potentate, easily subvert and abolish the Turks, without any disturbance; yea, and would render the whole Signiory thereof to such a noble actor. I do not see in that small judgment, which by experience I have got, but the redemption of that country were most facile; if that the generous heart of any Christian prince, would be moved with condign compassion to relieve the miserable afflicted inhabitants.

William Lithgow

Of the Turkish army

And besides there is another reason of the depopulation of these parts; to wit, when the great Turkish army, is to march to a far country to make wars, then must their vulgar subdued peasants, perhaps twenty or thirty thousands go along with them, to carry their victuals, and all manner of provision, being taken from the plough, and constrained to this servitude, and notwithstanding the half of them never returns again: Partly, because of the change of food, and air, and partly because of their long travel and insupportable service, both in heat and cold: And to these of the first reason, there is another perpendicular cause; to wit, that the whole commerce of all commodities in Turkey, is in the hands of Jews, and Christians, to wit, Ragusans [from Dubrovnik, Croatia], Venetians, English, French, and Flemings, who so warily manage their business, that they enjoy the most profits of trading there, disappointing the Turks own subjects of their due, and ordinary traffic.

The Turks have three things in their Armies which are very fearful, to wit, the infinite number of men, great discipline, and force of munitions: As for discipline, they are not only governed with great silence, and obedience, but they are ruled also with signs of the eye, and being tractable, they are tied to main conducements: And although their multitudes have often bred confusion to them, so that little armies have broke and overcome them; yet in their flight they are so fearless, that a small number can do them no absolute violence nor final overthrow: for as they assail, so they fly without fear.

The Turks have a custom, when they are masters of any province, to exterminate all the native nobility, chiefly these of the blood-royalty of the country: And nevertheless they permit to all and everyone of theirs to live and follow his own religion as he pleases without violence or constraint.

Traveling in Turkey

Among the Turks there is no gentility, nor nobility, but are all as ignoble and inferior members, to one main body the great Turk, lineally descending of the house of Ottoman [Osman]: whose magnificence, puissance, and power is such, that the most eloquent tongue cannot sufficiently declare: His thousands of Janissaries, Shouses, and others daily attending him: which are the nerves and sinews of the warlike body of his whole monarchy and imperial estate: His hundreds (besides his Queen) of Concubines, hourly maintained by his means, and monthly renewed: His armies, bashawes, emirs, viziers, sandjaks, garrisons, and forces here and there dispersed among his dominions, would be impossible for me briefly to relate.

The Persians differ much from the Turks, in nobility, humanity, and activity, and especially in points of religion: who by contention think each other accursed; and notwithstanding both factions are under the Muslim law. Neither are the sons of the Persian kings, so barbarously handled, as their; for all the brethren (one excepted) are only made blind, wanting their eyes, and are always afterward gallantly maintained like princes. And it hath oftentimes fallen out, that some of these kings, dying without procreate heirs; there have of these blind sons succeeded to the empire, who have restored again the seed of that royal family.

And now the great advantage, that the Turks have daily upon the Persians, is only because of their infantry, which the Persians, no ways are accustomed with, fighting always on horseback; neither are the Persians addicted or given to built forts, or fortifications, neither have they any great use of munitions, but exposing themselves ever to the field in the extreme hazard of battle, become ever doubtful in their victories: whose courage and valor cannot be paralleled among all the people of the Eastern world, as Babylon in their late and last fortunes may give sufficient testimony thereof.

Turkish mosques

The Turks have no bells in their churches, neither the use of a clock, numbering of hours, but they have high round steeples, for they contradict all the forms of Christians: when they go to pray, they are called together by the voice of crying men, who go upon the top of their steeples, shouting and crying with a shrill voice: God is a great God, and Mahomet is his Prophet, or otherwise there is but one God.

In Constantinople, and all other places of Turkey, I ever saw three Sabbaths together, in one week: the Friday for the Turks, the Saturday for the Jews, and the Sunday for the Christians: but the Turks' Sabbath is worst kept of all: for they will not spare to do any labor on their Holy Day. . . . In sign of reverence, and in a superstitious devotion, before they go into their Mosques, they wash themselves in a lavatory, beginning at the privy members, next their mouths, faces, feet, and hands. . . .

Of the Turks

The Turks which are born and bred in the lesser Asia, and east parts of Europe, are generally well complexioned, proportionately compacted, no idle nor superfluous talkers, servile to their grand signor, excessively inclined to venery, and zealous in religion: Their heads are always shaven, reserving only one tuft in the top above, by which they think one day to be caught to Heaven by Mahomet, and covered on all sides, counting it an opprobrious thing to see any uncover his head, they wear their beards long, as a sign of gravity, for they esteem them to be wise men, who have long beards: The women are of a low stature, thick and round of growth, going seldom abroad (unless it be each Thursday at night, when they go to mourn upon the graves of their dead friends) and then they are modestly masked: they are fearful and shame-fast abroad, but lascivious within doors, and pleasing in matters of incontinency; and they are accounted most beautiful, who have the blackest brows, the widest mouths, and the greatest eyes.

The other Turks which are born in Asia major, and Egypt, (I speak not of the Moors of Barbary) are of a greater stature, tan, cruel, a barbarous and uncivil people. The better sort use the Slavonian [Slavic] tongue, the vulgar speak the Turkish language, which being originally the Tartarian speech, they borrow from the Persian their words of state, from the Arabic, their words of religion, from the Greeks, their terms of war, and from the Italian their words and titles of navigation.

The puissance of the great Turk is admirable, yet the most part of his kingdoms in Asia, are not well inhabited, neither populous, but these parts which border with Christians, are strongly fortified with castles, people, and munitions: If Christian princes could concord, and consult together, it would be an easy thing in one year, to subdue the Turks, and root out their very names from the earth; yea, moreover, I am certain, that there are more Christians, even slaves and subjects to the great Turk, which do inhabit his dominions, then might overthrow and conquer these infidels, if they had worthy captain, governors and furniture of arms, without the help of any Christian of Christendom [Europe, but Western Europe specifically].

The true Turks wear on their heads white Turbans, save a few that are esteemed to be of Mahomet's kin, and they wear green sashes, being most part of them priests: the better part of the Turks in Asia, care not for fish, but these Turks which remain in Europe love fish better than flesh, especially at Constantinople or Stambol [Istanbul], where the best fish and most abundance of them are taken, that be in the world, and that in the Black Sea: They are ever desirous to seek advantage on their neighbors, which if they cannot by force, they will under color of truce, accomplish it with perfidiousness. And if their enterprises, find no happy event, they are never a wit ashamed to take the flight, yet are they generally good soldiers, and well taught in martial discipline: Their armies in marching, or camping (notwithstanding infinite multitudes) keep modesty and silence, and are extremely obedient unto their captains and commanders: When the great signor is abroad with his army at war, the Turks at home within towns, use great prayers, and fasting for him and them: They ingeniously describe the victories of their ancestors, and joyfully sing them in rhymes and songs; thinking thereby that fashion in recalling the valiant deeds of their predecessors, to be the only means to encourage their soldiers to be hardy, resolute and desperate in all their enterprises: They are not given to contemplation, nor study of letters or arts; yet they have diverse fair schools, where the public lecture of their legal laws are professed, and Muslimize. . . .

It is seldom, and rarely seen, that a Turk will speak with a woman in the streets; nay, not so much as in their Mosques one to be in sight of another; and yet they are Lords and Masters of their wives and concubines, from whom they receive as great respect, service and honor, as from their bond and bought slaves.

Discussion Points for *Totall Discourse of The Raree Adventures*

1. The author noted how Cyprus was divided between the Christian and the Turk—is this the case today, and if so, then why is that important?
2. Can you find any errors in how the author related the religious practices of the Turks?
3. Did the author's description of cross-cultural contact throughout the Mediterranean region add to your understanding of the heterogeneous nature of human existence? Or was it different?
4. Written in the early 1600s, this account represented something of an oddity, as the author seemed to infer that only if the Christian powers of Europe could unite, they could easily defeat the Turks. Do you really think that the Europeans could have beaten the Ottoman Turks so easily or was this just wishful propaganda?
5. What advantages in armed force did the author note of the Turks? How much do you think these things were true?

PART III: TRAVEL TO ASIA AND THE PACIFIC

Asia represented the crown gem in the European mind. Cross-cultural contact and international trade had occurred since the earliest civilizations and yet Europeans regarded the spices, jades, porcelains (during the Ming and Qing Dynasties), silks, and other luxury goods with great enthusiasm. Mongol conquest of Eurasia by Genghis Khan unified much of the overland trading routes and rationalized the exchange of goods from Asia to Europe, which only further excited Europe's idea of the Far East. Although Europe was decidedly poorer than much of Asia, Europe did seek actively to increase the trade networks running East to West. Venetian and Genoese colonists settled in the Black Sea area, and Jewish and Greek diasporas served as important links in the system, whereby goods would arrive in the Levant and then transit to Europe. Of course, what changed this arrangement in Europe was the discovery of an ocean route from Europe to Asia during the 1400s. Portuguese ships had begun sailing down the coast of Africa and deliberately surveyed and explored the land with each new voyage—much of this naturally came about because of the Portuguese desire for gold. As a fabled land rich with gold, the Kingdom of Mali under Mansa Musa (reigned 1312–37) inspired Europeans to design a way to obtain the riches of far-off lands, thanks to the story of his epic pilgrimage to Mecca laden with thousands of slaves and immeasurable riches. Portuguese sailing vessels made great headway and the voyages of Vasco da Gama created for Portugal the chance for global power. Portugal's small size and limited population, though, inhibited large-scale empire; instead, the Portuguese sought entrepôts off the coasts of Africa, India, and China to guarantee a secure trading opportunity abroad.

With Christopher Columbus's expedition to seek a direct westward route to Asia, the Spanish sought to join the Portuguese in overseas trade. Momentum already had shifted clearly from the Mediterranean Sea to the Atlantic Ocean, and the future of Europe rested with its most western countries. Italian, Greek, and Jewish traders who had long dominated commerce from the Byzantine and Ottoman Empires lost substantially once explorers found new trading opportunities and trade routes. While Columbus failed to find Asia, his discovery of the Americas for Europe altered the entire nature of global politics. This differed from earlier landings in the Americas because of the changed dynamic in intentions and increasingly interconnected world. Colonization of the Americas, alongside the high mortality rates among indigenous peoples and the repopulation of the Americas with African slaves for work on large plantations, created a completely new balance of power. Sugar, tobacco, furs, and, most of all perhaps, silver from the mines of Potosí in Bolivia, all moved across the globe on European ships. Tobacco would find its way into Europe and spread quickly to Persia and Arabia, smoked in a shisa, while silver would alter the economies of central Europe, Persia, and China.

Indeed, trade relations and the interconnectedness of goods united the world. While the Portuguese had first discovered Chinese tea in the 1500s, the tea market exploded thanks to the change in habits by the English; by 1793, the English imported more than a pound of tea per person per year, which increased the demand for sugar from planters in the Americas.[24] Bringing together such diverse crops from across the world pushed the boundaries of business, culture, and politics to new levels.

The great Indian harbor of Calicut attracted the attention of Europeans who sought ever-important spices such as pepper. As an aid to kill the rotten or rotting smell of meat and to enhance the overall flavor, pepper began as a luxury commodity thanks to early trade links with India. Arab merchants moved spices like pepper from Calicut to a port like Aden or Jidda on the Red Sea, then via camel caravan to Cairo, and thereafter via river barge down the Nile to Alexandria. From there, the pepper might have gone on a French, Genoese, or Venetian ship and off to the mainland of Europe. All the various middlemen each gained a commission and made the pepper tremendously expensive. Explorers like Vasco da Gama helped alleviate the high cost by providing a reliable and cheaper alternative by removing most of the middlemen. With a lower price, more people in Europe could afford the pepper and with increasing demand, control of India in the eighteenth century took root to guarantee a steady and inexpensive supply of commodities like pepper. Ludovico di Vartema traveled to Calicut in the early years of the sixteenth century and noted the allure of this exotic spice:

> Many pepper trees are found in the territory of Calicut: there are also some within the city, but not in large quantities. Its stem is like that of a vine, that is to say, it is planted near to some other tree, because, like the vine, it cannot stand erect. This tree grows like the ivy, which embraces and climbs as high as the wood or tree which it can grasp. . . . The leaves of these branches resemble those of the sour orange, but are more dry, and on the underneath part they are full of minute veins. From each of these branches there grow five, six, and eight clusters, a little longer than a man's finger, and they are like small raisins, but more regularly arranged, and are as green as unripe grapes. They gather them in this green state in the month of October and even in November, and then they lay them in the sun on certain mats, and leave them in the sun for three or four days, when they become as black as they are seen amongst us without doing anything else to them. And you must know that these people neither prune nor hoe this tree which produces the pepper.[25]

Europe's discovery of a direct route to India and China changed the world forever—the exploits of the daring men who ventured out reveal a great deal about this age of discovery.

First Reading:

Joris van Speilbergen, *The East and West Indian Mirror and The Australian Navigations of Jacob le Maire*, J.A.J. de Villiers, trans. (London: Hakluyt Society, 1906).

This first reading is from the diary of Jacob le Maire, a Dutch sailor who explored the Indian Ocean and proceeded to the various islands of Indonesia in order to unite with fellow explorer Joris van Speilbergen, who entered the same area from the opposite direction—that is, they both left Holland and le Maire went around Africa while Speilbergen sailed around Tierra del Fuego, at the southernmost point of South America. Dutch sailors like Speilbergen and le Maire featured prominently in the dramatic rise of wealth in Holland during the seventeenth century.

In 1602, Dutch businessmen gathered to establish the Dutch East India Company and thereafter did something absolutely ground-breaking for the development of modern capitalism—they made company stocks available for public trading. Such a bold move acted in contradistinction to the English East India Company, founded two years earlier, as the Dutch actions resulted in not only distributing the risk among more investors but also dividing the profits. As more Dutch invested in the company, they had more disposable income to reinvest in other business endeavors or to patronize the arts and education. By 1670, approximately 10 percent of Dutchmen were sailors and the Dutch ships—most notably, the fluyt, or lightly armed cargo cruiser—carried an enormous supply of Indian and Indonesian spices back to Europe. A more generous supply of such products drove prices downward and more people increasingly found themselves able to afford otherwise luxury goods. Owing to its smaller population than comparative countries like Great Britain, the joint-stock companies—not to mention insurance houses—greatly expanded the already rising middle class in Holland and created a legitimate identity for those who advocated efficiency, growth, and reform.

Of the trip

[W]e should try to get by a way other than the Strait of Magellan into the South Sea in order to discover there certain new countries in the south where it was thought great wealth could be got, or, if that did not succeed according to desire, that we should then sail along the great South Sea to the East Indies. There was great joy among the crew that day concerning this declaration, for they now knew whither they were being taken, and each one hoped to get something on his own account out of a prosperous voyage and to profit by it.

Portrait of Jacob le Maire

December

[Trying to leave an island,] the wind, fortunately for us in our position, was blowing westerly from the land, for had we had an east wind blowing at all freshly we should certainly have lost the ship. We found many eggs on the rocks there and caught fine mussels and fish, amongst others smelts sixteen inches long, wherefore we called this inlet Spierincx Bay.

On the morning of the ninth we again proceeded up stream under rail and came near Coninckx Island, so named by Olivier. The yacht got behind it and anchored, but we could not get inside with the Eendracht on account of contrary wind. Our men landed on the island, which was almost entirely covered with eggs. A man standing still, with his feet together, could touch with his hands fifty-four nests, each containing three or four eggs similar in shape to (but somewhat bigger than) plovers' [small wading birds] eggs. They belonged to the black-backed gull, and we brought them on board by thousands and ate them.

On the tenth our boat proceeded to the north bank of the river to look for fresh water, but could find none. The men dug pits, some of them 14 feet deep, but found all the water brackish [with some salinity], both on the high hills and in the valleys. In the evening they came on board again, bringing birds and eggs in great numbers.

On the eleventh the boat proceeded downstream to the south bank in order to look for water and human beings, but found only brackish water. We saw some ostriches and animals almost like deer, with very long necks, which were very shy of us. On the summit of the mountain we found some graves, consisting of a few heaps of stones, and as we did not know what these meant we overturned one heap and found under it the bones of human beings 10 and 11 feet in stature. They lay the dead down on the summit of the mountains and cover them with a quantity of stones, only to protect them from beasts and birds.

On the ninth there died Jan Cornelisz Schouten, skipper of the yacht and brother of our skipper, Willem Cornelisz. Schouten, after suffering more than a month from a very grievous malady. On the morning of the tenth after prayers had been read, the deceased was put overboard. After breakfast we saw land about three miles to the north-west and to the north-west by north of us; it was a low island, and not large. We also saw here a large quantity of gulls and fish, and shaped our course towards the islands, intending to get some refreshments there, but our ships could not land, as the sea was rough. Still, some of our men swam ashore, but found nothing that could refresh our sick, wherefore we went on until the fourteenth, when we saw an island, whereat we were all very glad. We proceeded towards it, changing our course, and towards the evening, when our vessel was still quite a mile from the land, a canoe came to meet us containing four Indians, who were quite naked and red of color, with very black and long hair. They kept a good way off the ship all the time, calling us and making signs that we should come ashore, but we could not understand them nor they us, although we called to them in Spanish, Malay, Javanese and in our Dutch language. In the evening, at sunset, we came near the land, but found no bottom nor any change in the water, although we got so close to the shore that we could have fired upon it with a musket, wherefore we turned seawards again, whilst the canoe went to the land, where a large number of Indians were on the beach awaiting it. A little while afterwards another canoe set out from the shore for the ship, but, like the other, would not board us. They shouted, indeed, and so did we, but we could not understand each other, and their canoe capsized before our eyes, but they soon had it righted again and were immediately in it with great rapidity. They kept on motioning us to the land and we them to the ship, but they would not come, wherefore we proceeded on our way and left the island, sailing south and sou'-sou'-west, in order to keep off the land. The island was not wide, but very long, being full of trees, which we took to be palmites and coker-nuts trees; it lies in latitude 15° 15' [this place cannot be determined with longitude, but the cities of Aden, Bangkok, and Manila lie approximately at 15° latitude], and has a white sandy beach. In the night we saw fires on the land in various places.

On the morning of the fifteenth, having proceeded about ten miles sou'-sou'-west during the night, we sailed along close to the shore, where we also saw many naked persons on the beach calling and shouting (so it seemed) that we should land. Again a canoe with three Indians put off to come to us; they also shouted, though, as before, they would not come aboard; but they rowed towards our shallop, close to which they came, and our men showed them every kindness, giving them some beads and knives, but they could not understand each other. Having been near the shallop a little while they left it and came so close to the ship that we threw them a line which they took, but they would not come aboard, though they did indeed get into our shallop, which returned from shore without having effected aught. However, after they had been a long time alongside of us at length got into the gallery and pulled the nails in the port-holes of the cabins belonging to the supercargo and the skipper, hiding them away and concealing them in his hair; they were very greedy after iron, indeed, they pulled at and thought they could drag out the bolts in the ship. We wished them to keep one aboard and send one of our crew ashore in the canoe in his place in order to make friends with them, but they would not. They were very thievish folk and went about quite naked; all they wore was a small strip of matting over their privy parts. Their skin was marked with various figures, such as snakes, dragons, and monsters of that kind, which stood out quite blue, as if they had been burnt in with gunpowder. We gave them some wine while we were sitting in the canoe and they would not give us back the pannikin [small metal cup]. We again sent our shallop to the shore with eight musketeers and six men with swords. Our underfactor, Claes Jansz, and Aris Claesz, the factor of the yacht, went too, in order to see what there was on the island, and in order to make friends with them, but as soon as they touched the beach and the men ran up through the surf, fully thirty Indians, armed with great clubs, came out of the bush and tried to deprive our men of their arms and to drag the shallop out of the water, taking also two of our people out of the shallop and intending to carry them into the bush. But the musketeers whose muskets were still dry fired three shots in the band, so that our men had no doubt that a few were shot dead or mortally wounded. They also carried long sticks with certain long spiked things at the end, which, so we thought, were the swords of sword-fish; they also cast with slings, but, thank God, wounded none of our people. They had no bows and arrows, as far as we could see. Our people also saw some women who fell upon the men's necks and shrieked; they did not know what this meant, but supposed it was to separate them. This island we gave the name of the Bottomless Island, because we could find no bottom there on which to anchor.

Shortly after, we found another island; there were many wild trees and inside it was also full of salt water. Our men, on returning aboard, were entirely covered with flies, to such a degree, that we could recognize no part of them; their faces, hands, boats, and everything, yea, even the oars, as far as they were out of the water, were all covered black with flies, a wonder to behold. These flies came on board with them and flew so thick upon our bodies and faces that we did not know where to hide from them, so that we could scarcely eat or drink. Everything was filled with them; we rubbed our faces and hands, hit and killed as many as we could. This lasted two or three days with great torture; then we got a stiff breeze, by which and by constantly pursuing them we got rid of them at the end of three or four days. We called this island the Island of Flies and proceeded thence in a westerly direction.

At noon, immediately after dinner, we saw a sail, which we took to be a barque, coming out of the south and running to the north across us. We at once headed for her, and when she got close to us we fired a shot from our bows over her starboard to get her to haul down, but she would not do it, wherefore we fired another shot, but still she would not haul down. We therefore launched our shallop with ten musketeers to take here, and whilst these were rowing towards her again sent a shot abaft her, but all without intention of striking or damaging here, but still she would not haul down, seeking rather to outsail us as much as possible. . . . When we approached her, and before our men boarded her, some of her crew sprang overboard from fright; amongst others there was one with an infant and another who was wounded, having three holes in his back, but not very deep, for they were caused by a grazing shot, and this man we got out of the water again. They also threw many things overboard, which were small mats, and amongst other things, three hens. Our men sprang on board the little vessel and brought her alongside of us without the least resistance on the part of her crew, as indeed they had no arms. When she was alongside of us we took on board two men who had remained in her and these immediately fell down at our feet, kissing our feet and hands. One was a very old grey man, the other a young fellow, but we could not understand them, though we treated them well. And the shallop immediately rowed back to the aforesaid men who had jumped overboard, in order to rescue them, but they got only two who were floating on one of their oars and who pointed with their hands to the bottom, wishing to say that the others were already drowned. . . . In the vessel were some eight women and three young children . . . both men and women were entirely naked and wore on a bagatelle over their privy parts. Towards the evening we put the men on board their vessel again; they received a hearty welcome from their wives, who kissed them. We gave them beads (which they hung around their neck) and some knives, and showed them every kindness, as they likewise did in turn to us, giving us two handsome finely-made mats and two coker nuts, for they had not many of them. This was all they had to eat and drink, indeed, they had already drunk the milk out of the nuts, so that they had nothing more to drink. We also saw them drink salt water from the sea, and give it, too, to their infants to drink, which we thought to be contrary to Nature.

Regarding a boarding of their vessel by islanders

In the afternoon the king came himself in a big sailing-prow, in shape as mentioned above, like an ice-sleigh, and accompanied by fully thirty-five canoes. This king or chief was called Latou by his people. We received him with drums and trumpets, whereat they were greatly astonished, as something they had never seen or heard. They showed us as much honor and amity, according to appearances, bowing their heads, beating their foreheads with their fists and performing other strange ceremonies. . . . This king could not be distinguished from the rest of the Indians, for he, too, went about quite naked, except by the fact that they obeyed him and that he had good authority over his men. We motioned the Latou to come over the side into our ship. His son came aboard and we treated him well, but he himself durst not or would not come; all of them, however, made signs that we should come to the further island with our vessel, that there was enough of everything to be got.

On the morning of the twenty-third there came some forty-five canoes alongside of us in order to trade, accompanied by a fleet of some twenty-three small sailing vessels, shape like ice-sleighs; each of these had, on an average twenty-five men aboard, two small canoes having four or five, and that without our knowing what they had in mind. The canoes still kept on trading with us, exchanging coker-nuts for nail, and still acted as if they were great friends of ours, but we subsequently found out otherwise. They still kept on making signs that we should sail to the other island. When we had had our breakfast we weighed anchor and set sail in order to proceed to that other island. The king, or chief, who had come near our vessel the previous day, also came towards us in a small sailing vessel, and they shouted very loudly all together. We would have like to have had him on board, but he would not, whereat we were not easy in our mind, fearing some evil, especially as all the small vessels and canoes kept close around our ship, and the king got out of his vessel to sit in a canoe whilst his son sat in another. Immediately after this they beat a small drum which had been left in the king's vessel, and then all the people began to shout, which seemed to us to denote that they would all attack us together in order to take our ship; and, indeed, the little vessel out of which the king had got, came up to us at a speed so swift that it seemed as if she wished to run us down, but she struck our ship with such force that the two prows of the canoes that protruded underneath were broken into splinters, those men who were on her (amongst whom there were some women, too), springing into the water and swimming off to windward. The other began to throw stones at us most bravely, thinking to frighten us thereby, but we fired upon them with muskets and three guns (charged with musket balls and old nails) so that all the people in the little vessel that lay alongside of us sprang into the water.

May 1616

On the morning of the thirtieth, as we were drifting along in a calm, many canoes came alongside filled with blacks, who, as they approached us, broke their asagays in pieces upon their heads, in token of peace, but not one of them brought us anything, although they wanted everything. They appeared to be better and more civilized folk than the last, for they covered their privy parts with small leaves and had a handsomer kind of canoe, adorned fore and aft with a little carved work. They are very proud of their beards, which they powder with chalk as well as the hair of their head. Upon the three or four islands from which these canoes came there were many coker-nut trees.

July 1616, near New Guinea

On the eighth we anchored in 70 fathoms, about a gun-shot distant from the shore. Some canoes came alongside there with a funny kind of people, who were all Papoos [natives of Papua], having short hair, which was curled, and wearing rings through their noses and ears, with certain small feathers on their head and arms, and hog's tusks around their neck and on their chest as ornaments. They also ate betel-nuts and were afflicted with various deformities; one squinted, another had swollen legs, a third swollen arms, and so forth, whereby it is to be presumed that this must be an unhealthy country, especially as their huts stand upon piles about eight or nine feet from the ground.

On the fifteenth . . . the skipper rowed to land with the skiff and the shallop, well equipped, intending to fetch a number of coker-nuts which grew in great quantities on these island, but when they reached the shore the blacks lay in the wood near to where we were, being terribly on their guard, and pelted us very fiercely with darts so that some sixteen of our men were severely wounded, one being shot right through his arm, another through his leg, a third in his neck, hands, or other parts.

Perceptions of the natives *See Key for details

On the morning of the seventeenth two or three canoes full of blacks came alongside, threw some coker-nuts into the water above stream and made signs for us to fetch them out, whereby they sought our friendship. . . . On the eighteenth we continued to barter for bananas and coker-nuts, as well as for a little cassavy and papede, which is also obtained in the East Indies. We saw some herbs here which we thought must have come from the Spaniards. Nor were these people very curious concerning the ships, as the preceding ones had been, for they were able to speak about the firing of big guns and gave the island upon they lived, and which was the most easterly, the name of Moa; the other, lying opposite, they called Insou, and the farthest, which was rather a high island, lying some 5 or 6 miles from Nova Guinea, that they called Arimoa.

Encounter with islanders

On the twenty-third we had good weather and a fine breeze. . . . There also came some blacks from another island who brought us some food supplies; they also had a specimen of Chinese porcelain, of which we got two saucers by barter, so that we presumed that Christian vessels had been here, especially as they were not so curious about our ship. They were a different kind of people from the last, yellower in complexion and taller in stature; some had long hair, some short, and they also used bows and arrows. They were very eager after beads and iron-work and wore sticking in their ears rings of green, blue and white glass, which we presumed they got from the Spaniards.

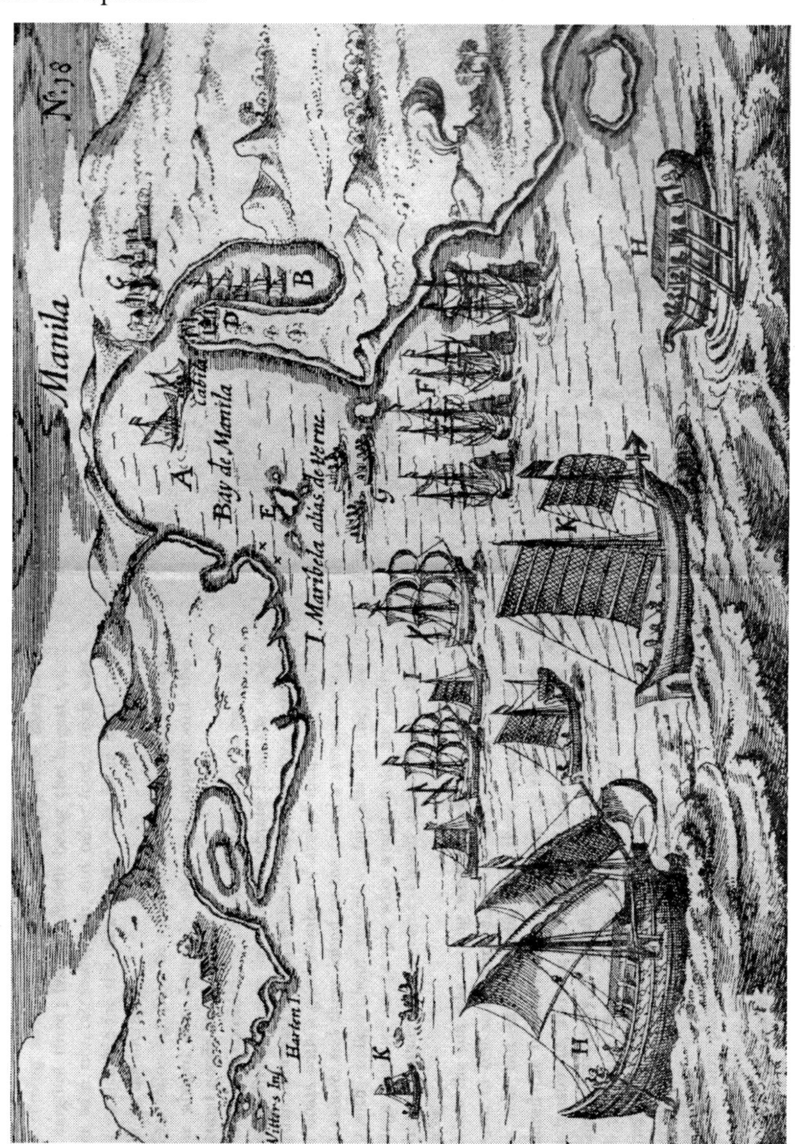

Mix of Dutch and Asian ships

August 1616

On the fifth we proceeded towards the land which we had on the previous day taken to be islands. . . . They [natives] brought us naught but a sample of Indian beans and peas, together with some rice, tobacco, and two birds of Paradise, one of which, colored white and yellow, we got by barter. We could understand these people fairly well, for they spoke Malay well, with which language the supercargo of the yacht, Aris Claesz, was well acquainted. There were some who also spoke a few words of Spanish, and amongst other things they also had a hat of Spanish felt. Their clothing consisted of certain bright-colored cloths around their waist and a few wore silk breeches of various colors; some, too, had turbans on their heads, and these, they said, were Turks or Moors. Some wore gold and silver rings on their fingers and all had jet black hair. . . .

[In October, they reached the island of Java, where they found Dutch ships in the new trading settlement established there by the Dutch East India Company]

Discussion Points for *Australian Navigations*

1. Think about the system of communicating with the various indigenous peoples. What do you think about how the Dutch sailors conducted themselves and what they lost in their strained dialogues.
2. What sorts of misperceptions do you think the Dutch made about the peoples they encountered?
3. What do you think was striking in how the Dutch described the indigenous peoples on the various islands they encountered (skin color, tattoos, rings, hairstyle, etc.)?
4. Much of the exploration in the South Seas done by the Dutch was ground breaking for Europe. Dutch sailors discovered and mapped Australia and named that continent along with New Zeeland. Only later, in fact, more than a century later in some cases, did English sailors like Captain James Cook discover some of these same places and anglicize the names [New Zeeland to New Zealand]. What do you imagine the Dutch thought when they saw otherwise uncivilized islanders with Chinese porcelain or so-called Spanish goods? What sense of competition do you think the Dutch had with the other naval powers operating in Asia?
5. It seemed that the contact between the Dutch and the islanders rested on weary foundations. Why do you think both sides resorted so quickly to violence and ill-opinions? Would that happen today, for instance?

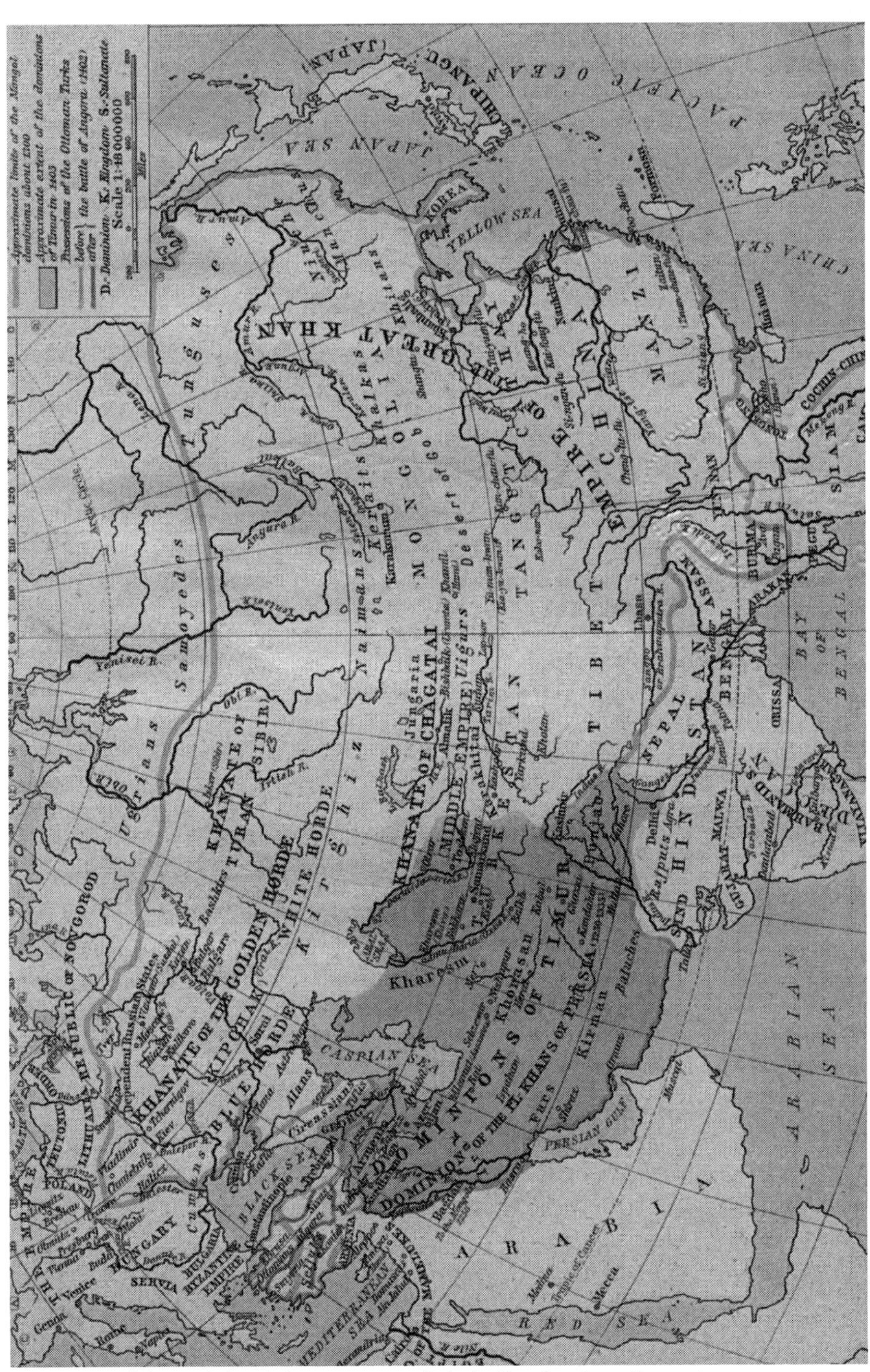

Mongol dominions across Asia in the fourteenth century

Second Reading:

George Makepeace Towle, *Marco Polo: His Travels and Adventures* (Boston, MA: Lee and Shepard, Publishers, 1880).

No traveler commands more widespread fame than Marco Polo, as his trip to Asia in AD 1271 and time at the imperial residence of Kublai Khan has stood the test of time. Interesting of course, was how the American version from 1880 began his story in the preface: Marco Polo was, ostensibly, of a "bold spirit and a curious mind," when he left his "beautiful Queen City of the Adriatic [Venice]" to live among a "far-off Asiatic people, and at a court of barbaric and yet splendid pomp."[26] Despite the otherwise exciting text of his journey, George Towle turned what he saw as "monotonous translation" into an "entertaining story" by which young readers could appreciate this history—moreover, Towle seems to have fit nicely as a nineteenth-century character concerned with supporting jingoism among a new generation.[27] Marco Polo, as Towle reminded us, was "heroic" because he was "in all things manly, brave, persevering, intelligent, and chivalrous."[28] While not the exact account from his own perspective, pieces of this journey still unveil important aspects of any account of Asian travel.

In the Middle East

He found Bagdad to be not only full of ancient monuments, but a very thriving and busy place, ruled over by a caliph, who had a large and valiant army. It produced a bewildering variety of cloths, such as silk, gold cloth, and brocade, and it was a fine sight to see the men and women of the higher classes, arrayed in these splendid tissues, as they strolled on the river bank, or lolled in their luxurious balconies, that overlooked the Tigris. It was while in this famous place that Marco heard a story which gave him an insight into Oriental character. About forty years before there had been reigning at Bagdad, a caliph who was very avarice, and also very rich. He had a lofty tower, which was said to be piled full of gold and silver. A Tartar prince came with a great army, attacked Bagdad and took it, and made the caliph a prisoner. When he saw the tower full of treasure, the Tartar conqueror was amazed; and ordering the captive caliph into his presence, said, "Caliph, why hast thou gathered here so many riches? When thou knewest I was coming to attack thee, why didst thou not use it to pay soldiers to defend thee?" The caliph not replying, the Tartar went on, "Now, caliph, since thou hast so vast a love for this treasure, thou must eat it!" He caused the caliph to be shut up in the tower, and commanded that neither food nor drink should be given to him; for, he said, he must eat the gold, or nothing. The poor caliph died in the tower some days after, of starvation, though surrounded by heaps of treasure, that would have bought food for a mighty army.

Marco had by this time picked up enough of the language of the region to converse with the natives; and nothing pleased him more than to wander about the bazaars and shops, and to find some talkative Mussulman, who would sit and tell him stories. In this way, he heard many tales which were scarcely less romantic than those of the Arabian nights.

Upon reaching Cathay – Yuan China

After passing across the great Gobi Desert, where he endured many hardships, and once came near being lost . . . Marco encountered a very different country and people from those he had seen before. Before he had met with Turcomans only; for the most part fierce, wandering tribes, given to plundering and murder, and going from place to place, without any settled home. Now he found himself among a quiet, busy, and to a large degree civilized people, the greater portion of whom seemed to be farmers, devoted to the tilling of their fruitful and abundant yielding lands.

Instead of tall, large-featured, heavily bearded Turcomans, the people were short and squat, with squinted eyes, high cheek bones, hair braided in long queues behind, and a peculiar yellow complexion.

They were, indeed, Chinese. Their loose costumes, their hats turned up at the brim, their small shoes turned up at the toes, their taste in dress, marked them as a quite distinct race from the inhabitants of the mountain regions Marco had not long before traversed. Instead of the plain mosques, too, with their glaring white exteriors, their bare interiors, and their big bulblike domes, Marco now saw gorgeous temples, decked out both inside and out with the greatest profusion of ornament, and containing huge idols that fairly glittered with gilding and gems. . . . Instead of the worship of Mohammad the Prophet, the people were Buddhists, and paid their devotion to the countless idols everywhere set up.

In Tibet

Marco was very much struck with the wealth and rich productions as well as the picturesque aspect of Thibet [Tibet]. He found gold very plenty, so plenty that many of the commonest people wore golden ornaments on their arms and around their necks. Cinnamon was one of the most valuable resources of the country; and the women displayed a great deal of coral on their persons. Thibet was full of wizards and astrologers; but Marco thought them, unlike those of Kambalu [imperial court where he stayed with Kublai Khan] wicked men, who served rather the devil than mankind.

He saw many very large dogs in the country, which seemed to him as big as donkeys, and which were excellent hunters; and he was amazed at the height to which the canes grew in the jungles. These canes were used by caravans who passed through the jungles at night, to make fires with, and thus to keep off the lions, tigers, and bears that prowled in the dark, dismal swamps.

In Hangzhou, China

He was told, and could almost believe it, that the walls around Kinsai [Hangzhou] were no less than one hundred miles in circumference; as he neared the gates, the buildings stretched out on every side as far as the eye could reach, presenting the same idea of vastness which London now does to the eyes of the approaching traveler. He found it harder to believe that there were at least twelve thousand bridges within the limits of the city, all built of stone, beneath many of which ships of the largest size could pass.

As he passed through the streets of Kinsai, he wondered more and more at the great wealth and extreme beauty and activity of the place. Many trades were evidently pursued there; for great warehouses and factories covered block after block, and long lines of bazaars bordered the sidewalks, or ran through the center of the broad avenues; while palatial residences, belonging to the merchants, crowned the hills above the business quarter.

Marco, a comely young man of twenty-three or four, could not fail to remark that the women of Kinsai were "of angelic beauty," and that in their apparel they were as elegant and showy as the ladies of the European courts. The men were tall and stalwart, and full of vigor and enterprise in their movements. The streets, in whatever direction Marco turned, were well paved with large stones; and he observed, at brief intervals, large square buildings which, he learned, were the public baths. Of these he was told there were no less than four thousand in the city, in each of which a hundred people could bathe at once; and now Marco was at no loss to account for the very neat appearance that all the natives made.

Upon leaving Hangzhou

It was time for Marco to think of returning to the khan's court, and reporting the result of his errand to the western provinces. As he reflected on all that he had seen and heard, he could not but be astounded at the wonderful civilization, riches, and activity of these far Eastern peoples, of which Europe had scarcely heard, and certainly of whose great skill in the arts and industries Europeans had not the faintest idea. He cast his eyes in the future, and foresaw the time when all these marvels would become known to the Western world; he pictured to himself the immense trade which would grow up between the West and the East—what luxuries, comforts and adornments Europe would sooner or later derive from Asia.

In Japan and Indonesia

He found them [Japanese] a people with lighter complexions than those who dwelt on the main land, and better looking. Their pleasant manners, too, pleased him. Like the Tartars and the Chinese, they seemed very rich, and especially to have an abundance of gold. He saw a palace on the first island at which he landed which appeared to be fairly plated with gold. Even the pavements of the palace blazed with the rich metal. The Japanese also had plenty of precious stones; and among them Marco saw for the first time red pearls, which struck him as very beautiful.

After a long voyage Marco found himself among that famous group of islands that lies in a long, almost parallel line, along the southern coast of Asia. He landed on Java, which was then a powerful and independent kingdom, with a prosperous trade with India and China. The Java merchants sent their pepper, nutmegs, cloves and other rich spices to the continent, and received back grain and silks. Marco was amazed at the busy aspect of its towns and the wealth of its people. He was still more deeply interested in Sumatra, which he soon afterwards visited, and which seemed to him even richer in commerce and in natural productions. In some parts of the island he found the people very wild and barbarous; and while sojourning in one of the interior towns, he amused himself by witnessing a wild elephant hunt. The rhinoceroses there were the largest and most ferocious he had ever seen, with big black horns in the middle of their foreheads, and a most-forbidding aspect. There, too, he saw the greatest multitude of monkeys of all shapes, sizes and colors, whose antics among the branches of the forest trees he watched with much glee.

Among the tribes inhabiting Sumatra, Marco found some who were cannibals; and so much afraid were the Tartars who came with him that these cannibals would catch and roast them, that they built huts of wood and twigs on the seashore, so as to defend themselves from them if attacked. In one of the tribes, if a man fell sick, his family sent for a magician and asked him if the invalid could recover. The magician, after performing incantations over him, pretended to be able to predict this. If he foretold that the man would die, the relatives made haste to strangle the sufferer, to cook his body, and invite all their friends to feast upon it. They were very careful to eat him completely up, for they believed that otherwise his soul would be in torment; and having collected the bones, they placed them in a large, beautifully ornamented coffin, which they hid away in a cavern in the mountains.

On another island, which Marco visited after leaving Sumatra, he saw some huge orangutans, which, it seemed, the natives believed to be hairy wild men who dwelt in the woods.

Ceylon

After leisurely cruising for some time among the islands in this vicinity, Marco at last came to that famous and lovely island which we know as Ceylon. The loveliness of the place was in striking contrast with the barbarous aspect and character of the natives, who, Marco noticed, went almost naked, and roamed about their picturesque mountains and forests just as if they were wild beasts. . . . But savage as these people were, Marco was amazed at the number and beauty of the gems they possessed. Chief among these were rubies . . . Sapphires, topazes, amethysts and diamonds were also abundant.

India

The people [of Maabar, India], he perceived, went naked, except that they wore a piece of cloth about their middle. The same was true of the king himself; but to make up for want of clothes, the dusky potentate fairly glittered with rich jewelry. He wore an enormous necklace of rubies, sapphire and emeralds; and from this was suspended a long silk chord, on which very large pearls were strung. On both his arms and legs were heavy jeweled and golden bracelets.

This king had no less than five hundred wives, and freely appropriated the wives of any of his subjects when he happened to take a fancy to them; and the despoiled husbands were obliged to submit to their loss with a good grace. The king had a numerous body guard, armed to the teeth, who attended him where he went, and protected his palace at night.

Culture and society of the Hindus

Marco found the Hindoos, like most of the Orientals he had seen, very much under the influence of magicians and astrologers. They were very superstitious, and there were many omens the warnings of which they always took care to obey, believing that if they did not do so, misfortune would fall upon them. A man who set out on a journey, if he met with what he considered an evil omen, would turn back and go straight home again, no matter how near he might be to his destination, or how pressing the business. The day, hour and minute of the birth of every child were recorded, simply to enable the magicians to make predictions concerning his future life.

Intelligent as the Brahmins seemed, they were as completely under the influence of superstition and magic as the lowest and most ignorant of their country folk. When a Brahmin merchant was about to make a bargain for some goods, he rose at sunlight, went out, and caused his shadow to be measured. If it was of a certain length, he went on with the trade; if not he postponed it to another day. This is perhaps the origin of the Eastern greeting, "May your shadow never be less!"

Off Africa in Zanzibar

Crossing to the main coast of Africa, Marco passed through the country of Zanzibar, where he saw negroes of gigantic size, quite terrible to behold, who could carry as much in their arms or on their shoulders as any four common men. They were very black and savage, and went quite naked; their mouths were huge, their teeth very regular and glistening white. The women struck Marco as singularly hideous, with their big eyes and mouths, and their coarse, clumsy shapes. He heard that this people were very warlike, and fought on the backs of elephants and camels, fifteen or twenty men being mounted on each animal; and that their weapons consisted of staves, spears, and rude swords. As they went into battle, they drank a very strong liquor, which they also gave to their elephants and camels, rendering both the beasts and their riders extremely fierce and bloodthirsty.

In Ethiopia (Abyssinia)

The young traveler observed all that he saw and heard with the keenest interest; for he wished to carry back as minute an account as possible of this land of sable Christians. He soon learned that it was ruled over by a powerful emperor, under whom there were six kings, each of whom reigned over the six large provinces into which Abyssinia was divided. Three of these kings were Christians, and three were Mohammedans, the subject of each being of the same faith as their sovereign. The emperor himself was a Christian. Marco also found that there were many Jews in Abyssinia: but they were not at all like the long-nosed, keen-eyed, heavily-bearded Jews whom he remembered at Venice.

Very different, too, were the Christian customs of this half-savage country from those to which he was accustomed at home. The Christians distinguished themselves from the Mohammedans and Jews, by having three marks branded on their faces; one from the forehead to the middle of the nose, and one on each check; and it was the branding of these marks with a red-hot iron which constituted their baptism.

Discussion Points for *Marco Polo*

1. Do you think this account—prepared by an American author in the 1880s—is any more or less worthwhile than the supposed first-hand accounts in this reader? Why or why not?
2. Do you note a preoccupation with the people, landscape, technology, or riches of the places that Polo visited? Explain.
3. What part of this journey most intrigued you? His work in China, travels by sea, time in Africa, or something else?
4. How do you account for the biases unveiled—namely, when he compared Jews in Ethiopia with those in Venice? Was that Marco's prejudice or possibly an addition by the author later?
5. How does this short account of India (land of the so-called Hindoos) compare with Niebuhr's version earlier?

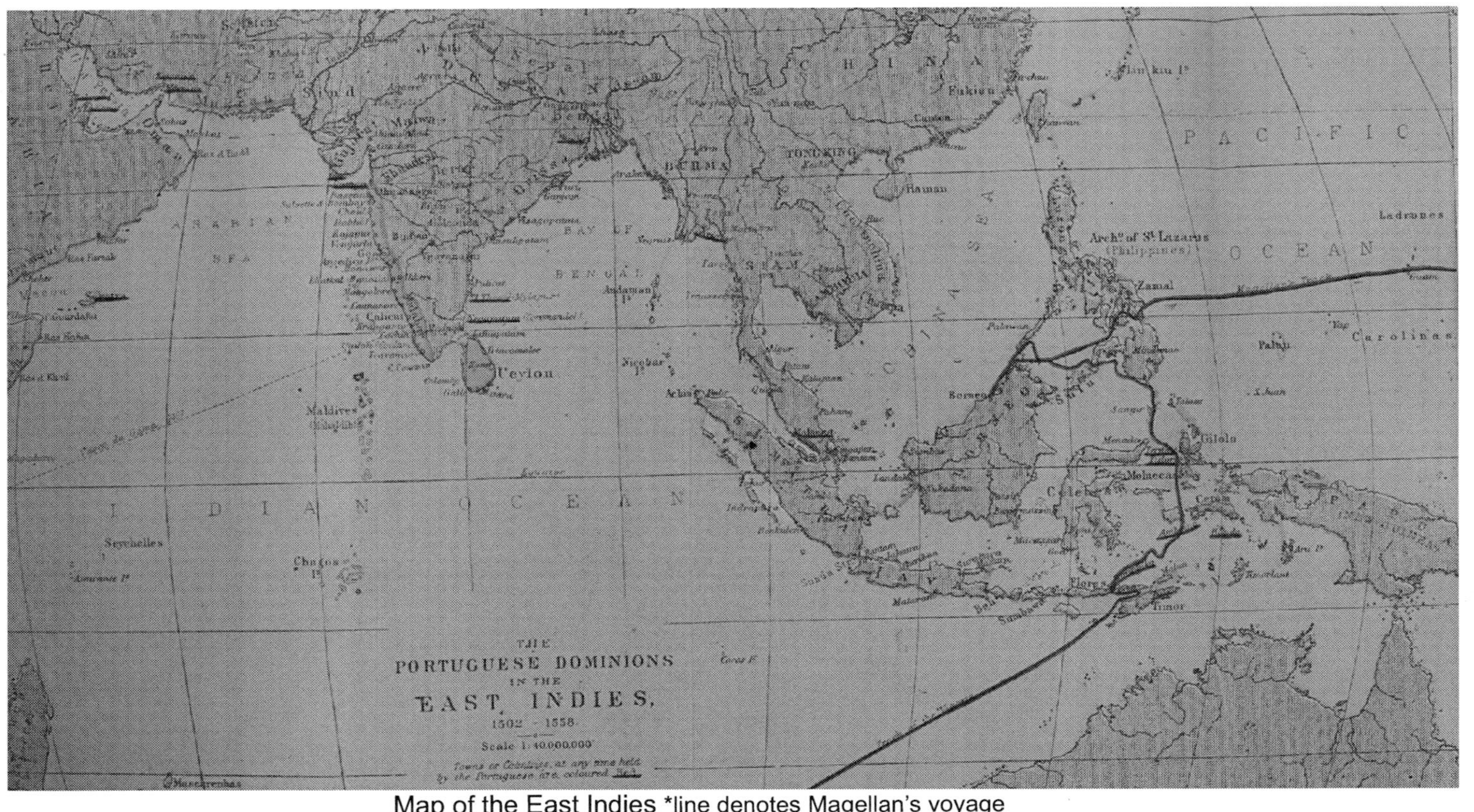

Map of the East Indies *line denotes Magellan's voyage

Third Reading:

Thomas Henry Grattan Esmonde, *Round the World with the Irish Delegates* (Dublin: Sealy, Bryers and Walker, 1892).

The introduction to this piece of travel literature called on the "gentle reader" to come on a trip, because, the author noted, "I'll do my best to amuse you. I'll make the way as short and as easy as I can." Besides general amusement, the author promised a visit to that "dark, romantic continent" of Africa as part of a mission to advocate as spokesmen of Irish liberty.[29] As a self-proclaimed Irish evangelist, Mr. Esmonde ventured to parts of the British Empire in its heyday to meet with Irishmen and speak on behalf of the Irish cause of liberty. Irish indeed comprised a sizeable number of the colonists abroad, from southern Africa to New Zealand and Australia. But the question whether their disposition had improved upon leaving Ireland remained. For some, of course, the chance of a new life awakened them and the new opportunities meant new fortunes and a better life. For others, though, going abroad—especially still within the British Empire—meant much of the same prejudice and dismay under London's rule as before. Hoping to garner contributions to the cause of independence, this Irish adventure certainly raised awareness of nationalism and Irish independence.

New Zealand

Of all our journeying that, perhaps, to which we look back with the pleasantest recollections was our journeying to New Zealand. Whether it be owing to the influence of climate, of scenery, or of the friends we met and made, I cannot say; but we look back to the home of the warlike Maori with a sentiment into which gratitude and kindness enters much, both on our own personal account and on account of the profitable prosecution of the purpose that took us there.

New Zealand has oftentimes been called the Switzerland of the Southern Hemisphere. It well deserves the name. A more majestically beautiful, or more wildly picturesque country is difficult to conceive. Almost every region I have every visited was represented to me somewhere or other in Maoriland. Switzerland and Italy in its glaciers and its lakes: Mexico in its changeful coloring and its stately mountain spires: Ireland in its flashing rivers, its brown heathery manuka scrub, and its waving billows of emerald bracken; England in its tidy farms, with their neat fences and their perfect farming; New South Wales, Florida, or the tropic isles of the Pacific in its gorgeous wealth of evergreen. To describe New Zealand is beyond the compass of this chapter. I may be allowed, however, a few words upon its hot lake district—one of this world's greatest wonders.

I started for New Zealand's wonderland. After an enchanting two days' drive from Napier, we made our first halt upon the sounding shores of Lake Taupo—an island sea of six hundred square miles, overhung on the far horizon by a white-headed mountain barrier. There we found ourselves in a centre of volcanic activity. All about us were hot springs—mud and water geysers, fumaroles—natural steam escapes—and boiling pools. Many of these hot springs and lakelets [small lakes] were heated to a temperature far above boiling point by subterranean fires. The water geysers flung up scalding jets thirty to forty feet into the air. The mud-holes bubbled and boiled, and seethed and snorted with horridly uncanny voices. . . . We spent two or three days here, bathing in luxurious natural hot baths, and then drove on forty or fifty miles to Ohinemutu, by the classic waves of fair Lake Rotorua. We had there, and on a grander scale, a repetition of Taupo's marvels. Hard by is a Maori settlement, called Whaka-rewa-rewa—about the most curiously-situated hamlet in existence. It is actually built among an aggregation of active, never-sleeping geysers. Of these some are diabolically alive; smoking and spitting and hissing and snorting day and night; throwing up columns of water and sulphurous vapor unceasingly; while their roaring silences every other sound.

About the native houses—"whares," as they are called—are burning pools and many colored mud holes, into which occasionally Maori babies fall, and get boiled or baked, which occurrence nobody seems to mind, nor is anybody in the least surprised. Least of all does anybody seem ever conscious in the least degree of the weirdness and general instability of the situation.

As for the New Zealanders, we found them most hospitable of the hospitable; kindliest of the kindly and generous beyond thanking in the expression of their sympathy with Ireland. In no other part of the globe have I seen so proportionately magnificent a generosity towards her cause as I have among the miners of the West Coast.

The South Seas Islands

The South Sea Islands! We have often read of them, and of South Sea Bubbles, and of Captain Cook, and D'Entrescasteaux; of Bougainville, and of La Perouse; of beachcombers and of buccaneers; of pearls and palms; of corals, cyclones, cannibals, and of all the other daring and venturesome men and strange, scarce credible things and scenes which have woven round those far-off islets a many-tinted halo of semi-mythical romance.

At Hapaai—among the crowd of natives assembled on the coral beach to greet us on our landing—were two white men. Of those, one was a western Irishman, from the county Mayo, all the way, who gave me £5 for the Irish evicted tenants. Blessings on his generous heart. At Vavau I met another Irishman from the county Dublin, one of the half dozen white citizens of the chief town there, who does a roaring trade in glassy beads and gaudy calicoes among its dark-skinned population.

Maori villagers in New Zealand

My visit to Vavau left a lasting impression on my mind. It is one of the most beauteous spots on the broad bosom of the Pacific. . . . It was a romantic arrival. All round us varied forms of rocks and islands, covered with tropical vegetation, cast dark shadows on the deep, still waters. Not a cloud dimmed the glory of the starry heavens; not a ripple stirred the waters underneath; while a religious silence brooded over the whole, and made us feel like intruders in some mystic and sacred place.

Next morning we awoke in fairy-land. An archipelago of volcanic rocks and cliffs, rising precipitately from a sea intensely clear and unfathomably deep. These islets, everyone crowned with a crown of brilliant green, which contrasted with the white rock walls and the blue of the ocean at their feet and the bluer sky overhead, with an effect too beautiful to be rendered.

That afternoon, I went in a canoe to explore one of the many wondrous caves in which the islands abound. My boatman was a native, cheery and good-natured, with a voice soft and musical as a woman's, and the "torso" of a HERCULES. He paddled me some four miles to the Ana-peka-peka, a cavern upon whose beauties a poet could expatiate everlastingly. . . . The paddle in my comrade's hand gleamed silver azure in the water, and the myriad gorgeous things that clustered round the buttresses of the walls glowed with more colors than I can name.

Of the people

In the center of these villages is an open space called the "Mali," where the folk assemble whenever—which is fairly often—there is occasion to discuss matters of public importance. The King, or head chief, presides; and each subordinate chief addresses the congregated audience in turn, through his "talking man." A good "talking man" is an influential personage. Every chieftain has one as an indispensable adjunct to his household. The debates of these South Sea Parliaments are conducted in accordance with strictest rule and certainly with far more decorum than even the deliberations of Britain's Imperial Legislature.

The native houses are more picturesque, clean, and comfortable. They are usually shaped like the back of a tortoise. They are built upon a wooden framework, most ingeniously designed, fastened together with rope made from cocoa-nut fiber. Not a single nail, or iron of any sort, enters into their construction. This framework is thatched with cocoa palm leaves, most neatly interlaced; and the walls, which rise some six or seven feet to the eaves, are covered with plaited palm-branches, so designed that they can be drawn up in panels like Venetian blinds to admit the breeze from whatever quarter it may blow. Inside, the walls are bare, if it be an ordinary house. If the house of a chief, they are artistically draped in folds of "Tappa" or "gnatu"—native cloth—manufactured by beating from the steeped bark of the Chinese mulberry tree, and painted in very effective, if rude, designs in black and white and yellow and brown. The interiors of the houses are spotlessly clean.

When a stranger enters he is at once greeted with cries of "Talofa," "Alofa," "Aloha"—*i.e.*, Good-day;" literally, "My love to you." A roll of matting is spread for him upon the small, black pebbles, of which the floor is made, and he is invited to seat himself. Young cocoa-nuts, full of a delicious, cool, clear liquid, are brought to him to drink; and luscious bananas for him to eat. Such bananas! We never see the like elsewhere. Cigarettes of native-grown tobacco, rolled in bits of banana-leaf, are handed round.

If the master of the house desires to do his visitor special honor "Kava" is ordered to be prepared. Kava is the national drink. It is made from the dried roots of a shrub, which is carefully cultivated. These roots are cut into small pieces and grated—in the good old days they were masticated—into a large wooded bowl, standing on many legs, and sometimes richly carved. When enough has been grated water is added; and when the compound has been strained and cleaned by an elaborate and graceful process of every particle of woody fiber, it is Kava as it is drunk. When the beverage has been thus concocted the maker announces the fact; whereupon all the company clap their hands. An attendant then stands up with a cup of polished cocoa-nut in his hands, and says solemnly to the host, "The Kava cup is full. To whom shall it be brought?" . . . The ceremony is most interesting from first to last. Unfortunately, like many another of the ancient native customs, it is gradually being shorn of the details of its celebration under the influence of our so-called "civilization." As to the Kava itself, it looks like muddy water, and tastes like soap-suds. They say, however, that it is very good, and that the liking for it is easily acquired by practice. I found it abominable. It is intoxicating, and has a curious effect when taken to excess—a fitting one, perhaps, for an antipodean drink—in that the tippler loses his feet instead of his head, and while he keeps his senses is bereft of his understanding.

Another charming South Sea custom is the "Siva" or native dance. I was present at several of them. The best was one organized for my entertainment at Apia, by a Samoan chief—a judge, and one of King Malietoa's Cabinet—called by the musical name of Leapai Tuletefuga. These sivas used to be given upon grand occasions, such as marriages in high life or returns from victorious wars. . . . Kava had been duly drunk, and we lighted our cigarettes. Then the dance began. The dancers were divided into parties. Each party was ushered in in order at the opposite end of the edifice, and went through their several figures, while all the native community of Apia gathered round. The actors were arrayed in native gala dresses of vari-colored woven leaves. Round their heads they wore crowns of flowers, and round their necks strings of glistening with cocoa-nut oil. . . . Various chants, marvelously harmonized, were sung. The dancers waved their hands and arms to the singing with graceful motions; sitting at first, then standing; slowly to begin with, then more and more rapidly; finally going through all sorts of figures, with the most extraordinary agility, and still more extraordinary facial and bodily contortions; the whole to the most perfect time, and each figure to a different song.

Village in the South Seas

The Tongans and Samoans are delightful people. They are of the same stock as the New Zealand Maories. Their hair is straight and as long as ours. It is naturally black, but by bleaching with coral lime it turns to a ruddy golden hue, which contrasts with their coppery skins with pleasing effect. They are tall in stature and splendidly built. They are brave, chivalrous, cheerful, thoughtless as children. . . . They have no care for the morrow. Nature does everything for them. Heaven will always provide them with cocoa-nuts without any trouble on their part. Fruits in abundance grow wild. Their main industry is the making of tappa and their main occupation the cultivation of the taro—a species of yam. They are law-abiding under their own laws. They are peaceable nowadays. The Tongans used to be cannibals, but they are such no longer. All they require is to be let alone. But in comes the white man with his "civilization" and the million plagues and vices which follow him; with his book and his brandy, his dollars and his rifles; he robs the aborigines, and teaches them to rob; demoralizes them, destroys them; and, doubtless, before many generations have passed away the places of these interesting, kindly islanders will know them no more.

Take, for instance, the case of Samoa. There you have a group of fertile and lovely islands inhabited by a friendly, peaceful people. A German firm gains a footing there; cheats two or three chiefs out of portions of their land—of which by native law they cannot dispose—plants cocoa-nut trees, forms plantations, to which they import hundreds of natives from other islands to work as slaves. They then give the Samoans to understand that their own country is theirs no longer, but belongs to the German Kaiser. The Samoans don't see this. They are then called "Rebels," as we have seen other races similarly circumstanced likewise styled. Soldiers are landed to shoot them down; but the Samoans with their clubs and spears hunt the soldiers back into their ships. Then there is a great outcry. "Massacre of Europeans by South Sea Savages." "Horrible atrocities," and so forth . . . "These white martyrs must be avenged!" . . . Native villages are shelled and blown to atoms. Native women and children are massacred. All in the sacred names of law and order. . . . The murder is done in the cause of civilization and of humanity.

And so the game goes on. When, fortunately for Samoa, another white power steps in. America objects to this spreading of German civilization. England, under a Tory Government, has acquiesced in the atrocity. But America will not, and America stays Germany's hand. A conference of white power is called. . . . The conference confers; talks platitudes; draws up a "Constitution" if you please, framed on the latest European patent, for these South Sea Islanders; and tells them they may have this grand machine as an earnest of the white man's anxiety to civilize them. This grand machine is, of course, to be worked by white officials, whose salaries, equally, of course, these South Sea Islanders are to pay. A constitution for Samoa! What a glorious proof of the white man's generosity and magnanimity and philanthropy. What a boon! What a blessing to a nation of wayward islanders, who, to be sure, never asked for one, never wanted one, but only wanted, and only want still, to be left alone! And who, uncivilized as they are, are clever enough to perceive that this grand constitution is only an engine for fleecing them more easily and more strictly in accordance with humanitarian principles. And this is how those things are done! 'Tis philanthropy! 'Tis civilization! 'Tis Christianity! But is it not monstrous that great, civilized, and so-called Christian empires, with thousands and thousands of square miles of territory at home, should be so possessed of the demon of universal plunder that they cannot allow even a handful of harmless creatures at the other end of the earth to live in the land the Almighty has given them, in peace and in their own way?

Discussion Points for *Round the World with the Irish Delegates*

1. This expedition clearly had a different purpose than the others that we have examined. How would you compare it to the other readings? Is it more trustworthy, more honest, more sympathetic, or the same?
2. What sense do we get from how the South Sea Islanders lived? Was it a simple existence—indeed, that of a "thoughtless child"—or more complex?
3. Why might an Irishman have taken the position that Esmonde did in his account of so-called civilizing missions across the world?
4. As Edmonde noted, American diplomacy intervened in the German conquest of Samoa but what do you think about that intervention? Was it for humanitarian reasons or do you suppose that larger politics had a hand in such actions? Specifically, Esmonde contrasted America's actions with the Tory Government of Great Britain. What does all of this say about where sympathies or understandings lie in politics?
5. What about the colonists/imperialists—people left Europe to settle areas like New Zealand, Australia, and South Africa; do you think the author thought those people were just as bad as the policies of the government or were they less guilty of destroying indigenous life?

Fourth Reading:

Jared Sparks, *The Life of John Ledyard, the American Traveller; Comprising Selections from his Journals and Correspondence* (Cambridge: Hilliard and Brown, 1828).

While Europeans otherwise predominate in this reader, we cannot forget the role that Americans played in the exploration of the world. American frontiersmen won fame for their bold conquests over the Native Americans as they settled across the continent during the nineteenth century. As the first major expansion westward, the Louisiana Purchase from Napoleon Bonaparte in 1803 signaled the move towards the Pacific Ocean. Foreign policy then grew to a so-called manifest destiny to inhabit all of America; such a policy meant not only purchasing land but also fighting wars or threatening war, as was the case with the conquest over Mexico in 1848 and the establishment of a secure border with Canada in the Oregon territory. Dominance over Mexico seemed too easy for the Americans, who had a more unified mission and vision of expansion alongside perhaps the most important aspect of all—an ever-increasing population thanks to immigration from Europe. Native Americans also fared poorly at the hands of the Americans who viewed their indigenous brothers as uncivilized nomads who had little claim to the land. Such a perception was all too common in comparison with how Europeans understood their exotic neighbors in the Middle East or Africa; the difference for the Americans was that they fought for the same contested space and then dominated the Amerindians.

Once the Americans reached the Pacific Ocean, though, historian Frederick Jackson Turner formulated his so-called frontier thesis, which linked westward expansion to the American way of life. With no more contiguous land to accumulate the Americans had lost their entrepreneurial and inventive spirit according to Turner. In contrast, vigorous proponents of expansion—perhaps none more outspoken than Theodore Roosevelt—vowed to continue America's drive westward into the Pacific Ocean. With an ocean-going navy (and, thanks to developments like the isthmian canal in Panama), the Americans could project power outward towards Asia. Hawaii, the Philippines, and China (not to mention Japan) all became fair markets for the Americans. Thus, a character like John Ledyard stands out not for his unique adventures but rather as a typical American who sought adventure, markets, and power.

Travel with Captain Cook

The last expedition under [British] Captain Cook, and the one in which our traveler was engaged, left England on the twelfth of July, 1776. It consisted of two ships, the Resolution and Discovery, the former commanded by Captain Cook, and the latter by Captain Clerke. After touching at Teneriffe, they proceeded to the Cape of Good Hope, and came to anchor in Table Bay, where they were to refit, lay in a new stock of provisions, and prepare for encountering the inconveniences and dangers of a long voyage in the great Southern Ocean, with the certainty that many months must elapse, before thy could hope to arrive again in a port of civilized people.

Several days were passed here in getting all things in readiness; the men of science employed themselves in short excursions into the country; provisions were collected by the proper officers, and the sailors were busy at their daily tasks. Last of all were taken on board various live animals, designed to be left at the islands where they did not exist, making, in connection with those brought from England, a motley collection of horses, cattle, sheep, goats, hogs, dogs, cats, hares, rabbits, monkeys, ducks, geese, turkeys, and peacocks; thus, says our voyager, "we resemble the Ark, and appear as though we were going as well to stock as to discover a new world." Aesop might have conversed for weeks with such a congregated multitude. The monkeys and peacocks seem to have been out of place in this assembly of sober and useful animals, and in the end they did little credit to their community. The monkeys never ceased from mischief, and the gay attire of the peacocks tempted a chief of Tongataboo to steal and carry them off.

On the first of December, Cook departed from the Cape of Good Hope, and proceeded in a southeasterly direction, intentioned to shape his course around the southern extremity of New Holland [Indonesia]. After sailing twenty-five days and passing two islands, the tops of which were covered with snow, although it was mid-summer in those latitudes, he came to anchor at an island, which had been recently discovered by Kerguelen, a French navigator. A bottle was found suspended by a wire between two rocks, sealed, and containing a piece of parchment, on which was written in French and Latin an account of Kerguelen's voyage and discovery. The island was desolate, without inhabitants, trees, or shrubs. A little grass was obtained for the cattle, and a species of vegetable was found resembling a wild cabbage, but of no value. It rained profusely, streams of fresh water came down from the hills, and the empty casks were replenished. The shore was covered with seals and sea-dogs, the former of which, apparently unconscious of danger, were killed without difficulty, and they afforded a seasonable supply of oil for lamps and other purposes. Vast flocks of birds hovered around, and the penguins, so little did they understand the character of their visitors, would allow themselves be approached and knocked down with clubs. Man was an enemy, whose sanguinary prowess these tenants of the lonely island had never learnt to fear, and the simple penguin received his death blow with a composure and unconcern, that would have immortalized a stoic philosopher.

The ships being moored in this bay, called by Tasman, who discovered it, Frederic Henry's Bay, the sailors were sent out in parties to procure wood, water, and grass, all of which existed there in great plenty. No inhabitants appeared, although columns of smoke had been seen here and there rising through the woods at some distance, affording a sign that people were in the neighborhood. After a day or two the natives came down to the beach in small parties, men, women, and children, but they seemed the most wretched of human beings, wearing no clothes, and carrying with them nothing but a rude stick about three feet long, and sharpened at one end. Their skin was black, hair curly, and the beards of the men, as well as their hair, besmeared with a red oily substance. They were inoffensive, neither manifesting fear, nor offering annoyance to their visitors. When bread was given them, it was thrown away without being tasted, although they were made to understand that it was to be eaten; in the same they did with fish, which had been caught in the harbor; but they accepted birds, and intimated a fondness for that kind of food. When a gun was fired, they all ran off like wild deer to the woods, and were seen no more that day; but their fright was not of long duration, for they came again the next morning with as little unconcern as ever. In all respects these people appeared in the lowest stage of human advancement. "They are the only people," says Ledyard, "who are known to go with their persons entirely naked, that have ever yet been discovered. Amidst the most stately groves of wood, they have neither weapons of defense, nor any other species of instruments applicable to the various purposes of life; contiguous to the sea, they have no canoes; and exposed from the nature of the climate to the inclemency of the seasons, as well as to the annoyance of the beasts of the forest, they have no houses to retire to, but the temporary shelter of a few pieces of old bark laid traversely over some small poles. They appear also to be inactive, indolent, and unaffected with the least curiosity." Cook remarked, that the natives here resembled those, whom he had seen in his former voyage on the north part of New Holland, and from this and other circumstances it was inferred, that New Holland from that point northward was not divided by any strait.

On Van Diemen's island are now some of the most flourishing settlements in the British dominions. The wilderness is disappearing before the strong arm of enterprise, and under the hand of culture the hills and valleys yield in abundance all the products, common to similar latitudes in the north. Emigrants from England annually flock to that country, invest their capital in lands, and engage in agricultural pursuits. Towns have been built, and commerce established. Wheat, maize, wool, cattle, and other articles, are largely exported, and there is hardly recorded in history an instance of a new colony having increased so rapidly in numbers and wealth. The wild men, like our North American Indians, retreat and leave their native soil to a better destiny.

When Cook had provided his ships with wood and water, they were unmoored, and their course directed to New Zealand. . . . In the character of the inhabitants are exhibited contrasts never perceived in any other people. They are cannibals, devouring human victims with eagerness and delight, ferocious beyond example in their wars, deadly in their revenge, and insatiable in their thirst for the blood of their enemies; yet, they have many of the opposite traits, strong attachment to friends, with a quick sensibility to their sufferings, and grief inconsolable at the death of a relative; nor are they devoid of generosity, or unsusceptible of the tender passion. Living as they do in a temperate climate, they are an athletic, hardy race of people, whose progress in refinement bears no proportion to their natural powers of body and mind; and thus no proper balance being maintained, the contending elements of human nature, the propensities, passions, and affections, short forth into the wildest extremes.

When Cook was at New Zealand he was greatly assisted in his intercourse with the people by Omai, a native of the Society Islands, whom he had taken to England on a former voyage, and who was now returning to his country, loaded with presents from the king, and other persons whom curiosity had drawn around him, in Great Britain. Although Omai had never before seen a New Zealander, yet the language so much resembled his own, that he could easily converse with the inhabitants. As he knew English, he thus became a ready interpreter. This was an advantage, which Cook had never been able to enjoy on any former occasion.

Having above spoken of Omai, the native of the Society Islands, whom Cook had taken with him to England on a former voyage, and who had received every possible advantage for becoming acquainted with the habits, arts, and enjoyments, of civilized life, the reader may be curious to know, in what manner he demeaned himself when he returned to his native country, and what were the prospects of his being benefited by his acquisitions and experience. . . . The subsequent fate of Omai is not known, but had his knowledge, his efforts, or his example produced any valuable effects in his native island, the monuments of them would have been obvious to future voyagers. There has never been a more idle scheme of philanthropy, than that of converting a savage into a civilized man. No one attempt, it is believed, had ever been successful. Even Sampson Occum, before his death, relapsed into some of the worst habits of his tribe, and no North American Indian of unmixed blood, whatever pains may have been taken with his education, has been known to adopt the manners of civilized men, or to pass his life among them. The reason is sufficiently plain, without resorting to natural instinct. In a civilized community, a man who had been a savage, must always feel himself inferior to those around him; this feeling will drive him to his native woods, where he can claim and maintain an equality with his associates. This is the universal sentiment of nature, and none but a slave can be without it. When a man lives with savages, he will assume the habits of a savage, the light of education will be extinguished, and his mind and his moral sense will soon adapt themselves to his condition.

Discovery of Nootka Sound, 1788

Description of the peoples of Nootka Sound, in present-day Canada

"I had no sooner beheld these Americans, than I set them down for the same kind of people, that inhabit the opposite side of the continent. They are rather above the middle stature, copper-colored, and of an athletic make. They have long black hair, which they generally wear in a club on the top of the head. . . . They also paint their faces with red, blue, and white colors, but from whence they had them, or how they were prepared, they would not inform us, nor could we tell. . . . We saw them make use of no coverings to their feet or legs, and it was seldom they covered their heads. When they did, it was with a kind of basket covering, made after the manner and form of the Chinese and Chinese Tartars' hats. Their language is very guttural, and if it were possible to reduce it to our orthography, it would be very much abound with consonants. In their manners they resemble the other aborigines of North America. They are bold and ferocious, sly and reserved, not easily provoked, but revengeful; we saw no signs of religion or worship among them, and if they sacrifice, it is to the god of liberty."

On the Tartars

"The faces of the Tartars have not a variety of expression. I think the predominating one is pride; but whenever I have viewed them, they have seen a stranger. The intermixture by marriage does not operate so powerfully in producing a change of features, as of complexion, in favor of Europeans. I have seen the third in descent, and the Tartars prevailed over the European features. The Tartars from time immemorial (I mean the Asiatic Tartars) have been a people of a wandering disposition. Their converse has been more among beast of the forest, than among men; and when among men, it has only been those of their own nation. They have ever been savages, averse to civilization, and have never until very lately mingled with other nations, and now rarely. Whatever cause may have originated their peculiarities of features, the reasons why they still continue is their secluded way of life, which has preserved them from mixing with other people. I am ignorant, how far a constant society with beasts may operate in changing the features, but I am persuaded that this circumstance, together with an uncultivated state of mind, if we consider a long and uninterrupted succession of ages, must account in some degree for this remarkable singularity.

"Mr. John Hunter of London has made, or is making, some anatomical examinations of the head of a Negro, which is said externally at least to resemble that of a monkey. If I could do it, I would send him the head of a Tartar, who lives by the chase, and is constantly in the society of animals, which have high cheek bones; and perhaps, on examining such a head, he would find an anatomical resemblance to the fox, the wolf, the bear, or the dog. I have thought, that even in Europe mechanical employments, having been continued for a long time among the same people, have had a considerable influence in giving a uniform character to their features. I know of no people, among whom there is such a uniformity of features, (except the Chinese, the Jews, and the Negroes) as among the Asiatic Tartars. . . . Whether in Nova Zembla, Mongolia, Greenland, or on the banks of the Mississippi, they are the same people, forming the most numerous, and, if we must except the Chinese, the most ancient nation of the globe. But I, for myself, do not except the Chinese, because I have no doubt of their being of the same family.

"I am now at Kazan [south of Moscow, Russia, on the Volga River]; it is nine months since I left this place on my tour eastward, and I am nine times more fully satisfied, than I was before, of some circumstances mentioned in my diary in June last. As I was fond of the subjects I have been in pursuit of, I was apprehensive that I might have been rash and premature in some of my opinions, but I certainly have not been. I am not fully convinced, that the difference in color in man is solely the effect of natural causes, and that a mixture by intermarriage and habits would in time make the species in this respect uniform. I have never extended my opinion, and do not now, to the Negroes; but should I live to visit them, I shall expect to find the same data, leading to the same conclusions, namely, that they are like the other two classes of man, which I call by the general terms of *white people* and *Indians*. There are many reasons, that rise naturally from the observations on my present voyage, which induce me to think so, yet I still wish to have better. I expect, however, the result will be, that I shall find the same causes existing in Africa to render the Negro blacker than the Indian, as in Asia to render the Indian darker than the European.

Discussion Points for *Life of John Ledyard*

1. How did his trip with Captain Cook relate to other accounts of the peoples of the South Pacific?
2. What do you think of his views on race? Who exactly were the Tartars according to Ledyard?
3. What significance was his statement on measuring the heads of people? How might that practice have influence other so-called scientific endeavors or ideologies of the nineteenth century?
4. During the Enlightenment, philosophers highly regarded education as a way to uplift all people. What kinds of things did you recognize in his description of Omai, the islander who was supposedly civilized through learning and then returned to barbarity?
5. Do you think his views on race and the origins of skin color stood out as exceptional during his time or were they common?

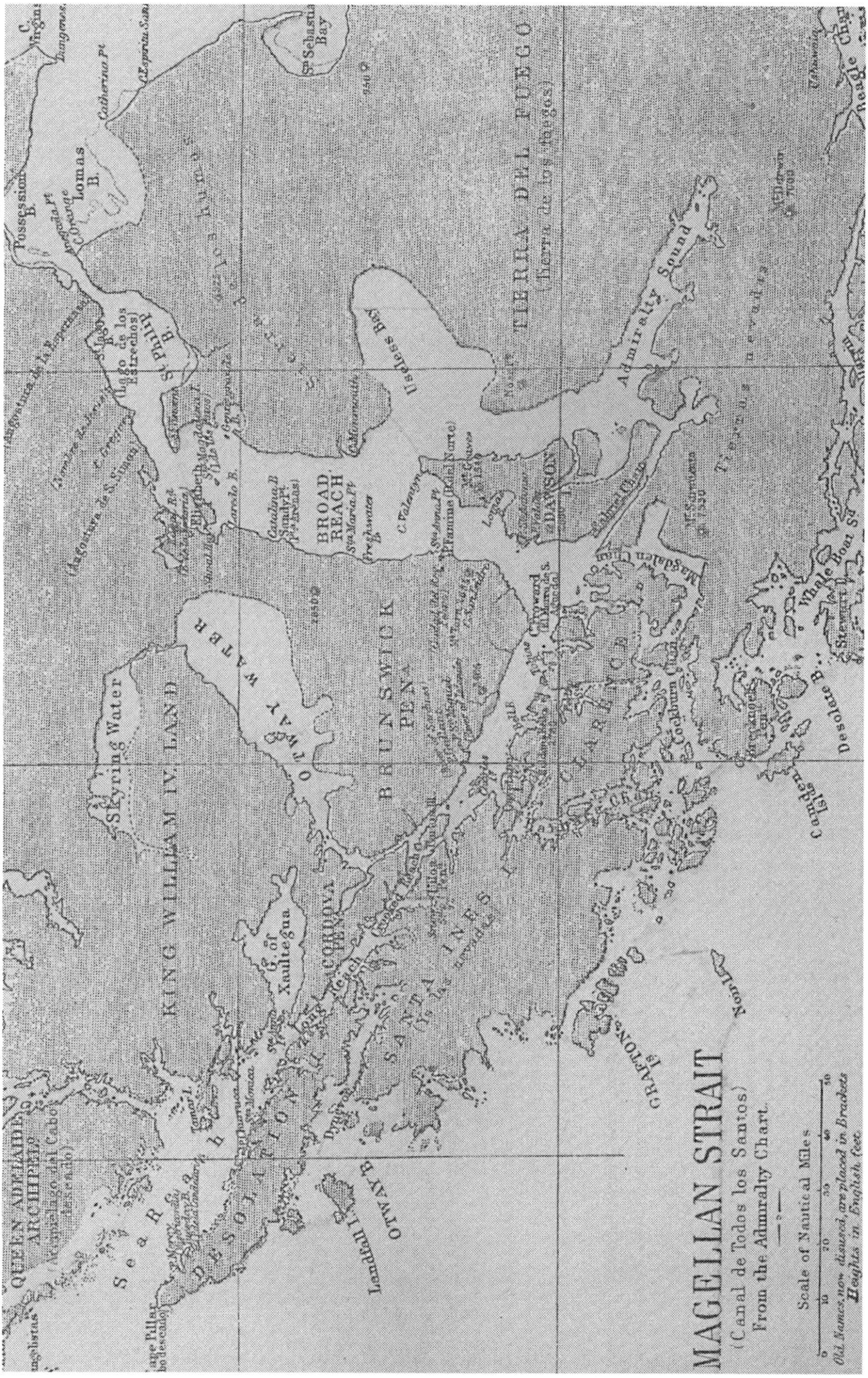

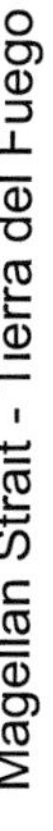

Magellan Strait - Tierra del Fuego

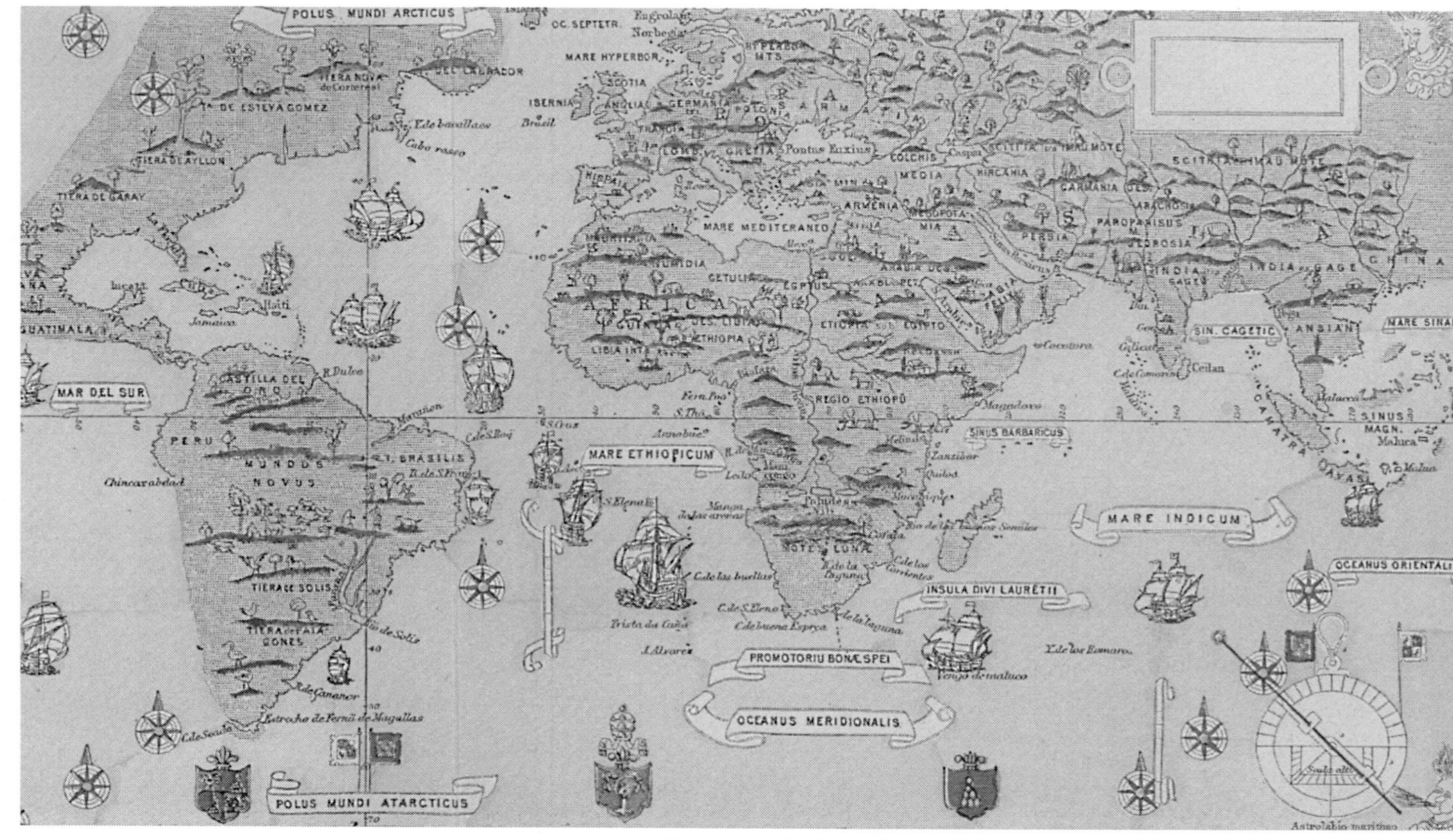

World map in Magellan's time

PART IV: TRAVEL TO CHINA

China long intrigued Europeans from virtually all perspectives—cultural, economic, political, and social. Traveling to the so-called Far East preoccupied countless adventurers, merchants, and missionaries, who all saw grand opportunities for themselves. A view on the culture of China thus created an excitement by Europeans who wished to describe this far away land in all its peculiarities. By the nineteenth century, the idea of opening up European goods to the vast population of China drove merchants and politicians alike to push for exploration, trading rights, and other benefits—all in the name of the market. Such a mind-set excited the Americans, too, who after the closing of the frontier at the end of the 1800s, sought further expansion outward.[30] Missionaries also saw in China the potential to convert millions—as a result, both Catholic and Protestant missions dotted the Chinese landscape. Trade conflicts between Europeans/Americans and Chinese strained relations in the stagnating Qing Empire and led to such conflicts as the Opium Wars. While European might during this period was not as great as people generally surmise, the Europeans did take advantage of the significant rifts within Chinese society (merchants in Canton and Qing bureaucrats in Peking). Outside of the business world, missionaries created tremendous stresses in China; originally when Jesuits like Matteo Ricci went to China in the 1600s, they focused on converting the Confucian elite in the hope that those elites would adopt Christianity and pass it down to the peasant masses. While a trusted notion for Europeans, this top-down approach to conversion did not work so well in China; as a result, Christianity did not become a force there until the nineteenth century. But Christians had grown so successful that the Taiping Rebellion (1850–64) took the form of anti-Qing zeal combined with a bastardized version of Christianity. Millions in China died during the course of the conflict and weakened the Qing Empire even further, leaving it almost totally reliant on outside power (including the Japanese and Americans). Religious conflict again came in 1910, having sparked the ill-fated Boxer Rebellion.

A general infatuation ran through the Westerners' political interests in China owing in part to the vast cultural differences with Europe. Early descriptions of China detailed the types of housing, hygiene ceremonies, costume, and diet. Strangeness no doubt sold more than a few copies of books. In a description of Hangchow, in central China, an author pointed out how in the beginning of the twelfth century cannibalism had developed in the north, owing to violent wars and famines. These cannibals had migrated later to Hangzhou and opened restaurants that supposedly served human flesh: "Dishes made from the flesh of women, old men, young girls and children each had a special name, and were served in the same way as mutton, human flesh in general being euphemistically called 'two-legged mutton.'"[31]

Besides the exotic nature of the Chinese, Europeans desired trade, especially the fabled luxury items of silk, jade, and porcelain. Indeed, in 1600, Asians produced 60 percent of the world's commodities but by 1900, following the boom in European growth that accompanied the agricultural, industrial, and technological revolutions, Asia accounted for only 10 percent of global output yet had 60 percent of the world's population.

In *Four Hundred Million Customers* (1937), Carl Crow explained through his experiences in China just how complex business was in a foreign land. Crow began his book by noting the general perception of the Chinese as stingy: a foreign merchant had come to him and declared that "'I suppose the Chinese will buy anything, provided the price is cheap enough.'" While not without its caveats, the author noted that indeed, "No one gets more enjoyment out of a bargain than the Chinese, or will search further or haggle more ardently to get one." But, more importantly, Crow observed that "no one will more stubbornly and successfully resist attempts to sell him something he does not want, no matter what the price may be."[32] While much of his story rested on his time as an advertising executive catering to foreign companies in China, his ideas of the Chinese nonetheless took the form of vague generalizations. Such was the case when he declared that a weight-loss company approached him with a seemingly perfect product for China. Yet, as Crow conceded, there were no fat women in China: the Chinese husband, it seemed, never had to "face the problem" of a fat wife, because "his wife never allows herself to get fat. They never go on a diet or take reducing exercises to restore their girlish figures, because they never lose them." This was, Crow declared, because foreign women dress to please other women while the Chinese women dress to please their husbands.[33] Alongside the notion that the "Chinese believe that everything they eat has some medicinal value," outside perceptions helped to forge an entire mind-set regarding how best to market goods to the Chinese.[34] Crow's title no doubt was the gorilla in the room—400 million customers. What business in America or Europe would not want the opportunity to peddle their products to so many people? Of course, actually figuring out the countryside, the people, the market, and the politics would take quite a long time.

First Reading:

Archibald R. Colquhon, *Across Chryse, Being the Narrative of a Journey of Exploration through the South China Border Lands from Canton to Mandalay* (New York: Scribner, Welford, & Co., 1883).

In this reading, the author traveled throughout the southwestern portion of China, which bordered British Burma, Siam, and French Indochina. He had the official clearance from the Chinese government and moved about with an armed guard and interpreter. With a general description of the people, the land, and the opportunities for business, this reading shows some of the diversity among explorers—namely, while a man like Marco Polo might have had business on his mind when he journeyed to Asia, he did not survey the land and people with a mind to expanding direct European control. Marco Polo, along with most of the other explorers collected in this reader, stood out as true adventurers, while Mr. Colquhon was simply a business traveler. More businessmen would follow in Colquhon's footsteps as economic opportunities blossomed throughout the world by the twentieth century.

Aborigines in W. Yunnan

Meeting with Chinese notables

He [a Chinese prefect] seemed, like other officials, to be greatly shocked, when he was told that I was unmarried at thirty-five years of age, and evidently looked on the pleas which I gave—such as my foreign residence—as so many plausible pretexts. He regarded my bachelorhood as something uncanny. I had no idea how very awkward it is to be asked point-blank why you have never married, especially by a Chinaman, to whom marriage at an early age is an imperative duty.

I had brought with me and showed the Prefect a specimen of Hoang-nau, a Tongkinese remedy, for the plague, leprosy and other maladies, which was a gift from Sir Harry Parkes; but I could neither in Canton nor elsewhere ascertain that the drug was known. The luncheon was finished by a bowl of soup, with some flour and meat-balls floating in it, which took the place of the cup of rice that usually terminates a Chinese dinner.

Tiny cups of some good sort of sam-shu, or rice wine, were served and replenished as often as drank; and we had to place reins on the rapidity with which the General would have compelled us, by emptying his own cup, to drain ours. He seemed greatly amused when we pleaded our inability to compete with him. It tickled him greatly that such notable drinkers should be vanquished.

Chinese buildings

It is curious that the noble limestone and conglomerate, which are so plentiful in this neighborhood, are used almost entirely on the causeways, protective walls and foundations of buildings, in blocks of rubble. The dwellings and public structures are, excepting their bases, entirely of wretched sun-dried bricks, of huge size and of the rudest manufacture. A white plaster covers these mud walls, but only in the case of the houses of the wealthier people and of the public buildings. The conglomerates met with in the causeways along the I-long lake, especially near Shih-ping, worn to a polish by the feet of travelers, are most beautiful and variegated, and present natural mosaics which would in Europe be employed to grace some public structure or the palace of some wealthy citizen. Here they lie neglected, and the mud, bricks and plaster, partly on account of their less cost, but also possibly because they are not natural. . . .

This northern margin along which our road lay was studded with villages, some of which were of considerable size, and the whole margin being under careful cultivation. Fruit and flower trees give a setting to the picturesquely dilapidated villages, and, with the verdant vegetation along the water edge, impart a cultivated and smiling aspect to the beautiful spot. The hills on both sides slope down close to the lake, the northern edge being broken up by little promontories which gave a variety to this bank, which is seemingly wanting on the southern shore.

Poppy is grown in great quantity in this neighborhood, and we saw families—from grandmamma, with her wrinkled face and bent frame, to tiny dots—who were made to assist in these beautiful fields, which are fated to help in the work of causing so much misery. The peasantry are honest, hardy people, who show no trace of being addicted to the horrible practice, and from all accounts but a small number of the aborigines indulge in opium, though so large a number live by producing it.

The Lo-lo women . . . wore silver ornaments in profusion, the most remarkable being a silver-worked cloth band, hanging over the forehead, and a rectangular one on the side of the hair. Earrings of massive filigree, and finger-rings rudely made, as well as bracelets . . . or simple bangles, were largely worn. In one place we met at least sixty men and boys carrying bags of rice in the same fashion that the bandywallahs do in India.

The country in this neighborhood is largely inhabited by Lo-los, and the Shih-ping and Lin-an women of that tribe are reported to be exceptionally good-looking. But we saw nothing to make us accept this verdict. Fairly good-looking and pleasant, stout, strong wenches, they presented none of the marked good looks which we had noticed in the Kai-hua aboriginal people.

We passed a Chinese lady on horseback who—modest creature that she was—sheltered herself from the rude gaze of the western barbarians by manipulating her umbrella! I knew enough of woman's nature—seeing there were none of her sisters about to criticize her conduct—to feel sure she would have a peep before she turned the corner, and I halted to satisfy myself. I was gratified by a glimpse of as ugly a face as I had seen throughout our Yünnanese travels!

Market in W. Yunnan

In Yuan-kiang

The town of Yuan-kiang has but little trade, and what there is comes from the Shan country through Ssu-mao and from Man-hao. Man-hao is a pretty place, in which but little business is done; a small import traffic passes through it and Men-tzu, the latter being the last Yünnanese town of any importance near the frontier.

The principal objects of import are small foreign goods brought from Hong-kong and known locally as "Canton goods." The transit trade of Yuan-kiang and Men-tzu consists mainly of metals from Western Yünnan, Puerh tea and cotton from the Laos or Shan country, which comes through Ssu-mao along the road which we traveled. Men-tzu is a busier place than Yuan-kiang.

The Pai are the principal aboriginal inhabitants neighboring the river. We saw many of them at Yuan-kiang.

The other tribes along the river, to the south of Yuan-kiang and in its neighborhood, are nearly all different in names and costumes from those described or before met by us. Some of them are still under their aboriginal chiefs. Besides the Pai, the Lo-lo and Poula whom we had before seen, we came across the Min-chia, "native families," the So-be, Po-winni, Hei-winni, Sansu, as well as several others.

Of these the Pai are the best off, and the most civilized. They cultivate opium largely in this district. The others are all very poor, the So-be are the poorest. They cultivate red rich, and an inferior kind of opium in patches, but live principally by the sale of firewood and charcoal. Very little opium is grown to the south of the Yuan-kiang river, and we hardly saw any after leaving Shih-ping on our way southward. We met a party of the Han-pai at the river ferry. The women were handsome and picturesque, active and graceful.

Of trust and bias

Travelers in these parts cannot be too careful in accepting information of the most ordinary kind without testing it by every means in their power. I have constantly been given by numerous people the wrong name for villages, streams and, more often still, for the tribes. The fact became more and more apparent that they know little, and that lying comes most easy to them. It saves them a world of trouble to call every aboriginal tribe Lo-lo or I-jen, or by the first name that occurs to them. The officials even know nearly as little as the lower classes regarding these people and care less. The aborigines are all rude, uneducated, uncivilized savages to them, and not worthy of any notice of any sort. They would as soon think of studying the animal kingdom, and of that they know nothing.

It is very hard to gain information where its only sources are innkeepers, muleteers and traders. The aboriginal people in the Ssu-mao district offer few points of difference from those met at Puerh and Talan. Towards the Mekong, beyond the Chinese frontier—which lies two days' south of Ssu-mao—a number of tribes exist of whom little is known. A visit to this region of the Mekong would clear up a great deal of mystery.

Supposedly a typical Muslim face in Yunnan

We noticed some savage women toiling along under loads of firewood, which were more fitted for beasts of burden. They were dressed in short dark dresses, cut open in front and displaying a more than liberal amount of bosom and waist, and had very short trousers resembling short bathing-drawers, which gave full play to a vigorous pair of legs. They had no head-dress, and carried their loads by thongs over their foreheads. . . . If more attention has been given to the attire of the fair sex in Yünnan, and throughout my narration, it is because their costumes were more varied than those of the men, and not solely because I naturally was inclined to admire the last and fairest of Nature's works.

Power of narcotics

The predatory nature of our police escort was shown in their knack of buying things from some passing peddler, such as brown sugar, sweetmeats or tobacco, and in the great reluctance with which they handed over their cash. This I invariably made them do, to their great disgust. . . . These locusts—soldiers and police—are dreaded by all the country people. They are all confirmed opium-smokers and generally good-for-nothing rascals, yet good-natured withal. Their invariable excuse for opium-smoking is the pestilential nature of their climate—a plausible pretext for a pleasant and most dangerous vice.

The Oni, and even the Han-jen of these valleys and most of the aboriginal people, are rice-spirit drinkers, but they seldom indulge except on some special occasion and after the day's work is done. The amount they can drink is incredible, and they show only a slightly flushed face as a sign of their libation.

A broad, strapping fellow—a policeman—who was with me lay down on a bed at eleven o'clock, when I halted, and never left his opium-pipe until three o'clock, when I was about to start. He then—but not till then—thought of something to eat.

Chinese street scene

Trade among peoples

Notwithstanding the richness of the country, there is hardly any trade. This is partly due to the late Mahomedan rebellion and the plague which followed it. But these are certainly not the only causes. *The chief reason lies in the want of com-*

munications. Not only is there an absence of any trade approach from without, but intercommunication within the province between town and town is rendered practically impossible by the absence of good roads. All merchandize has, for this reason, to be carried on the backs of porters, mules or ponies, and the cost of such conveyance over long distances is enormous.

In the plains the products are rice, maize, peas, beans, opium, tobacco and sugar. Most of the European fruits—such as apples, pears, plums, peaches, chestnuts, etc.—are found; while on the hillsides roses, rhododendrons and camellias of several varieties are seen growing freely. Quite one third of the cultivated area is devoted to poppy, which is partly used locally by the Chinese valley dwellers but mostly exported to the neighboring provinces. The aboriginal tribes manufacture opium for sale, but do not use it. Occasionally two poppy crops are grown in the year, but usually a pea crop succeeds the poppy in May. The Yünnan opium finds a ready sale in the other provinces on account of its superior quality.

As regards the use of opium, I am of opinion that it has a most injurious and evil effect upon the Chinese, especially on those living in the highlands, where they seem to consume more than in the plains. The aborigines, who drink a rice spirit but who avoid opium, present a great contrast to the Chinese in respect of appearance and activity.

But, much as I deplore the widespread practice of opium-smoking, I do not see how it is to be stopped. The Government issues edicts prohibiting the cultivation and importation of the drug, but is powerless, I believe, to deal with the question so as to effect any reform. Within the walled prefectural cities, and indeed under the very walls of the yamen or official court, we often found the poppy growing.

In view of this it is impossible not to believe that the stoppage of the introduction of Indian opium into China would mean no diminution in the consumption of the drug. It would simply mean an increased area laid under cultivation in China itself.

The ill-effects of opium were chiefly made apparent to us through our close intercourse with the people on the march, in the inn or in some peasant's house. But we constantly met mandarins [Chinese officials] being carried in their sedan-chairs under the influence of the drug, lying sunk in a heavy sleep while they were conveyed over some precipitous road.

A significant fact was that nearly all the mandarins we met, and with whom we exchanged presents, made their first inquiry as to whether we had any European medicine for the cure of the craving of opium.

The population of Yünnan is probably not less than four millions, having sunk to that figure from fifteen millions through the devastations of the civil war and the plague.

On technology

Exploration of the country to the east of the Mekong would be well worthwhile, as nothing is known of it. In time it might be feasible to construct a railway up a branch valley to Ssu-mao, or some other town on the border of Yünnan, and so induce the Chinese to carry it forward into their country. Should this railway through the Shan country to the frontier of South-west China be constructed, it will prove, I make bold to predict, the starting-point, of what will be the greatest railway system on the face of the globe.

Only by thus showing the Chinese the effects of a railway, on a large scale, will they be led to open out their own country, containing a population of about one-third of that of the whole world. By such communications, once begun, railways in China will increase with rapidity hitherto unknown, even in America.

[Railroads, the author noted, worked in British Burma; some reasons, therefore, for railway expansion in China.]

That railway extension to South-west China has been advocated by both English and Indian commercial bodies, and by the local Government administrators.

That the railway under discussion would not only open up the north of Siam, the Siamese and the Independent Shan country, but also the richest part of South-west China.

That experience has shown, in many quarters of the globe but nowhere so markedly as in Burmah, that *new markets can be created, nations and tribes have to be trained to become buyers and sellers*. What are at first considered luxuries soon become necessaries.

Some millions of people are there to be clothed with British piece-goods, and to receive the manufactures of England. In return they will give us the finest tea drunk in China, cotton, silk, petroleum and the most useful and precious metals, to an extent which will be enormous with European skill shall effect their development.

The field for a new market has been shown, I trust, to be worth securing and, with the French pressing upon our flank at Tonquin [Tonkin, or the Vietnam/Laos area more generally], there is no time to be lost. Exploration is what is required to inform us as to the best means of securing this new market for British industry.

The political difficulties—the barriers imposed by man—are now practically removed. Those of nature will be overcome by that energy and perseverance, science and capital, which have before overcome infinitely greater obstacles. British commerce will thus secure a fresh market of the first importance.

On the issue of Christian missions

From Mr. Clarke's [missionary who worked in southwest China] great experience of the people, he has come to the conclusion that to obtain real converts it is necessary to commence with the children. It is a growing belief amongst missionaries, so far as my experience goes, that it is nearly useless to endeavor to convert the Chinese, when once impregnated with the strange mixture of superstition and religion which exerts such a firm sway over them.

This, however, is not the case amongst the aboriginal races of Indo-China, as has been found by the American and Roman Catholic missionaries, especially amongst the Karens in Burmah. In Zimme, likewise, the American Mission has found a fruitful friend. The extension of missionary work to North Siam, the Independent Shan country, South and South-west Yünnan, will ere long be found possible, I hope. The kindness which we met with from these aboriginal people, their frank and simple ways, unsteeped as they are in Buddhism and Confucianism, lead me to think that most excellent results may be looked for in this direction.

Mr. and Mrs. Clarke's mission in Tali

The happy influence which Mr. Clarke has already obtained over the Chinese in Tali, as shown by their allowing their children to attend his school, must be great.

We were much pleased to see that he was on very friendly terms with some of his neighbors, who often called on him to have long talks.

Power of language

[After some difficulty] . . . I deposed the interpreter, and told him he should be dismissed at Chü-tung or Tali, and that he was no longer to serve me. To attempt to reach the Irrawadi [Irrawady River] with the tin-chai was out of the question. I told him that he might travel with us to Chü-tung, but he would be employed by me in no way and that he was never to address me. From that day I never spoke to him again.

We had often felt the great disadvantages and danger of traveling with a native interpreter in China, and in the Chinese borderlands especially. The importance of having either a knowledge of Chinese yourself, or a European companion who knows the language, should be strongly impressed upon all future travelers.

We started from Yung-chang on a dark, threatening morning, and before we had crossed the plain the rain came on heavily and lasted for several hours, drenching us thoroughly. I had for the previous two days had a bad attack of fever and ague, the result of a wetting which I had received before we reached Yung-chang, and now I had to struggle along, my head bursting and my bones racked with terrible pain. This made our difficulties all the more harassing.

On arrival at our halting-place, Shui-chai, I had to turn in at once and load myself with every imaginable covering, while I drank "pain-killer" in hot tea, which eventually brought out a profuse perspiration. It weakened me terribly, but the fever was checked. This drastic remedy, rough-and-ready as it may seem to the European reader, had often saved me before from a severe bout of fever.

Gender and assimilation

It is curious to note that the women of all the aboriginal tribes are the most conservative. It is they who last of all consent to abandon their national dress. Perhaps this may be due not a little to the pardonable vanity and coquetry of the fair sex, who are naturally reluctant to abandon their picturesque costumes for the doll-like and inelegant Chinese dress.

The longer one spends in Yünnan, the more one notices how the women of the aborigines are markedly free from the nauseous prudery of the Chinawoman. . . . In other words they are simple, natural, honest, good-hearted creatures, and form a bright contrast to their Chinese sisters.

It is a thousand pities that custom is fast driving them to adopt that most horrible, hideous and senseless fashion, the club foot! We have more than once seen so-called Lo-lo women with "the golden lily foot," [Colquhon was referring to foot-binding practices of the Chinese] whose poverty compelled them to wear jackets so tattered and torn, as not properly to cover their persons. Strange travesty of fashion! The Chinese, by means of opium and their superior civilization (Heaven save the mark!) are rapidly demoralizing all the aboriginal people. The savant who would study any of those interesting tribes must make haste, or he will find nothing left but a sorry imitation of the Chinese. The sooner missionary labors are commenced in the field, the easier and more effectual will the work of conversion be.

Divide and conquer

When Yünnan was conquered by the Chinese, all the aboriginal tribes, one after another, submitted to the yoke except the Man-tzu and the Lo-los, who took refuge in this high ice and snow-lands of Ssu-chuan, where they have found themselves safe from Chinese interference ever since.

In this desolate region the people live on the only produce cultivable, namely rice and black wheat, and they rear herds of goats and sheep; the flesh of these animals is their main source of food. These tribes are the dread of their Chinese neighbors, whom they hate with an implacable hatred, caused not a little by the treatment occasionally received by them from the Chinese mandarins, whose fair words and promises have always been the forerunners of treachery of the basest sort to the aboriginal tribes.

Fearing neither cold nor hunger, the Man-tzu are possessed of extraordinary vigor and power of endurance, and make sudden *razzias*, or raids, upon unsuspecting villages with marvelous rapidity. In this way they surprise houses, plunder and murder the old and feeble, and carry off the rest into slavery. In the fastnesses of Liang-shan the captives are sold for a few pieces of silver and employed as herdsmen. Many are said to be thus carried off each year.

Discussion Points for *Across Chryse*

1. During his trip across the southwestern hinterland of China, the author noted the presence of non-Chinese (that is, Han Chinese). What do you think this meant for the governing Chinese and for the potential for European penetration of the area?
2. The author mentioned the presence of missions but doubted their success in all areas. How would success be measured? Why would some people be more apt to convert than others?
3. Is trade, as the author noted, something that can be taught, thanks to things like railroad connections? How important was a railway for the author and what do you think it symbolized?

4. Who seemed more responsible for the opium trade, the British merchants or the Chinese? Why? What sorts of ill-effects did opium have for the people in China?
5. What differences did the author note existed between the Chinese women and women from other ethnic groups? With which group did he sympathize the most, and why?

Chinese student

Second Reading:

Robert Fortune, *Three Years Wanderings in the Northern Provinces of China* (London: John Murray, 1847).

Robert Fortune's account of his travels through China shows an interesting perspective on what the people of China looked like and how they behaved. He first arrived in the southern part of China and used that area as a baseline to judge the remainder of the country. One fascinating aspect was his description of a battle with Chinese pirates and how, in the end, it was his superior Western thinking that had naturally prevailed.

Of Hong Kong

Since the island of Hong-kong has been ceded to England, the foreign population in it had been much changed. In former days there were only a few mercantile establishments, all known to each other, and generally most upright and honorable men. Now people from all countries, from England to Sydney, flock to the Celestial country, and form a very motley group.

Viewed as a place of trade, I fear Hong-kong will be a failure. The great export and import trade of southern China must necessarily be carried on at Canton, as heretofore, there being at present at least, no inducement to bring that trade to Hong-kong. It will, nevertheless, be a place of great importance to many of the merchants, more particularly to those engaged in the opium trade; and will, in fact, be the head-quarters of all houses who have business on the coast, from the facilities of gaining early information regarding the state of the English and Indian markets, now that steam communication has been established between this country and the south of China. Moreover, with all its faults, its importance may yet be acknowledged in the event of another war. Our countrymen cannot have so entirely forgotten the kind of protection which used to be afforded them by the Portuguese at Macao, as to make them wish to be put in the same circumstances again; and it is of no little importance to know that their lives and property are safe under the British flag, which has . . . "braved a thousand years / The battle and the breeze."

Namoa is the name of a small island about halfway between Hong-kong and Amoy, and it is well known as one of the stations where the contraband trade in opium is carried on between foreign vessels and the Chinese smugglers. At this time I was fresh from England, and full of all the notions which we form there of the sacredness of the Chinese empire. I then thought that, although I might perhaps get a view of the celestial country, no barbarian feet would be allowed to pollute the sacred soil. Great was my surprise and pleasure when I found the captains of vessels wandering about all over the island unmolested. . . . They seemed quite the lords of the soil, and were not subjected to the least annoyance from the natives.

Since this port [Amoy] has been thrown open several foreign merchants have established themselves, and the trade, although small when compared with that of the more northern port of Shanghae [Shanghai], is still considerable. Indian cotton, cotton twist, long cloths of English and American manufacture, and opium seem to be the principal articles of import, if we except the Straits produce, which is chiefly brought in their own junks. Since the arrival of the British Consul the opium ships have been removed from the harbor, and now lie just outside its limits, where the Chinese smugglers are allowed to visit them with impunity.

Unfortunately for the trade at Amoy, the exports of which we are most in need—I mean teas and silk—are not so easily brought to it as to the northern port of Shanghae. . . . Native gold, in bars, is sometimes brought in considerable quantities, to pay for the cotton and opium, and is I believe considered a very pure quantity.

Shanghai

Being now well acquainted with the country in the immediate vicinity of Shanghae [Shanghai], I was anxious to extend my researches into the interior, particularly as far as some hills which were said to be about thirty miles distant, in a westerly direction. It was extremely difficult to gain any information on this subject from the Chinese, who were particularly jealous of foreigners going any distance inland. Their suspicious feelings had also been much increased at this time, by the indiscretion of some of our own countrymen, who had hired a boat and gone a considerable distance up one of the rivers, taking soundings with bamboo poles, in the manner of the Chinese. The authorities suspected that they had some particular object in view in ascertaining the depth of the river, and immediately complained to Captain Balfour, the English consul, who was consequently obliged to notice the circumstance.

I reached a small town in the vicinity of the hills about two o'clock in the afternoon; the pony having had nothing to eat since we left Shanghae, was much exhausted, and I was therefore anxious to procure a feed of corn for him at some of the shops. The news of the presence of a foreigner in the town spread like lightning, and I was soon surrounded and followed by some thousands of people of both sexes, young and old, who were all anxious to get a glimpse of my features of dress. Their behavior on the whole, however, was civil and respectful, and the only inconvenience I had to complain of was the pressure of the crowd.

The natives in this part of the country were vastly surprised when they saw me for the first time; at the different villages and towns, men, women, and children of all ranks lined the banks of the canals as my boat passed along, and often requested me to come out in order that they might have a better opportunity of seeing me.

When I left my boat for the purpose of ascending the hills, my boatmen used to make a good deal of money by allowing the people to go in and inspect my little cabin. . . . It is a remarkable fact, however, that nothing, as far as I know, was ever stolen from me at this time, although several hundred persons visited my boat in my absence. The boatmen must either have been very sharp, or the people must have had a superstitious dread of the property of a foreigner: to put it down to their honor is, I am afraid, out of the question!

Mode of travel

I was, of course, traveling in the Chinese costume; my head was shaved, I had a splendid wig and tail, of which some Chinaman in former days had doubtless been extremely vain, and upon the whole I believe I made a pretty fair Chinaman. Although the Chinese countenance and eye differ considerably from those of a native of Europe, yet a traveler in the north has far greater chance of escaping detection than in the south of China, the features of the northern natives approaching more nearly to those of Europeans than they do in the south, and the difference amongst themselves also being greater.

In Fuzhou

Banking is carried on to a greater extent in Foo-chow-foo [Fuzhou] than in the other towns which I have visited. Paper notes are a common medium of exchange, in which the people have the greatest confidence, preferring them to dollars, or "cash." Some of the notes are as low as four hundred cash—about eighteen pence English money; others are for very large sums.

The people here are generally much cleaner in their habits, and appear to be a more active race, than those in the northern towns. In fact, they approach more nearly to the natives of Canton than to any other, in these respects. I was much surprised to find them consuming beef, and even milk, in considerable quantities; articles which are never used by the inhabitants of the other districts where I have been: indeed, everywhere else the Chinese are wont to express their astonishment when they saw the English using such articles of food.

Piracy

The Chinese sailor never goes to sea without first presenting an offering to the gods to propitiate [appease] them, in order that the voyage may be a speedy and successful one. Accordingly, on this day the cabin of our junk was set in order, and the tables covered with dishes of pork, mutton, fruits, and vegetables. Candles and incense were burned upon the tables for a short time, and the whole business had something solemn and imposing about it. The cook, who seemed to be the high priest, conducted all the ceremonies.

Early on the following morning, the whole fleet was in motion, starting altogether for the sake of mutual protection. The wind and tide were both fair, and we proceeded along the coast with great rapidity, and were soon out of sight of the Min and its beautiful and romantic scenery. The plan of mutual protection soon seemed to be abandoned, and the vessels separated into threes and fours, each getting on as well and as fast as it could. About four 'clock in the afternoon, and when we were some fifty or sixty miles from the Min, the captain and pilot came hurriedly down to my cabin and informed me that they saw a number of *Jan-dous*, right ahead, lying in wait for us. . . . By the aid of a small pocket-telescope, I could see as the nearest junk approached that her deck was crowded with men; I then had no longer any doubts regarding her intentions. . . . I knew perfectly well, that it we were taken by the pirates I had not the slightest chance of escape; for the first thing they would do would be to knock me on the head and throw me overboard, as they would deem it dangerous to themselves were I to get away.

The shot from the pirates fell considerably short of us, and I was therefore enabled to form an opinion of the range and power of their guns, which was of some use to me. Assistance from our cowardly crew was quite out of the question, for there was not a man amongst them brave enough to use the stones which had been brought on deck; and which, perhaps, might have been of some little use when the pirates came nearer.

The pirates now seemed quite sure of their prize, and came down upon us hooting and yelling like demons, at the same time loading their guns, and evidently determined not to spare their shot. Theirs was a moment of intense interest. The plan which I had formed from the first was now about to be put to proof; and if the pirates were not the cowards which I believed them to be, nothing could save us from falling into their hands. Their fearful yells seem to be ringing in my ears even now, after this lapse of time, and when I am on the other side of the globe.

[The pirates fired their last shot, at point-blank range, but the crew on board ducked on the author's command and thereafter rose to shoot back at the pirates.]

Had a thunder-bolt fallen amongst them [the pirates], they could not have been more surprised. Doubtless, many were wounded, and probably some killed. . . .

They were so completely taken by surprise, that their junk was left without a helmsman; her sails flapped in the wind; and, as we were still carrying all sail and keeping on our right course, they were soon left a considerable way astern.

With the captain, pilot, crew, and passengers, I was now one of the greatest and best of men in existence. They actually came and knelt before me, as to some superior being, and expressed their deep and lasting gratitude, which, however, did not last long.

Discussion Points for *Three years Wanderings*

1. How did he compare the people of the south and north of China? Which did he prefer?
2. What about the Opium trade—how did Chinese cooperation seem to play a role in its trafficking?
3. Were the Chinese trustworthy in his opinion? Even after a positive experience (with no one having stolen his possessions) he commented on the so-called general nature of the Chinese. What grounds do you think he had for that?
4. What do we see from his account of Chinese piracy? How did the Chinese sailors deal with it and why? Even though he acted differently, the Chinese apparently lauded him as a hero. Why?
5. How well do you suppose he blended in—as he suggested he did—as someone from northern China?

Buddhist priest in China

Third Reading:

Reverend J. Macgowan, *Sidelights on Chinese Life* (London: Kegan Paul, Trench, Trübner & Co., Limited, 1907).

Finalizing the dedicated account of China, this piece by a member of the London Missionary Society shows a different perspective during an era of imperialism, jingoism, and Social Darwinism. While some men focused on merely making money in the so-called Celestial kingdom, others availed themselves the opportunity that European power provided to truly uplift and civilize the poor non-white masses. No less sincere about their project than anyone else at the time, these missionaries served an important role in bringing one of the foundations of European civilization to China—Christianity. Despite Islam having already prospered across much of Asia, including in parts of China, Christian missionaries took their charge from the earliest days of European adventure to save souls in Christ's name. Late nineteenth-century imperialism afforded missionaries even more promise of success as an increasing European control over Asia would mean greater opportunity for conversions. While some Asian countries—notably the Philippines—had become largely Christian by the 1800s, areas like China allured Americans and Europeans alike. Both Catholic and Protestant missionary societies had thousands of representatives in China to take advantage of the increasingly lucrative opportunities—just like Carl Crow's idea of 400 million customers, these men and women no doubt saw 400 million converts.

The Chinaman

The Chinaman's mind is a profound and inexplicable puzzle that many have vainly endeavored to solve. He is a mystery not simply to the foreigner, who has been trained to more open methods of thought, but also to his own countrymen, who are frequently heard to express their astonishment at some exhibition of character, that has never occurred to them during the whole of their oblique life. A Chinese cook who was living in an English family, and who found life so intolerable through some petty devices and schemes of his fellow-servants that he was compelled to resign his situation, was so taken aback by the ingenuity and skill of the maneuver that had been employed to oust him from his employment that, with flashing eyes and a face flushed with excitement, he said: "I know the Englishmen well, I can accurately gauge his mind, and I can tell exactly how he will usually act; but my own countrymen are a mystery to me that I do not profess to be able to comprehend."

[In determining the motives of the Chinese,] The eyes are liquid and childlike, and just that touch of sadness that harmonizes with his sorrowful feelings has laid its lightest shadow over his features, and you begin to feel that you have been doing the man an injustice by doubting him.

It is the unexpected that so often happens in Chinese life that has given such an air of mystery to this strange and wonderful people. The very opposite virtues and vices seem to flourish and exist in the same individuals. The Chinese, for example, in ordinary and everyday life have no sense of truth. It is not that they are any worse than other nations of the East. The moment you pass through the Suez Canal and have come upon the confines of the Orient, you realize that truth as it is looked upon in the West does not exist in all the vast and glowing regions beyond.

Chinese gentleman

Family life

One very unpleasant evidence of this is the frequency with which wife-beating is carried on by all classes. The Chinese, who adopt ten when they wish to give an idea of comparative numbers, declare that in six or seven families out of ten the husbands regularly beat their wives. Sixty or seventy percent of the husbands treating their wives in this rough and brutal manner is a terrible commentary upon the home life of the Chinese, and yet no one, as far as my observation goes, ever expresses any condemnation of the custom. It seems to be considered as an inalienable right that has come down from the ancient past, before the civilization of the sages had begun to touch their forefathers with their humane teachings, and with the intense conservatism of the Chinese, the husbands continue to exercise it, whilst the great public looks on and takes no step to stop the barbarous custom.

Chinese eating rice and drinking

There is nothing in the world that a Chinaman dreads so much as being laughed at. He can stand a great deal, but that stirs his soul in a way that transforms the solemn, staid-looking Celestial into a raging wild beast. "If that is all my neighbors have to be amused at," he said, whilst passion was tearing his soul with a perfect storm of fury, "I can soon prove to them that they are utterly mistaken, and I will show them in a most convincing manner that they have been so."

There is no Bible, of course, and not a single book in the home, and if there were the mothers could not read them. It will be seen, then, that the machinery in the West for the training of the children does not exist out here. There is no God, no churches, no Sunday or Sunday schools, no pictures, and no special literature to influence the minds of the young to withstand the evil forces that grow rank and wild all around them in whatever grade of society they may happen to be. . . . It may be said without any exaggeration that it is in the home that the children learn the evils that cling to them all their lives, and that it is the mothers that are the principal teachers of them. Lying, for example, as a fine art is one that is indoctrinated by the mothers' example.

Of conversion

The Chinese are an exceedingly superstitious people, but they are capable of being intelligently religious when they become acquainted with the truths of the Gospel.

Until then all their offerings and ceremonies and ritual are performed, either to avert the sorrows that the supernatural beings might bring upon them, or for the purpose of putting the minds of their gods into such a pleasing state of satisfaction that they will be ready to send sons into the family and prosperity into the business, and riches and honor and a continued stream of blessings upon the home.

The Chinese on the whole are endowed with broad common-sense, and in anything that has to do with money-making or with commercial matters they are as wide awake and as shrewd as a canny Scotsman or a Yorkshireman. They are gifted too, with a keen sense of humor, and yet when they come to deal with the question of spirits and ghosts and ogres, they seem to lose their reasoning faculties, and to believe in the most outrageous things that a mind with an ordinary power of perception of the ludicrous would shrink from admitting.

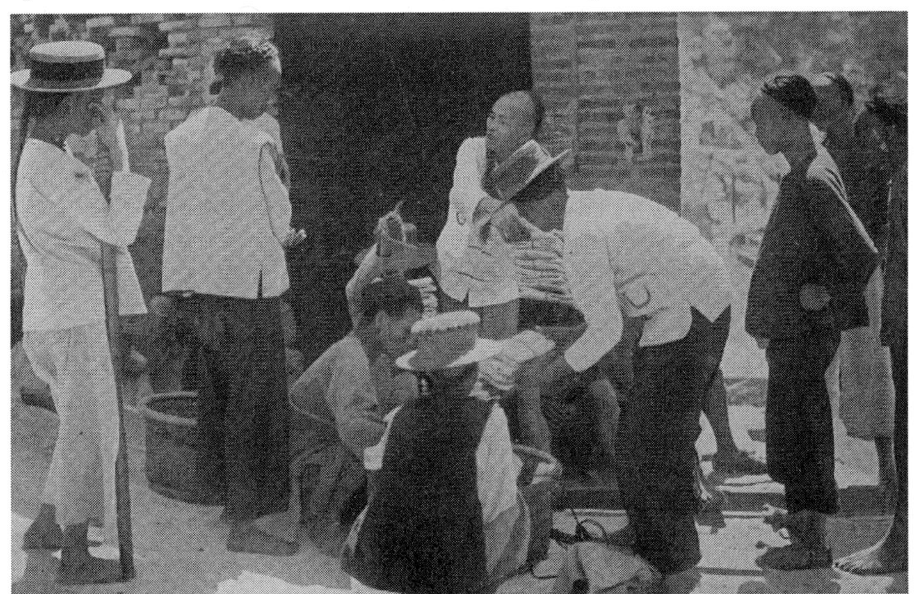

Chinese street scene

Superstition had been a most potent force during the whole course of Chinese history in preventing the development of the nation. The mineral resources of the country are exceedingly abundant, and if they had been rightly exploited, would have been the means of enriching great masses of people who are now in extreme poverty. . . . Now the one controlling reason why this great natural wealth, that God has put into the soil of this beautiful country for the service of man, is left untouched because it is believed that there are huge slimy dragons who lie age after age guarding the treasures of coal and iron, and that any attempt to take them from them would end in the destruction of the people of the whole region. The pickaxe and the shovel and the dynamite would disturb their slumbers, and, filled with passion and mad anger, they would hurl plague and sickness and calamites upon the unfortunate dwellers on the land. These unseen terrors, more potent than hunger and poverty and famine, have kept the mines unopened and the iron from being smelted, and have driven thousands of people into exile, very few comparatively of whom have ever come back to look upon the land of great mountains and peaceful streams, where untold riches lay ready for the gathering.

Refreshment stall

Of the city

The first street we travel along gives us a shock. Instead of the broad and spacious roadway along which the traffic is carried, we come into a narrow, dingy-looking artery which at its extreme breadth is not wider than twelve feet, and even that is not all available for the use of those that have to pass up and down it. The shopkeepers on both sides have put out their counters, on which they expose their goods, so that only five or six feet are left free for the use of the public.

We have not advanced far in our walk before we begin to be conscious of peculiar odors that seem to be the heritage of the East. The air is never fresh, but at corners of the street and indentations in the houses, and on the spots not actually in use, there are always accumulations of refuse and garbage that fester in the sun and send out the most abominable smells. But these are healthy and playful when compared with others that now and again seem to strike one as if with a sledgehammer and paralyze one for the moment.

These are caused by the foulness of the drain that lies underneath the center of the street. As the roads are so narrow and are occupied by houses on both sides, the only available place for the drainage of the city is right through the middle of the roadway.

Of privacy

Fortunately the Chinese do not believe in the privacy of the home as we do. They do not mind having the whole details of their daily experiences seen by everyone that cares to look. How they live, what they eat, and even the family jars [bedpans] that we try to hush up from the public are things that seem to be common property, and not to belong exclusively to this particular family who are most concerned.

The impression one gets from a look into these miserable homes is that the Chinese idea of comfort differs essentially from our own, and that they can put up with a vast amount of discomfort such as would drive an Englishman mad. Their houses are filthy dirty and untidy. The wife after a few weeks of married life loses the trim, neat appearance she had as a young girl. She drops naturally into the slattern ways of the women who are her neighbors, and ere long dust and dirt and cobwebs, and frowsy and untidy garments, are the leading features of the home.

It would be unwise to infer from this state of things that the Chinese are unhappy, or that they are conscious that their surroundings have something in them to induce melancholy or discontent. The ideal of the West is cleanliness, a thing that the East never seems to aim at, or to even dream of. This great city through which we are walking is an example of this latter statement. Its streets are unswept from one year's end to the other. Heaps of rubbish festering and fermenting in the sun and exhaling the most unpleasant odors meet you at every turn. The drains are badly made and left absolutely to themselves until, choked up, they are opened for repairs, when the hidden compressed effluvia send their noxious vapors into the homes around.

The people are highly unclean in their persons. They never bathe, and even in the homes of the rich the bathtub is an unknown luxury. The face and hands are about the only parts of the body that on ordinary occasions ever make the acquaintance of water. Their clothes, too, from a Western standpoint, are anything but satisfactory.

Morality

China is a country full of lofty ideas. These are found in the writings of the sages. They are pasted up in crimson strips of paper on the doorposts of the houses and shops in every city in the Empire. They are found staring at one over the temples of the gods, and on the lofty doors of the Yamens, so that one would suppose that these latter were churches where the highest morality and the profoundest of theological teachings were being daily expounded. There is no place indeed that is considered so bad a public sense of decency would demand that they should be excluded from it. Low, miserable opium dens, and houses of ill-fame, and gambling hells, and homes that are the abode of thieves are adorned with the most exquisite sentences full of the highest morality, and seemingly culled with the greatest care from the vast repertory that the language contains, as if to condemn the very vices that are rampant within.

Young Chinese scholar

Another very objectionable feature of Chinese life is the passion that everyone seems to have for gambling. There are sections of people in England who are as much addicted to this vice as are the Chinese, but there are vast numbers who have never had anything to do with games of chance, and who would be horrified if they were asked to do so. Now, in this land there is no class of people similar to those. High and low, rich and poor, seem to have the gambling spirit in their very blood, and, like the craving in the opium smoker, that must be satisfied at all hazards, so the cards and the dice must be fingered to allay the passion that is burning within their hearts.

Of opium

People who have been jealous of English honor have tried to prove that the opium was in common use amongst the Chinese before the ships of England appeared before Canton with their deadly cargoes, but this is an absolute mistake. Isolated travelers from India may have brought some for their own individual consumption, but the drug was unknown and unused by the Chinese people. That this statement is true is proved by the fact that there is no word in the language of this people for opium, for the only one that has ever existed is the one that attempts to give the sound of the foreign name that those who produced it in other lands gave it. If the thing had been an indigenous product, the Chinese would have had a name for it that would have had no flavor of a foreign land.

It has been a most disastrous thing for China that the one nation that has championed opium and has made treaties for its sale in this land, and that in the interests of its merchants and for the sake of its Indian revenue, insisted upon these treaties being carried out, should be England. If it had been a smaller Power the Chinese Government might have successfully resisted the attempt to force upon it a trade that was inevitably bound to degrade and demoralize its people. But England, the mighty power of the West, whose guns had thundered over Canton, and had waked the echoes of the Yangtze, and had even sounded through the capital of the Empire, was one that China dared not contend with, and so it has come to pass that the country that has always professed to be the refuge of the oppressed and the freer of the slave, has been the one to bind the shackles of opium on a people that, whilst they have fallen under its spell, yet feel the profoundest indignation against the Power whose legislation has helped enslave them.

This terrible evil [opium addiction] exists throughout the length and breadth of the Empire, and there is no power outside of Christianity that seems to be able to cope with it. Human affection, and sense of honor, and pride of race, all succumb before the touch of opium. The Church of Christ in China alone possesses the one motive that will enable the victim to bear the agony of giving up the habit, of that will restrain the man that is tempted from indulging in it, and what is supreme affection and fidelity to Christ his Savior. The same mysterious power that has touched the men of other lands in the most intense and unwavering devotion to Him, has in countless instances kept men in this old Empire of China from the seductions of the pipe, and has made them bear heroically and without flinching the bitter pains that opium makes its victims endure before it will lose its grasp upon them.

Discussion Points for *Sidelights on Chinese Life*

1. The author seemed to tell a different story of opium compared to the others before. It was the British who held sole responsibility for the proliferation of the drug, according to the reverend. But, do you think that he might have had a bias?
2. How curious is it that nothing in the so-called Oriental character is strong enough to resist opium? What does Macgowan suggest is the only remedy for addiction? Does his logic carry through? Can the origin of sin really contain its saving grace?
3. Do you think the author's description showed that he admired the Chinese? Or, in contrast, did he look down upon them? Why?
4. A popular joke among Europeans was that the British believed that soap equaled civilization. How much of an emphasis did the author place on smells and cleanliness and how did that compare to what other authors noted? Why might the accounts differ?
5. Did the author trust the Chinese? How did he view them and evaluate their personal and family lives? What makes you think that he might have been mistaken?

PART V: TRAVEL TO THE AMERICAS

Triumph over the Moors in 1492 finalized the unification of the two kingdoms of Castile and Aragon and created a powerful Spain under King Ferdinand and Queen Isabella. Despite the victory in Grenada, the new Spanish kingdom lacked a meaningful political and religious mission, not to mention the critical amount of debt that accumulated in the final war over Grenada. A desperate economy, too many unproductive noblemen, and little in the way of manufacturing or industry, the Spanish sought to find a direct trade route to Asia and extend outwards, taking advantage of the recent spirit of conquest. Because their Portuguese neighbors were already well on their way to mapping the African coast, the Spanish bet on Christopher Columbus to reach the Indies and rob the traditional Muslim merchants of their erstwhile monopoly on trade between East and West.

Columbus sought a route to the Indies by sailing west, and in the process bumped into the Americas. From that point onwards, travels to the Americas not only created a completely new global economy based on cheap agriculture and minerals but also deeply changed the European psyche. With notions of the endless frontier and starting life anew, thinkers began philosophizing over the repercussions of America's discovery and their notions of mankind in the so-called state of nature. But when Columbus had set foot on the island of Hispaniola in 1492, no one could have imagined the vast amounts of goods and diseases that would thereafter traverse the world's oceans. Cocoa (as chocolate) naturally sweetened the desires of Europe's masses while potatoes became a cheap staple in northern Europe; yet, more important products like tobacco would create a far larger footprint across the globe. Europeans might have fancied rolling tobacco leaves into cigars but Muslims in the Ottoman and Safavid Empires slowly smoked their tobacco in the shisha, or water pipe. Other addictive substances, like the caffeine found in coffee, thrived in South America, and redefined methods of socialization, work-ethics, and tastes.

Moreover, Adam Smith's legendary concepts that formed the nucleus of modern capitalism won over the world following the publication and distribution of his three-volume collection, *Wealth of Nations* (1776). Intellectual notions from the likes of David Hume and John Locke also fueled people in the New World to seek political change. As perhaps the first professional revolutionary in modern time, Thomas Paine's wildly popular pamphlet, *Common Sense* (also 1776), struck a chord among colonists who saw themselves as the domesticators of an untamed and unpopulated wilderness. In addition to bringing Enlightenment philosophy to layman's terms, Paine had likened Americans to the brave frontiersmen who would forge ahead with building a new society premised on self-governance:

> In order to gain a clear and just idea of the design and end of government, let us suppose a small number of persons settled in some sequestered part of the earth, unconnected with the rest; they will then represent the first peopling of any country, or of the world. In this state of natural liberty, society will be their first thought.[35]

Notwithstanding that the United States of America would arise from Britain's thirteen colonies and dominate the Western Hemisphere, other peoples in America had profound influence in shaping Western and global civilization since Columbus's exploits of 1492. Haiti's revolution emerged as a powerful force in European and American politics despite its humble roots as a slave rebellion. Moreover, the demise of Spain's empire at the hands of the greedy Napoleon Bonaparte left much of Central and South America manuevering for independence by the second decade of the nineteenth century. Men like Simón Bolívar sought to unite South America but poor infrastructure, rough terrain, and competing viewpoints between the various domains prevented that vision from reaching reality. President James Monroe's docrtrine of 1823, which vocalized Washington's sphere of influence over the Americas, began a longstanding special relationship from Hudson Bay to Tierra del Fuego.

Map of North America

First Reading:

Alonzo de Guzman, *Book of the Life and Acts of Don Alonzo Enrique de Guzman of Seville*, Clements R. Markham, ed. (London: Hakluyt Society, 1862).

Once the Moors had conquered the Iberian Peninsula in AD 711, the struggle to remove them grew intense and helped created a Spanish identity that later crystallized within the larger European intellectual advancement. We see here with Alonzo de Guzman just the sort of man who began his young adulthood as an impoverished nobleman and sought action first against the Moors in Europe, and then in the New World, in search of fame and fortune. The experience that he gained fighting and dealing with the Moors shaped his ability to interact with folks in the colonies—including the Spanish who were already there and the various indigenous peoples. His journey was both extraordinary for the times, owing to its diversity and expansiveness, and typical for a man of his rank in Spanish society.

From the foreword

The present work was composed by a knight, in imitation of that of Caesar. This knight left his country to acquire glory and renown in foreign lands, that his name might be had in perpetual memory. In this work will be found many things very healthful for the soul, and for the honor and safety of the body. . . . Know then, O most inquisitive reader that, if you are curious to learn the transactions of the governments of this world, I am able to say, with truth, as regards this my writing, that I saw what I wrote, and I wrote what I saw.

His early exploits

In the year 1518, being eighteen years of age and nearly nineteen, I found myself fatherless and poor of estate, though rich in lineage, with a mother, who was a very talkative yet honest, good, and pious woman. She was not able to provide for me, seeing that I was growing up, though not of an age to marry, and so from necessity I married. Oppressed with poverty, and desirous of riches, I determined to go in search of adventures, and set out from the city of Seville, which was my native place, with a horse, a mule, a bed, and sixty ducats. I resolved to write down all that happened to me, and not to record anything which is not worthy of credit. My name is Don Alonzo Enriquez de Guzman. I am a descendant of the Count of Gijon, who was son of the King Don Enrique, of Castile. My mother was named Doña Catalina de Guevara.

[After having gone to serve in the royal court and failed, he became a soldier.[35]]

We disembarked on an uninhabited island called Formentera, where we found the people whom we were to join from Barcelona, consisting of five thousand foot soldiers and four hundred men at arms, and three hundred light infantry, under the command of Diego de Vera, a veteran knight. In a few days we sailed for the island of Sicily, where we were joined by Don Diego de Moncada, prior of Messina, of the order of St. John, who was appointed captain-general of the army. He was quartered, with the cavalry, in a town called Trapani, and the infantry were encamped at a distance of four or five leagues [approximately 14–17 miles], at a place called Marsala, with Diego de Vera as lieutenant-general. We were thus encamped for five months, during which time I will first tell you what happened to myself, and then what befell the army.

I, being of tender of age, though self-willed, having left my mother's house and come to a land of strangers, who shut their doors in my face, was taken very dangerously ill during two months. I had made no friends, because, during the voyage from Barcelona, I was so indignant and enraged at the treatment I had received, that I avoided everyone. When I recovered, and had spent all my small supply of money, I desired to go to Marsala, where the infantry were encamped, to join the company of Captain Villaturiel. When I made as if I was going to pay for my lodging, the people, as I had made no complaint of my poverty, declined to receive payment, solely on account of my youth, and my weakness. I begged for food from door to door in the daytime, but I fared very ill at night, as the people closed their doors early. In this manner passed a month, when I began to collect faggots of wood and to sell them at a tavern, and in this way passed another month. At last I fell in with a knight of Seville named Gonzalo Marino, captain and alcaide of Melilla for the Duke of Medina Sidonia, who came here to accompany the captain-general, Diego de Vera having command of the infantry, and Gonzalo Marino of the cavalry. This knight said that he was a friend of my father, and my fellow townsman, and he desired that I would honor him by using person and his estate. He took me to his lodging, clothed me, and took me to the captain-general, speaking very highly of me, and after twelve days they gave me a company of infantry and made me a captain. Fifteen days afterwards the said Gonzalo Marino died, whom may God pardon, and soon afterwards the army set out, to drive the Moors from the island of De los Gelves.

We sailed in a great fleet of ships, and with the same number of men as I have before stated, for though some had died, yet others had arrived to take their places. We were delayed longer than we expected by calms and light winds. On our arrival the Moors were prepared to receive us, numbering thirty thousand on foot, and thirty horsemen, there being few horses on the island, and the Moors not having had any opportunity of obtaining them. We jumped on shore, and, forming an encampment near the beach, passed the night there. Next day we began our march, in order of battle, with great confidence and certainty of success, which was the cause of all our misfortunes; for having marched two leagues [7 miles] without meeting any enemy, we began to think that there was no danger. We then advanced without any caution, some picking figs and others dates, for the country is thickly covered with palm trees, while others entered the houses of the natives in search of plunder, but only found a few jars of honey and raisins, which the people had not had time to carry off. We were in this state of disorder, when the Moors suddenly appeared, on all sides, twenty thousand in the front, five thousand in the rear, and thirty horsemen on our flank, led by a Moor, dressed like one of our hermits and riding on a donkey. Firm in their false faith, they came on with such determination to die, that I really believe they desired more to be killed themselves, than to kill us; for they rushed upon our pikes with open arms, as soon as they had hurled the stones and lances which they held in their hands. The said hermit and one thousand four hundred Moors were killed, and five hundred of our people and seven hundred of the cavalry, which were those who did not run away. I escaped, though wounded, with two or three others, the captain-general, and Diego de Vera. We assembled with great fear, because the advantages which we possessed in arms, were counterbalanced by their knowledge of the country. After we had rallied, we again embarked, and sailed to an uninhabited island called Favignana, two or three leagues [7–10 miles] from Trapani, on the coast of Sicily, where we were dismissed.

On a voyage to the Indies

As I left Spain a banished man, in disgrace with the Emperor; and as I am naturally of a quarrelsome as well as merry disposition, I determined, in order to avoid the chance of suffering as a I had formerly done, to disarm both myself and my followers, and thus I mixed with the sailor lads as one of themselves. I ate their salt fish with them, on my knees, and allowed them to share my fowls; because I thought I might benefit by their speaking well of me, and that they would report my peaceful and jovial conduct on their return to Seville. One morning, when I rose from my cot, and came on deck, I found the captain of the ship with a sword by his side, which he had not worn until now, and several men armed with darts on the main topsail yard. I said to the captain, "O great Captain, what is the matter?" He replied that several French ships were reported to be in these seas, coming from Brazil, and that he wished to be found ready for them, and not to be caught like a pig. I was amused, and called to my lads to bring me my sword, and to get theirs. He replied, very haughtily, that I must do no such thing, for that he had been watching me, and had seen cause to suspect that I wanted to seize the ship, for that I could have no other motive for making the sailor lads my companions and equals.

I answered: "Sir, you may make your mind easy, for I swear by God, and by my habit of the order of Santiago, that you may sleep in peace and have pleasant dreams, for I have no such intention. Free yourself, good Captain, from this delusion." He said that he was not satisfied, for that he had been told that I intended to cut the halliard, which is the rope that supports the mainsail, and to kill him, and all his friends. I soon saw that no one had told him this, but that he had invented it to conceal his folly and to hide his fear. All that I did to assure him he took offence at; and there was a great commotion in the ship, but at last he was pacified.

We continued our voyage until we came in sight of some islands, one of which is called Anguila; another, Sombrero; a third, Anegada; and some others, the Virgin Islands. From the Canary islands to these islands, we had gone eight hundred leagues [2,762 miles] over the sea, suffering hunger and thirst, and seeing no land for twenty-five days. We came to an anchor off one of these islands, which are in the Indies, and inhabited by fierce and warlike men, called Carribs. They fight with each other; and when they take or kill their enemies, they eat them. If the prisoner they capture is thin, they make a hole in the ground, and fatten him in it, and afterwards eat him. The hands and feet are considered the most dainty morsels, and these they give to those whom they desire to please. These Carribs are fierce, and can defend themselves with arrows; and, as their land does not yield gold, the Christians have passed it on one side, and pressed on; and we did so also, coming to an island inhabited by Christians, called San Juan de Puerto Rico.

Puerto Rico is a fertile island, containing two large Christian towns, called Puerto Rico and San German. The distance between one and the other is twenty leagues [69 miles] by land, and a day and a half's voyage by sea from Puerto Rico to San German, but at least a month's voyage from San German to Puerto Rico. There are many fruits in the island: some called batatas; other ajis; others piñas; others, pitahayas; others, guayavas; others, mamayas; others, cococos; others, platanas; but the only fruits which have been introduced from Spain are citrons, oranges, melons, cucumbers, lettuce, cauliflowers, pomegranates, and figs. There is a fish here called manati, the size of a bullock, and tasting like veal; and it comes out of the sea to browse on land. It looks like a calf in the face, but its eyes are smaller, resembling those of a goshawk. These beasts are very fat, and the flesh is eaten roasted with sauce. If a man did not see the manati taken out of the water, he would think the flesh was that of a bullock, especially after it is cooked. I am sure that there is no good Christian who, if he did not know beforehand, would not think he was eating beef, even if they assured them it was fish. I also saw turtles of the size of large wheels, and these also taste like meat. In this island there are no flies, no lice, no fleas, no bugs, and no water lizards, nor other evil insects; but there are rats and great land lizards. There are plenty of sheep and cattle, and several gold mines. All the Indians are either dead, or have escaped from the island, except a few whom the Christians retain as slaves.

We were here for eleven days. I found many sons of servants of my ancestors, especially of the family of Medina Sidonia, who received me with much honor, and entertained me with bull fights, and tilting matches. The water is very good, though it is brought from a distance of about half a league from the town. In this town of Puerto Rico there is a very good church, and a monastery of Dominican friars, who are very devout. The monastery and church are built of stone and mortar, and roofed with tiles; but all the houses, except one or two, have their walls and the floors of the upper stories of wood, and the roofs of tiles. There are between four and five hundred inhabitants, and they all have very good houses in the country, which they call estancias. We sailed from Puerto Rico to the island of Española [Hispaniola, or today Haiti and the Dominican Republic].

On a voyage to Peru

I sailed from the island of Española on my way to Peru, and arrived at the port of Nombre de Dios, in the province of Castilla del Oro [lit. region of gold]. The native name of the place means Bones, and it was so called on account of the number of people who have died there. Of the six horses which I landed at this port, I sold three, and sent three by land to Panama, a port on the shores of the South Sea [Pacific Ocean]. I traveled across the land to Panama, a distance of eighteen leagues [62 miles]. For the first seven the road passes between two high ranges of hills, densely covered with forest, along the banks of a river which was nearly dry, the water reaching to the hocks of the horses, but in some places to the girths; and, to those who travel on foot, it is a very weary journey. For the last eleven leagues [39 miles] the road is better, though there are several rivers to pass. There are three inns on the road, one called Capira, the second La Junta, and the third La Venta de Changres, because here they disembark from another deep river called Changres.

I must now tell you what I saw in this province of Castilla del Oro, and what I thought of the Indians, and afterwards, if I live, I will tell you about Peru. The Indian people appeared to me to be like what we should have been, if Adam had never sinned. They neither sin, nor know how to sin; they feel neither envy nor malice; they have no money amongst them, nor do they require any; and, as to clothing, they go about as their mothers bore them, excepting a small cotton cloth between the legs. They are very timorous respecting all things in the world, excepting death, for they know not that there is any other world either for rewards or punishments. They are very loyal, and will suffer floggings, tortures, and death before they will say a word which might do harm to their masters or their country.

In this land of Panama there are many parrots as large as crows, tigers, turtles, and animals called yayanas, the size of large cats, which are very good to eat, as well as their eggs, of which they each have twenty or thirty. There are also wild pigs in the forests, somewhat smaller than those in Castile, with their navels on their backs. I say this, because I have seen them; for I shall tell no lies, because I must give an account to God of what you may here read. There are bats which, when they succeed in finding any part of a man uncovered, suck the blood until he dies. The land is very fertile and densely wooded, and the reason of this is partly because the people neither sow nor gather in harvests, and partly because the rains are very heavy. It is always very hot, and there is no cold either in winter or summer. The bread is made from roots, and they take very little trouble either in sowing or gathering them, using no iron tools, but merely working with poles and by hand; thus the people can live without much labor, if we would leave them alone.

To sail in the South Sea is like navigating a smooth river without wind. December, January, February, and March are the best seasons for navigating. I sailed from Panama on the 20th of March, with three horses, the passage costing me four hundred and fifty castellaños de oro for the horses, twenty for my slaves, and one hundred for my own passage and for my cabin, with very good ship's stores. Two days before I embarked in this port of Panama, I received a letter from a very good friend of mine, advising me to return, saying that I wanted more wealth than was reasonable, seeing that I have 150,000 maravedis of rent, and that I ought not to go in search of more.

Arriving in Peru

The Indians of this land of Peru are a gentle and peaceful people, living on such light food as gourds and batatas, cooked with a sort of spice called aji, which they use in all their dishes. Occasionally they eat meat and fish. The meat is from a strange kind of sheep, which can go without eating for fifteen days. The chief of these Indians was Atabalipa [Atahualca], who, as I have been told by many witnesses, only wanted Christianity to make him worthy of being a king. There are not so many ants in Spain as there are Indians in this country. This Atabalipa, when he was taken prisoner and put to death by the Spaniards, was about thirty years of age, of middle height, somewhat fat, with a round fair face, and the manners of a gentlemen. He was served by women and not by men; and he wore a fringe on his forehead, in the manner of a crown. No one approached him without bringing a present in token of submission; and, though those who came were great nobles, they entered with the present on their backs, and without shoes. He was carried on men's shoulders when traveling, and roads were made five hundred leagues long [1,726 miles], and broad enough to allow ten horses to ride abreast, the ground being as smooth as the palm of the hand, with a wall on each side, and trees in double rows to rows to keep off the sun. Atabalipa was so intelligent, that in twenty days he understood the language of the Christians, and learnt to play at chess and at cards. He was the son of a great king of a province called Cuzco, and of another called Quito, named Guaynacapa, who reigned over more than fifteen hundred leagues [18,987 miles, *sic.*] of country.

He marched with a great army, establishing his authority through the country, until the arrival of the Christians caused him to return. . . . He was taken, and put to death in the following manner. The Christians arrived within a league and a half of the Indian army, and they then sent ten men on horseback to say that they wanted not their gold nor their silver, nor to do them any injury, nor to subjugate them; but that they only wished to be their friends and brothers. These envoys tried to frighten the Indians with their horses, which caused much terror to men who had never seen such animals before; and they forced their horses' heads over the head of Atabalipa, when he was sitting in state, so that the breath from their nostrils moved the fringe on his forehead. The Spaniards were astonished that, though he had never seen horses before, he was not in the least terrified, nor did he even raise his head; but he heard what they had to say, and replied that if the Christians desired to be the friends and brothers of the Indians, they should return all the gold they had robbed from his vassal at Tumbez: he also said that he desired their friendship, and that he would visit them on another day.

Accordingly, he came with a great multitude of people, and a friar came out to receive him with the commandments of the Christian faith, which many of us do not know as well as we ought, and, telling Atabalipa that the book contained the decrees of God, he put it into his hand. Atabalipa took it, and threw it on the ground, saying—"I neither understand, nor do I desire to understand, what you say; but you have robbed my vassals; and when you have returned to them their silver and gold, I will be your brother and friend." Then the rascally friar, who was certainly a peace breaker, began to call with a loud voice, saying—"Christians! I call upon you to avenge this insult to the faith of Jesus Christ." The soldiers obeyed, killed a great number of the Indians, and imprisoned Atabalipa.

In Peru

I arrived at a city in Peru, inhabited by Christians which is called Piura, fifteen leagues [52 miles] from the port where I had disembarked. They did not build the town on the sea-shore, because there is neither water, nor wood, nor grass for horses. The Judge and Regidores of the town sent me all kinds of refreshments when I was three leagues [10 miles] off, and my entrance took place at sunset, as they had arranged.

The great city of Tumbez is inhabited entirely by Indians. It is on the sea-shore; and in it there is a great house, belonging to the lord of the country, with walls built of adobes, like bricks, very beautifully painted with many colors, and varnished, so that I never saw anything more beautiful. The roof is straw, also painted, so that it looks like gold, very strong, and very handsome.

The distance from this place to Cuzco is three hundred leagues [1,035 miles], and along the whole way there is a straight smooth road, passing amongst very lofty naked mountains, bare of grass or trees. On the coast there is an infinite quantity of sand, and when the wind raises it, it looks like clouds of snow. The road is bounded on each side by walls, two yards thick, and six in height. In some parts there are rows of trees which yield a fruit like that of the carob tree. Every three, or at most every four leagues [10–14 miles], there is a house which the Indians call tambo, but which we, in Spain, should call an inn. These tambos are well built, for the use of the lord of the land when he travels from the great city of Cuzco to Tumbez. I have already said that this Lord was called Guaynacapa, and that he was the father of Atibalipa.

Seventy leagues [241 miles] from Piura, and near the sea coast, there is a city which, in the language of the Indians, is called Chimu, and by the Spaniards Truxillo. Another eighty leagues [276 miles] further on, there is another city inhabited by Christians, two leagues [7 miles] from the sea shore, called by the Indians Lima, and in our language, the City of the Kings. Here I arrived very tired, with swollen ankles. I was cured by a woman who was married, honest, and ugly; and she suggested to me the following reflections. He who is not married, should not seek for a pretty woman, but for an ugly one, for the following reasons. First, because the ugly woman is free from two inconveniences, namely, annoyance from the attentions of other men, and from the love of her own husband; for he knows that, as she has no other resource, she must love him, and therefore gives her no trouble. But the pretty woman loves her husband for the first year, and runs after other men all the rest of her life; who have more use of her than her own husband.

At this time I was suffering from a most dreadful toothache, and as the object of this book is to relate all the troubles I had to encounter, I will first tell you how I cured the toothache, and afterwards I will relate what passed between the Governor and myself.

To cure the toothache take some aji, which we call Indian pepper, and apply it to the tooth; then put some hot olive oil in a cloth, and squeeze it over the place. This pain is so common and yet so terrible, that a remedy for it is almost so valuable as a remedy for loss of life or honor.

I set out from the City of Kings well supplied with horses, servants, and provisions, and the distance to Cuzco is one hundred and thirty leagues [448 miles] over the most rugged mountains that can possibly be imagined. The object of my journey was the conquest of a province called Chiriguana, which I was unable to effect, as you presently see, owing to the rising of the Indians.

I arrived in this city of Cuzco, tired and worn out by the long and rugged road, and the difficulty of getting provisions; for we had to take what we wanted from the Indians, and they killed one of my slaves, who had cost me six hundred castellaños. This city is built in a valley, and the houses are very lofty, with walls of hewn stone, strongly and beautifully worked. At a distance of three casts of a sling from the city, near some very high hills, there is a great fortress, which is no less beautiful than strong, all of quarried stone. The Indians have a youth of twenty years, a little more or less, for king, named Capa-ynga, which means, in our language, sole lord. He succeeded after Atabalipa, his brother, both being sons of Guaynacapa, who had a hundred sons and fifty daughters. The Indians adored their Guaynacapa, saying that he was a child of the sun; and they also worship his son Capa-ynga. These people have the following custom. At the age of fifteen years, they bore the ears of all their children; and this ceremony takes place every year, with the same solemnity as is observed in admitting to holy orders in Spain. On these occasions the youths promise three things—to worship the sun, to serve Capa-ynga, and to sow maize, which is their bread.

The Spaniards ill-treated the caciques and Indians, overworking them, burning them, and tormenting them for gold and silver; and one day Capa-ynga, on pretence of seeking for gold for Hernando Pizarro, the brother of the governor, who was that time acting as his lieutenant at Cuzco, left the city and never returned. He raised the country against us, and collected 50,000 armed men, the Christians not numbering more than two hundred, half of them being lame or halt. One day the Indians entered the city in the morning, by seven different points, fighting so fiercely, and burning as they advanced, that they gained half the city, and there was little left to burn, because the houses were thatched with straw.

God, and some force of our own, assisted us; but, in addition to the numbers and ferocity of the Indians, the smoke was so dense that we could not see each other. The conflict lasted from the morning of one day to the morning of the next. With the aid of God we at length drove the Indians back towards the fortress, where there was a captain of Capa-ynga, who was called Villa-uma. He was their Pope, and had charge of the house of the sun. We then assaulted and captured the fortress, killing 3,000 Indians; and they killed our captain, Juan Pizarro, a brother of the governor, a youth aged twenty-five years, and possessed of 200,000 ducats in money. During the combat in the city the Indians killed four Christians, besides more than thirty whom they killed in the farms of caciques, who were out collecting tribute.

The Indians of Cuzco are better dressed than those of any of the other provinces, both because it is colder here in winter, and because the land is more fertile, and the people are richer. They are much afraid of our horses, but their mountains offer an excellent means of defense against them. They have no defensive, but many offensive arms, such as lances, arrows, clubs, axes, halberds, darts, and slings, and another weapon which they call ayllas, consisting of three round stones sewn up in leather, and each fastened to a cord a cubit long. They throw these at the horses, and thus bind their legs together; and sometimes they will fasten a man's arms to his sides in the same way. These Indians are so expert in the use of this weapon that they will bring down a deer with it in the chase. Their principal weapon, however, is the sling, which I have delayed mentioning to the last. With it they will hurl a huge stone with such force that it will kill a horse; in truth, the effect is little less great than that of an arquebus; and I have seen a stone, thus hurled from a sling, break a sword in two pieces, which was held in a man's hand at a distance of thirty paces. The Indians also adopted the following stratagem: they made an endless number of deep holes, with stakes bristling in them, and covered over with straw and earth. The horses often fell into them; and the rider was generally killed.

I am able to certify that this was the most fearful and cruel war in the world; for between the Christians and Moors there is some fellow-feeling, and both sides follow their own interests in sparing those whom they take alive, for the sake of their ransoms; but in this Indian war there is no such feeling on one side or the other, and they give each other the most cruel deaths they can invent. After this there happened many things, which I remit to the chronicler who may hereafter write upon this subject.

Discussion Points for *Life and Acts of Don Alonzo de Guzman*

1. What can you say about how Guzman changed, if at all? Why?
2. Did the author have any compassion for the indigenous peoples of the Americas or were his views patronizing or demeaning?
3. How did the Carribs differ from the tribes the author encountered in Peru? How were they the same?
4. What sense do you have regarding the life of a Spanish warrior/adventurer?
5. Why do you think Guzman went to Peru and not another part of the Spanish Empire—Mexico perhaps? What forces brought him there?

Spanish conquistadors

Second Reading:

F.H.H. Guillemard, *The Life of Ferdinand Magellan and the First Circumnavigation of the Globe, 1480–1521* (New York: Dodd, Mead & Company, 1890).

As the epitome of the world explorer, Ferdinand Magellan accomplished much in his nautical career. Service to the crown of Portugal as an explorer and as a soldier provided Magellan useful experience before he vowed to circumnavigate the globe. Portuguese authorities denied his request for a commission, so he sought the backing of other patrons. Spain granted him the commission he needed and thus Magellan's famous voyage finished for the Spanish crown in 1522 what Columbus had dreamed of years earlier. While most of the men on the voyage did not survive the trip, including Magellan himself, they nonetheless proved the existence of a westward path from Europe to the Pacific Ocean.

Lisbon harbor

Rest

Returned once more to his native land, Magellan remained there for nearly a year. Whether he retired to his estate at Sabrosa or breathed the more stirring air of the court at Lisbon, we are not informed. But to one of his temperament—one who for seven long years had led a vivid life of adventure by sea and land, a life of siege and shipwreck, of endless war and wandering—a country existence must have become impossible. To be with his fellows, with men who had tasted of the sweets and bitters of the wider life, to be within reach of news from India, to watch the preparations for further and perhaps greater expeditions—this must have been to him as the breadth of life, and we cannot doubt that he remained in Lisbon. . . . It was to India, doubtless, that Magellan looked as the scene of his future success—to the Farther India of which Serrao had written to him, and of which he himself later said that he would find his way thither, "if not by way of Portugal, then by way of Spain." It was not, however, in India that he was next to serve. In the summer of 1513 difficulties arose with the Moors of Azamor in Morocco. In the time of Dom João II, a treaty had been concluded with them. Portuguese subjects resided in the city, their ships entered the harbor free of dues, and their goods passed the customs without charge. The peace remained unbroken until, tired of paying tribute, Muley Zeyam rebelled. Dom Manoel was not the monarch to leave an insult long without revenge. An armada was fitted out in Lisbon such as neither before nor since weighed anchor from the shores of Portugal.

The city [Azamor] was scarcely settled ere a series of "*entradas*" or armed reconnaissances was instituted, which, making their descent where least expected, greatly harassed the Moors and kept the country in a perpetual state of terror. In one of these, under the leadership of João Soarez, Magellan was wounded in the leg by a lance, which appears to have injured some tendon behind the knee in such a manner that he remained slightly lame for the rest of his life.

Voyage around the world – South America

The winter was not fairly established, and the cold became more severe. Nor was the weather they experienced such as to tempt to a renewal of their explorations along the coast. But the Captain-general [Magellan], anxious to learn something of the interior of the country, thought it advisable to dispatch a small expedition with that object. Four men only were sent. They were well armed, and were furnished with instructions to penetrate, if possible, to a distance of thirty leagues [103 miles], to plant a cross, and to put themselves upon a footing of friendship with any natives they might happen to meet. The nature of the country was, unfortunately, such as to render the expedition a failure. Neither food nor water was to be found. The men were forced to be content with the ascent of a high mountain at some little distance from the coast. Planting a cross upon its summit, and giving it the name of the Mount of Christ, they retraced their steps, and arrived at the ships, informing Magellan that the country was intraversable [*sic.*] and without resources, and appeared to be entirely without people.

It was not long before the latter piece of information at least was proved to be incorrect. The fleet had remained at anchor for weeks at Port St. Julian, and no trace of natives had been seen.

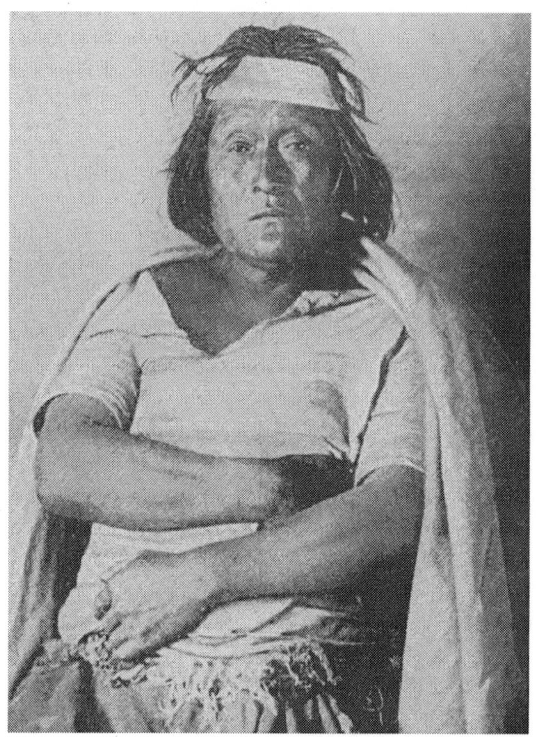

Man from Patagonia

One morning, however, the sailors were astonished by the appearance of a man of gigantic stature upon the beach, who sang and danced, pouring sand upon his head in token of amity. Magellan sent a man ashore with instructions to imitate the action of the savage, and, if possible, to make friends with him. This he succeeded in doing, and the newcomer was brought before the admiral. Spaniards and natives were equally surprised. The latter marveled, Gomara tells us, to see such large ships and such little men, and pointing to the sky, seemed to inquire whether they were not gods who had descended from heaven; while the Spaniards, wondering at the great stature of their visitor, concluded that they had come upon a race of giants. "So tall was this man," writes Pigafetta, "that we came up to the level of his waistbelt. He was well enough made, and had a broad face, painted red, with yellow circles round his eyes, and two heart-shaped spots on his cheeks. His hair was short and colored white, and he was dressed in the skins of an animal cleverly sewn together." This description given of this animal leaves no doubt that it was the guanaco. The skin of the same creature served to make boots for these people, and it was the unwieldy appearance thus given to the feet which led Magellan to apply to the race the name of Patagão. . . . The man seemed most peaceably disposed, though he did not lay aside his arms—a short, thick bow, and a bundle of cane arrows tipped with black and white stones. Magellan treated him kindly, and ordered that he should be given food. He was shown some of their objects for barter, among others a large steel mirror. So overcome was he on catching sight of himself, says Pigafetta, that he jumped backwards with an unexpectedness and impetuosity which overset four of the men who were standing round him. He was, nevertheless, not unwilling to accept a small mirror as a present, and some beads and bells having been added, he was put ashore under the care of four armed men.

A companion met him upon landing, and confidential relations having been thus established, the Spaniards had no difficulty in persuading the natives to visit their ships. Others, accompanied by their wives, were not long in showing themselves, and eventually several came on board. "The women," we are told, "were loaded by them with all their belongings, as if they were so many beasts of burden. We could not behold them without wonder." They were not so tall as the men, but much fatter, and had breasts half as long as a man's arm. With them "they brought four of those little beasts of which they make their clothing, leading them with a cord like dogs coupled together." The use of these, they said, was to tie up and entice others within range of arrows of the hunter, who was hidden near. The Spaniards were anxious to secure some of these guanacos, and getting together eighteen of the natives, set half of them to hunt on either side of the entrance of the harbor, but we are not told of the result of their endeavors.

Many visits were thus paid by the natives to the fleet, and Pigafetta was enabled to obtain a small vocabulary of their language. One of them, who seemed especially tractable and pleasing, remained with the ships some days. He was taught the Paternoster and Ave Maria, which he pronounced well, but in an exceedingly loud voice, and the priest eventually baptized him with the name of Juan Gigante.

The manners and customs of the Patagonians are described at some length by the supposed Genoese pilot as well as by Pigafetta. The fact that they devoured with great relish the rats which were caught on the ships filled the sailors with astonishment, which was not lessened by perceiving that they did not stop to skin them. Still more astonishing was their power of thrusting arrows down their throats without injury, which was apparently done more as a *tour de force* than for any definite purpose. . . . In spite of Magellan's fixed rule that the fleet should not be burdened with useless mouths, especially now that the rations had been reduced, he was so much struck with the *gigantes*, as they termed them, that he resolved to bring some of them back with him to Spain as a present to the Emperor. It was some little time before he was able to put his project into execution, for fifteen days elapsed before another native was seen. At length, upon the 28th July, four appeared upon the beach, and were brought on board the *Trinidad* [Magellan's flagship]. Magellan was anxious to keep the two youngest, but having an idea that their capture might not be an easy matter, he decided to use strategy rather than force. Loading them with presents, so that their hands were full, he then offered them a pair of irons, and, as they were unable to take them, showed them how they fitted upon the legs. A couple of strokes of the hammer riveted the bolts, and the two unlucky savages were prisoners before they realized their position. When they did so, they became furious, invoking Setebos, their Great Spirit, to their aid. Their two companions were conducted ashore with their arms bound by a party of men who were instructed to bring the wife of one of the captives, "who greatly regretted her, as we saw by signs." The huts of the natives were reached the same day, but as it was late, the pilot Carvalho, who was in charge of the party, decided on waiting till the following day. It happened that on the road one of their charges had attempted to escape, and in the struggle which ensued he was wounded in the head. His companions said nothing at the time, but next morning they spoke a few words to the women, and immediately all took to flight.

Passing the straits

The three remaining ships of the squadron, passing Cape Deseado, directed their course to less inhospitable shores and a warmer climate. Their passage of the strait had cost them thirty-eight days. Although its length was in reality not more than 320 miles, the many incidents that had arisen and the protracted time that they had spent within its limits led to exaggerate its size, and the distance from mouth to mouth was variously estimated at from 350 to 400 miles.

On reaching the Pacific, the other Patagonian captured in Port St. Julian died. He had been kept on board the flagship, and had apparently reconciled himself in part to his position. To Pigafeta he had become an object of curiosity and interest. "I conversed by signs or as best I could with the Patagonian giant we had on board, making him tell me the names of things in his language, whence I was able to form a vocabulary. When he saw me take the pen in my hand he used to tell me the names of the objects around us, or of some action he might imitate. . . . When he felt himself gravely ill of the malady from which afterwards died, he embraced the Cross and kissed it, and desired to become a Christian. We baptized him, and gave him the name of Paul."

Faring northward to escape the cold, the explorers encountered such favorable weather that the difficulties and privations they had passed through were well-nigh forgotten. The sudden, violent tempests had given place to steady winds which wafted [gently floated] them on their course over the surface of a placid sea, and thankful for their deliverance from their troubles they gave the name of the Pacific to the vast ocean which had afforded them so friendly a reception. "Well was it named the Pacific," Pigafetta writes, "for during this time (three months and twenty days) we met with no storm."

Discussion Points for *Ferdinand Magellan*

1. How did Magellan's method of dealing with indigenous peoples differ from that of other explorers? How was it the same?
2. Think about the way that explorers like Magellan named things. In Southern Chile, Tierra del Fuego—the land of fire—was logical because Magellan saw fires on the island the entire time the ships passed it. Other examples from the readings highlight this too. When we think of names of places in the United States, do we have a similar legacy from exploration?
3. Magellan was Portuguese but he served both the Portuguese and Spanish governments. How easy do you think this was and what do you think motivated such explorers? Was nationalism not an issue?
4. Besides exploring, what else did Magellan do while in Europe?
5. Jacob le Maire's account also noted that he found human skeletons from 10 to 12 feet long buried underneath heaps of rocks—how do you reconcile the notion that larger humans might have roamed the earth? After all, there are web sites like http://biblebelievers.org.au that describe how the existence of giant people verify stories from the Bible. Do such observations lend credibility or detract from the author's larger observations?

THIRD READING:

Eusebio Francisco Kino, S. J., *Kino's Historical Memoir of Pimería Alta, Pioneer Missionary Explorer, Cartographer, and Ranchman, 1683–1711*, Herbert E. Bolton, ed. (Cleveland, OH: Arthur H. Clark Company, 1919).

In contrast to the account by Guzman, who fought the Moors and then went to the New World in search of treasure and fame, we have this account of perhaps the most important Spanish constituency to reach the Americas—members of the church. Catholic missionaries worked to save souls for Christ and build the frontier into a working colony. Venturing out to the wilderness brought unique challenges and exposed the fathers to distinctive dangers, especially because they roamed as men of the cloth and not conquistadors. Father Kino traveled all over Northern Mexico into the American Southwest and played an influential role in building missions like San Xavier del Bac, just outside of downtown Tucson, Arizona. While Anglo-Americans eventually settled the West in the later 1800s, they certainly were not the first pilgrims. This powerful legacy of missionaries and how they worked to Christianize and control the indigenous populations form the basis of award-winning films like *The Mission* and *The Black Robe*.

Journey northward to the Sobaipuris

August 23, 1692. In spite of the obstacles which were present, and seeing that the whole of Pimeria was quiet, during the last part of August and the first part of September, 1692, I went in, with fifty pack-animals, my servants, and some justices, to the Sobaipuris, both of the north and of the northeast. The latter are in the valleys of the river of Quiburi, to the east, and the former are in the valley and river of Santa Maria, to the west. The journey to the former was more than eighty leagues by very level road. I found the natives very affable and friendly, and particularly so in the principal Rancheria of San Xavier del Bac, which contains more than eight hundred souls.

I spoke to them of the Word of God, and on a map of the world showed them the lands, the rivers, and the seas over which we fathers had come from afar to bring them the saving knowledge of our holy faith. And I told them also how in ancient times the Spaniards were not Christians, how Santiago came to teach them the faith, and how for the first fourteen years he was able to baptize only a few, because of which the holy apostle was discouraged, but that the most Holy Virgin appeared to him and consoled him, telling him that the Spaniards would convert the rest of the people of the world. And I showed them on the map of the world how the Spaniards and the faith had come by sea to Vera Cruz, and had gone in to Puebla and to Mexico, Guadalaxara, Sinoloa, and Sonora, and now to Nuestra Señora de los Dolores del Cosari, in the land of the Pimas, where there were already many persons baptized, a house, church, bells, and images of saints, plentiful supplies, wheat, maize, and many cattle and horses; that they could go and see it all, and even ask at once of their relatives, my servants, who were with me. They listened with pleasure to these and other talks concerning God, heaven, and hell, and told me that they wished to be Christians, and gave me some infants to baptize. These Sobaipuris are in a very fine valley of the Rio de Santa Maria, to the west.

San Xavier del Bac, Arizona

Second and third expeditions to the Sea of California

February, 1694. . . . I made another expedition to the same waters of the Sea of California, in company with Father Marcos Antonio Kapus, who was stationed in Cucurpe, and Lieutenant Juan Matheo Manje. We again saw very clearly the same California and its principal and larger hills. We named them San Marcos, San Matheo, San Juan (for the name of San Lucas is already given to the Cape of Californian), and San Antonio, as may be seen on the map. The natives of the nation of El Soba we found so friendly that, having come thirty, forty, and fifty leagues' journey from the north to see us, they gave us their infants to baptize.

A few months later I made another expedition with Lieut. Juan Matheo Manje, to this nation and to the sea, and we discovered the good port of Santa Sabina on the day of that saint.

During these months and the preceding ones there was built in La Consepcion del Caborica a capacious earth-covered hall of adobe and earth, and wheat and maize were sown for the father whom they were asking for and hoping to obtain.

Expedition to remove the body of Father San Xavier Saeta, who had died

Upon receiving the news, which I at once dispatched to the superiors and to the royal justice, the Señor governor of arms, Don Domingo Jeronsa Petriz de Cruzat, responded and came at once with the soldiers of his presidio and with many friendly Indians, and accompanied by Father Agustin de Campos and Father Fernando Bayerca, for the purpose of redressing the injuries and to remove the body of the venerable father to La Consepcion. But from everywhere around there the people fled through fear of the soldiers, whom they had never seen before. Having killed a boy, beaten an Indian woman, and taken captive three little children whom they encountered, they gathered up the bones and ashes of the venerable father, and various papers, books, and other trifles. Returning, the Señor governor observed the day of the Holy Cross in May in this new church of Nuestra Señora de los Dolores, confessing and partaking of the holy Sacrament in the morning, and in the afternoon we all proceeded to the nearby pueblo of Cucurpe. We bore the bones and ashes of the venerable father; and the Señor governor, to the great satisfaction of all, deigned to lead by the bridle the mule which bore the little box containing the bones of the venerable father. The following day the burial occurred, the father rector of this rectorate of Nuestra Señora de los Dolores, Father Marcos Antonio Kappus, singing mass.

Third expedition

July and August, 1695. Afterward, in July and August, there went inland three camps or garrisons, comprising one hundred and fifty men, with two hundred loads of supplies, and with many Indian friends from all parts, even from the Pimeria of the north itself, for besides the garrison of this Presidio of Sonora, that of the Presidio of Xanos entered under General Juan Fernandez de la Fuente; likewise, the garrison of the Presidio of El Gallo, under General Don Domingo Theran. These two garrisons passed through the lands of Hocomes and the hostile Xanos, in order to reach Pimeria, and in those lands, in the Serro de Chiguicagui, they found almost all the spoils of the many robberies which, during all these years had been committed in this province of Sonora and on its frontiers, including many arquebuses, swords, daggers, spurs, saddle-bags, saddles, boots, etc., whose theft many had so falsely imputed to the Pimas Sobaipuris.

There were also found the pieces, very recently broken, of the bugle which they took away from the bugler of General Quiros. Among these Hocomes were found the spoils of the soldier Juan de Ochoa, whom, a few weeks before, they had captured alive, killing his three companions, on the road between Guachinera and Guasavas. Many of these spoils, guns, saddles, etc., were redeemed, and truces were made with the enemy until they should come to the Pimeria, whither General Don Domingo Theran hurried, entering Tubutamma at night, without the other two garrisons knowing it, and killing fifteen or sixteen Pimas. Hereupon the people fled in all directions, just as they were about to deliver up the criminals to their deserved punishment.

Casa Grande ruins, constructed by the Hohokam, central Arizona

The garrisons, together with the friendly Indians, went up from El Tubutama to El Saric, and then descended to La Consepcion, a march of more than forty leagues, consuming fruitlessly many weeks time, because the people were still far away, until with great prudence, experience, and very Christian zeal, General Juan Fernandez de la Fuente, realizing that there was no rebellion among these Pimas, since in all this time they did not resist, oppose, or make war on anyone, anywhere, but merely fled through fear of the soldiers, and remained in retreat, endeavored to make peace, with the stipulation and condition that the Pimas and their chief captains and governors should obligate themselves to deliver up the principal malefactors in the murder of the venerable Father Francisco Xavier Saeta, and the Pimas joyfully accepted the proposal.

Catholic peace-agreements

General Juan Fernandez de la Fuente, seeing that all the Pimas, those who had retreated as well as those who had not, those of the west and those of the north, were falling in so amicably with his very generous and very Catholic proposals relative to the peace-agreements, his Grace summoned me to see that the truces were properly drawn up, so that we fathers should be safe, content, and satisfied. I went at once to El Tupo and La Consepcion, whither many natives of six distinct rancherias, or pueblos, presently arrived, on the twenty-fifth of August. Soon we came to the plains of La Cienega del Tupo; and on August 30, day of the most glorious Saint of the Indies, Rosa de Santa Maria, seven other rancherias or pueblos and many governors went down thither.

And after sundry very pacific and very Catholic talks on the part of the Company, and especially on the part of the generals, some very friendly, very excellent, and very Christian peace-agreements were drawn up in the name of God and the King, the Pimas very willingly obligating themselves promptly to surrender the principal delinquents to their merited punishment. And it was a source of most singular comfort, and edification, and tenderness to see those generals embracing those poor Pima captains and governors with such loving, Christian, Catholic embraces and friendly caresses. Thanks to the Sovereign Lord, some peace-agreements were drawn up and so well established and fixed that, by Divine mercy, they remained very permanent, to the great advantage of the province and to the great injury of our enemies, the Hocomes; and in due time these captains and governors fulfilled their promise, surrendering to the royal justice the principal delinquents. They were catechized, baptized, and prepared for death; but the very great and paternal charity of the father visitor, Oracio Polise, seeing them so humble and so repentant, obtained their pardon.

Letter from Father Anttonio Leal, 9 June 1695

I took great comfort from the pleasing reports with which the father visitor favored me, of the progress and increase of Christianity in the Pimeria, occasioned by the entry of your Reverence one hundred and fifty leagues to the north, and of the great number of heathen who anxiously sought the waters of holy baptism. But how could such ease be free from envy; and how could the Devil allow so many souls, which he held as his own, to escape him, without doing his utmost to block their pathway?

I have greatly regretted, and all greatly regret, that that revolt should have occurred among those poor creatures, although I hope in our Lord that it has been in all parts. However, my father, though the faith of our God has had such a setback, not for that has it been destroyed; and although the Apostles, disciples of Christ, and their successors in all ages, have died, si caro infirma spiritus promptus, those who have remained have again promptly kindled the fires of the Holy Spirit, reviving it from the deadest ashes. Your Reverence, whom it behooves not to give up—for the blood of our brother is to be the watering by which those new plants are to wax greater, and in heaven he is to be the patron of those poor souls—your Reverence has been and must be their apostle; and great will be the compassion which for some is suffered by others. Then, my father, the blood of Christ! Be not cast down, your Reverence, by what has happened, for it is the cause of God, and God will return for its sake and assist your Reverence, whom I pray Him to guard for me many years. Since, your Reverence, I have ever been your companion in desires whose fulfillment our Lord hath not granted me, may he make me a participant in your labors.

Journey to Mexico to obtain missionary fathers

Since the year before, and earlier, when from these coasts of this Pimeria we caught sight of California nearby, I had asked and obtained permission from the father provincial, Diego de Almonacir, to go to Mexico to discuss with his Reverence and with his Excellency the conversion of California and the extensive new lands of this mainland; but my going had been prevented by the royal justice and some fathers, the lieutenants, and citizens of this province, who reported to Mexico that I should be needed here, and that I was accomplishing more than a well governed presidio, etc. This year, 1695, however, in view of the very Christian truces which had been drawn up on the thirtieth of August in this Pimeria, and since the harvest of souls was so plenteous, so widespread, and so ripe, I determined, although some opposed me, to avail myself of the license, almost an order, which I had from the father provincial, and to go to Mexico for the good of so many souls in sore need; and so, setting out from these missions of Sonora on the sixteenth of November, 1695, in seven weeks and after a journey of five hundred leagues, I arrived at Mexico on January 8, 1696.

It was God's will that I should be able to say mass every day of this trip; and the three masses of the Feast of the Nativity I said in the new church of Nuestra Señora de Loreto of Guadalaxara. The same day on which I arrived at Mexico Father Juan Maria Salvatierra arrived by another route, while that morning the new government had been installed, Father Juan de Palacios having entered as provincial. I took with me to Mexico the son of the captain general of this Pimeria, and we received the utmost kindness and favors from the new father provincial and his predecessor, from his Excellency the Conde [Count] de Galves, and even from her Ladyship, the viceroy's wife, who were delighted at seeing new people who came from parts and lands so remote.

Opposition and rumors

Nevertheless, so great were the obstacles and the opposition against this Pimeria that they caused even the most friendly father visitor, Oracio Polise, to falter. It was again reported, but very falsely, as has since been seen, that the Pimas Sobaipuris were closely allied with the hostile Jocomes, and with the other enemies of this provinces of Sonora; and they were charged with stealing droves of horses, etc., and with having many large corrals full of them. It was falsely reported, also, that these Pimas were involved in the tumults and revolts of Taraumara, on the testimony of the Taraumares themselves, but the Taraumares could not have been speaking of the Pimas of this Pimeria, who are more than one hundred and fifty leagues distant from the Taraumares, but only of the Pimas near them, who are those of Tapipa and near Yecora. It had been said and reported, but very falsely, that the Pimas of the interior and their neighbors were such cannibals that they roasted and ate people, and that for this reason one could not go to them; but already we have entered and have found them very friendly and entirely free from such barbarities. . . . It was said and written to Mexico that I [Kino] lived guarded by soldiers, but I have never had, nor thanks to the Lord, needed such a guard.

Setting out from San Dionisio

In this first Rancheria of these Quiquimas, with the messages and little gifts which we had sent them during the months preceding, they received us with much friendship, asking us that we should remain some days with them. . . . The natives greatly wondered at many of our things, for they had never seen nor heard of them. They wondered much at the vestment in which mass is said, and at its curious sort of embroidery representing spring, and its skillfully woven flowers of different beautiful colors; and they would ask us to keep it on so that those who continually came to visit us might have the pleasure of seeing it. Also, it was a matter of much astonishment to them to see our pack-animals and mounts, for they had never seen horses or mules or heard of them. And when the Yumas and Pimas who came with us said to them that our horses could run faster than the most fleet-footed natives, they did not believe it, and it was necessary to put it to the test.

After crossing the Rio Colorado

As we crossed the river many more people came to us and there were dances and entertainments after their fashion. I preached to them through an interpreter, here and on the road, and in the afternoon, when, after about three leagues' journey, we arrived at the house of the captain of the nation [Quiquima, or chief]. In all parts the word of God and the Christian doctrine were well received. All the road was full of small but very continuous Rancherias, with very many people, very affable, very well featured, and somewhat whiter than the rest of the Indians. . . . [they live in the] most fertile lands, of most beautiful cornfields very well cultivated with abundant crops of maize, beans, and pumpkins, and with very large drying-places for the drying of pumpkins, for this kind lasts them afterwards all the year.

When, two hours before sunset, we arrived at the Rancheria and house of the captain, the captain of the neighboring Cutgana nation came also to see us, with a great following of people from the north and from the west, and with various gifts, and in particular with many blue shells from the opposite coast of California, and from the other or South Sea, giving us very detailed information in regard to them, and saying that they were not more than eight or ten days' journey to the westward, and that the Sea of California ended a day's journey farther to the south than where we were. . . . Besides, I sent them some messages in regard to Christian doctrine, and said that the purpose of our expeditions was the salvation of their souls, etc. And we left partially established some general peace-agreements among the Yumas, Pimas, Quiquimas, Cutganes, Hogiopas, and other nations, in order that all in their time might be very friendly and good Christians. I slept in a little house which they had made me, and almost all night they kept talking among themselves in regard to their very earnest desire to embrace our friendship and our holy faith.

Discussion Points for *Father Kino's Expeditions*

1. Notice how often he mentioned military and government figures in the selections—what do you think this says about how the Spanish colonized the lands they explored? What about the role of the church?
2. What sense do you have about how Father Kino regarded the Native Americans? Was he sympathetic to their needs or do you suspect that he considered them barbarians?
3. Recalling the U.S. Park Service caption from the introduction about how the Native Americans flocked to the Spanish missions for safety reasons, how do you imagine the hostility between Native American tribes really added to the conversion rates of missionaries? Do you think that certain tribes sought refuge with the Spanish and sincerely accepted Christianity?

4. How much of the attention that the Native Americans showed Father Kino do you suppose owed to curiosity and how much to a real affinity for Christianity? Or some other reason?
5. Father Kino mentioned little about the appearance of the natives and their food sources; this, of course, stands in contrast to most of the other accounts. Why do you think he failed to take a detailed look at the people? Was it because of his religious mission or something else?

PART VI: ADDITIONAL READINGS

On Africa

Africa had long hosted European visitors owing to its close proximity and integrated trade networks within the Mediterranean region. Egypt's great Nile River afforded some travelers the ability to reach Ethiopia and Sudan, just as missionaries or pilgrims had done when they brought Judaism and Christianity to East Africa during the twilight of the Roman Empire. Colonies of Greeks, Romans, and others dotted the North African shores and thus ensured a thorough connectedness between peoples on the two continents. With the advent of Islam, though, the character of the relationship between Africa and Europe changed and created a relationship based upon enmity and difference. Moors, Turks, Arabs all became synonyms for Muslims and the continued success by Islamic armies created a larger gulf that thereafter equated Muslims with barbarous infidels. With North Africa an entrenched Muslim domain, Europeans only really encountered sub-Saharan Africans in the 1400s, when Portuguese explorers slowly moved down the Atlantic coast. Prior to this Portuguese contact, tribes in Morocco dealt with Touregs—the Saharan nomads—to trade for salt, gold, and other sub-Saharan goods.

Early relations with Africans along the West Coast rested heavily on trade—including slavery, as the Portuguese brought a small number of people back to Portugal—with the construction of fortified trading ports. Colonies in the Americas changed the nature of the global economy, and the cash crops there made slavery virtually indispensable to facilitate growth to the economies of the European powers; that was, of course, because Africans provided the much-needed manpower to work the plantations of tobacco, sugar, and coffee. A direct trade route from Europe to India and China combined with the growing economic capital of the Americas, finalized the inter-connectedness of a global economy that greatly increased the living standards in Europe, which facilitated that continent's preeminence in world affairs until 1945.

Despite plenty of contact with Africans over the centuries, Europeans had failed to penetrate the interior of the continent, primarily because of disease. Most Africans and Europeans, through prolonged exposure, were immune and susceptible to essentially the same diseases. A major exception, though, was with malaria, which ravaged the Europeans, thanks to little prolonged contact with the infected insects. In contrast, Africans had developed an immunity—or, at least a higher level of tolerance—to various strains of the disease and thereby facilitated arguments calling for Africans to toil as slaves on Caribbean and South American plantations. Because Europeans could not tolerate malaria, their exploration into the African continent made little headway beyond a few days march from the sea until the last half of the nineteenth century, when quinine and other medical advances fostered healthier conditions.

A second major reason hindering earlier European contact and colonization was the failure of Western technology under exposure to humid jungles, dry deserts, or impenetrable rivers that often flowed out towards the oceans, (the latter rendered most sail-driven or man-powered ships essentially useless). Not until steamships could Europeans reliably sail upstream, but even then, the brutal climates wrecked frail technologies. Prior to complete brass-cased cartridges for firearms, Europeans had difficulty preventing misfires with their guns, which otherwise relied upon dry, yet exposed powder charges. Certain popular works of history and literature have tried to speak to this idea of technology as the boon to European advancement—in his book, *Guns, Germs, and Steel*, Jonathon Diamond argued that the Europeans developed as they did thanks to the happenstance of an adequate and nutritious food supply and other related cooperative conditions. Africans, in contrast, had to contend with fierce wild animals, relative inability to sow and store healthy crops, and a lack of mineral resources that would allow for steel production and industrialization.

Daniel Headrick's, *The Tools of Empire: Technology and European Imperialism in the Nineteenth Century*, also spoke to technological factors that coalesced for Europeans as the reasoning behind their ability to forcefully dominate other cultures across the globe, perhaps none so hazardous for the modern era than Africa. Late European colonization of that continent, combined with a relative decline in Europe's power during and after World War I, has led in part to Africa's general inability to stabilize and attain prosperity. Although European missteps in colonial policy proved devastating, they cannot account for the vast problems that plague Africa today. Just as in 1902, when Joseph Conrad wrote his chilling novella, *Heart of Darkness*, Africa remains a place on the margins of global politics.

Even in 1600, though, Europeans misunderstood Africa, precisely because they could not explore the territory. While they knew that Africa was larger than Europe, they assumed—based partly on accounts by Africans like Giovanni Leone (Al-Hassan Ibn-Mohammed al-Wezaz al-Fasi, or Leo Africanus)—that Africa was "in many places, uninhabitable," because of a "scarcity of water," or the "barrenness of the soil." Covered with unprofitable soil, dust, or ash, and subject to extreme heat, the "dangerous heaps of sand, which being raised by the wind, are driven up and down like the waves of a tempestuous sea."[36] With such a limited knowledge of the continent, moreover, geographers of the early sixteenth century imagined an Africa comprised of four parts: North Africa, Ethiopia, Libya, and the fourth, "land of the Negroes," a great unknown. Information was so scarce that the great Niger River (in present-day Nigeria) was supposedly "derived out of the Nile," which cosmographers believed was "swallowed up of the earth" and thus created a lake that served the Niger.[37] Indeed, it would take much time before the various superstitions, falsehoods, and misconceptions about Africa would cease.

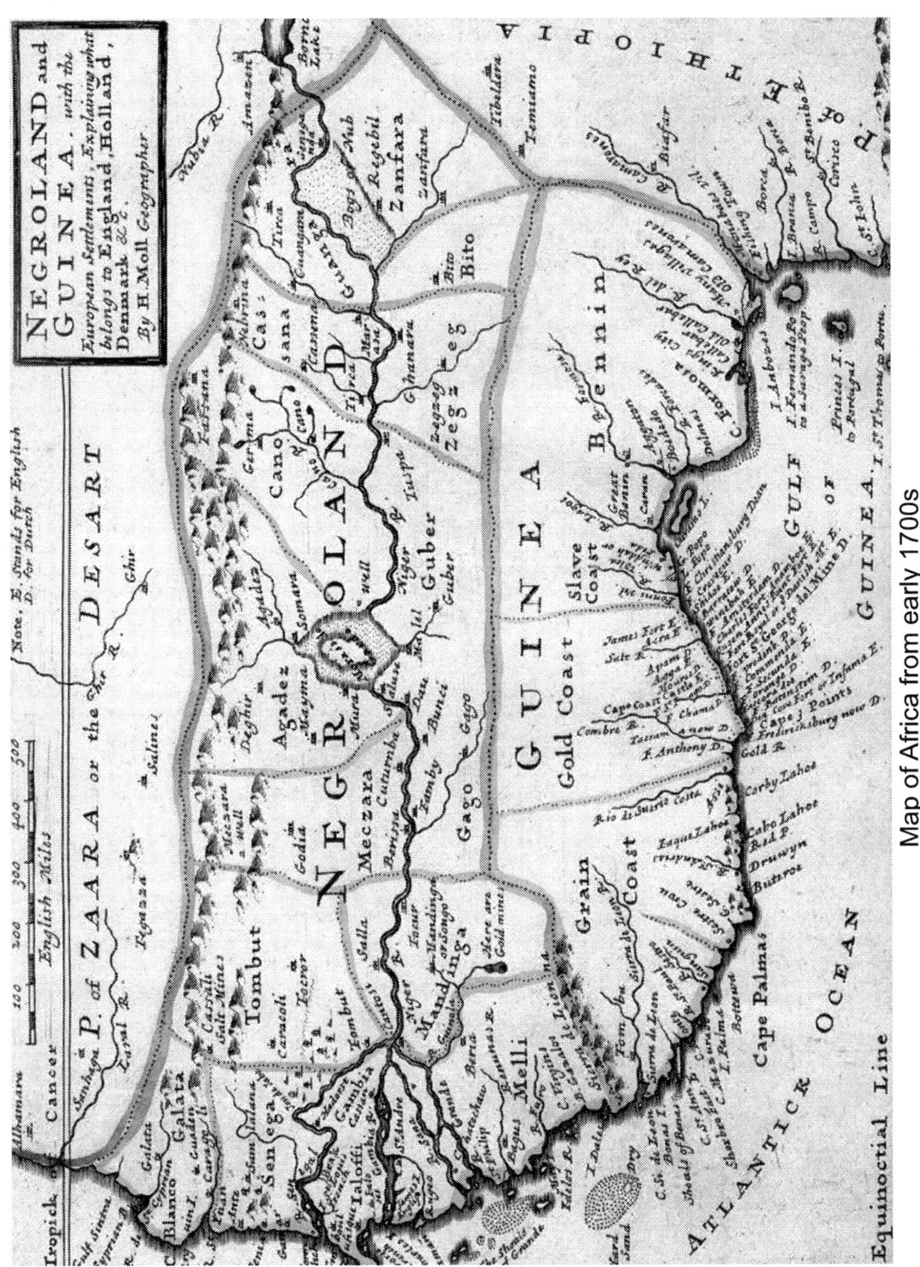

Map of Africa from early 1700s

Reading on Africa and the Slave Trade

Anthony Benezet, *A Short Account of that Part of Africa, Inhabited By Negroes* (Philadelphia, PA: Dunlap, 1762).

When Columbus landed on the island of Hispaniola and began an unprecedented European colonization of the Americas, he also jump-started an enormous move towards global capitalism, as the goods that crisscrossed the Atlantic Ocean proved pivotal in developing the modern economy. Unfortunately, people became just as important a commodity as the tobacco or sugar, as slaves both filled the population gap (with almost 80 percent of indigenous Americans dead by the end of the 1500s) and performed much the brutal labor involved with building colonies and harvesting cash-crops. Scholars have approximated that some 10 million slaves came to the Americas before slavery officially ended in countries like the United States and Brazil; the slave trade ended in the United States in 1808, but slavery as an institution ended only with the termination of the Civil War, while in Brazil slavery continued until 1888. Benezet's account below gives a landmark perspective from the 1760s, when the struggle over basic issues like whether slaves were human beings or not took place in England thanks to the growing presence of freed slaves like Olaudah Equiano and religious-minded abolitionists.

On human nature

And it must be acknowledged by every Man, who is sincerely desirous of becoming acquainted with himself, and impartially inspects his own Heart, that Weakness and inbred Corruption attend human Nature; which cannot be restored to its original Purity, but through the Efficacy of the Blood of Jesus Christ, our blessed Savior.

A lamentable and shocking Instance of the Influence which the Love of Gain has upon the Minds of those who yield to its Allurements, even when contrary to the Dictates of Reason, and the common Feelings of Humanity, appears in the Prosecution of the Negroe Trade, in which the English Nation has long been deeply concerned, and some in this Province [the thirteen colonies that later became the United States of America] have lately engaged. An Evil of so deep a Dye, and attended with such dreadful Consequences, that no well-disposed Person (anxious for the Welfare of himself, his Country, or Posterity) who knows the Tyranny, Oppression and Cruelty with which this iniquitous Trade is carried on, can be a silent and innocent Spectator.

The End proposed by this Essay, is to lay before the candid Reader the Depth of Evil attending this iniquitous Practice, in the Prosecution of which, of Duty to

God, the common Father of the Family of the whole Earth, and our Duty of Love to our Fellow Creatures, is totally disregarded. . . . It is also intended to invalidate the false Arguments, which are frequently advanced, for the Palliation of this Trade, in Hopes it may be some Inducement to those who are not defiled therewith to keep themselves clear.

Nor must we omit, in this dismal Account, the Weight of Blood which lies on the Promoters of this Trade, from the great Numbers that are yearly butchered in the Incursions and Battles which happen between the *Negroes*, in order to procure the Number delivered to the *Europeans*; and the many of these poor Creatures whose Hearts are broken, and they perish through Misery and Grief, on the Passage. May the Almighty preserve the Inhabitants of *Pennsylvania* from being further defiled by a Trade, which is entered upon from such sensual Motives, and carried on by such devilish Means.

By which it will appear, that the *Negroes* are generally a sensible humane and sociable People, and that their Capacity is as good, and as capable of Improvement as that of the WHITES. That their Country, though unfriendly to the *Europeans*, yet appears peculiarly agreeable, and well adapted to the Nature of the *Blacks*, and so fruitful as to furnish its Inhabitants plentifully with the Necessaries of Life, with much less Labor than in our more northern Climate.

As to the Account of the natural Disposition of many of the *Negroes*, and of the Fruitfulness of their Country, the aforementioned Authors, as well as many others, have wrote largely upon it. *M. Adanson*, in his Account of the Country and Natives of *Giree*, where he was so lately as the Year 1754, after giving an Account of the delightful Aspect of the Country, says; "The Simplicity of the Natives, their Dress and Manners, revived in my Mind the Idea of our first Parents; and I seemed to contemplate the World in its primitive State—they (the Negroes) are generally speaking, very good natured, sociable and obliging. I was not a little pleased (says he) with this my first Reception—it convinced me, that there ought to be a considerable Abatement made in the Accounts I had read and heard everywhere of the savage Character of the *Africans*—I observed, both in *Negroes* and *Moors*, great Humanity and Sociableness, which gave me strong Hopes that I should be very safe amongst them, and meet with the Success I desired in my Enquiries after the Curiosities of the Country."

Bosman, speaking of the *Negroes* of that Part of *Guiney* where he then was, says; "They are generally a good Sort of People, honest in their Dealings; others he describes as being generally friendly to Strangers, of a mild Conversation, courteous, affable, and easy to be overcome with Reason; in Conversation they discover a great Quickness of Parts and Understanding." He added, "That some Negroes, who have had an agreeable Education, have manifested a Brightness of Understanding equal to any of us."

A Brue, speaking of the People of *Benin*, says, "They are generally good natured and civil, and may be brought to any Thing by fair and soft Means. If you make them Presents, they will recompense them double. If you want any Thing of them, and ask it, they seldom deny it, even tho' they had Occasion for it themselves: But to treat them harshly, or think to gain any Thing of them by Force, is to dispute with the Moon." *Artus*, speaking of the same People, says, "They are a sincere inoffensive People, and do no Injustice either to one another or Strangers. He adds, that it is a capital Crime there to injure a Foreigner, which is severely punished.

Altho' the extreme Heat in many Parts of *Guinea*, is such, as is neither agreeable nor healthy to the *Europeans*, yet it is well suited to the Constitution of the *Negroes*: And it is to those Heats that they are indebted for the Fertility of their Land, which in most Places is so great, that with little Labor Grain and Fruit will grow in the greatest Plenty.

Andrew Brue, speaking of the great River *Senagal*, which runs many Hundred Miles within Land, says, "The farther you go from the Sea, the Country on the River seems more fruitful, and well improved. It abounds in *Indian* Corn, which is a never failing Commodity here—The Island of *Bifesha*, which is formed by an Arm of that River, abounds in *Indian* and *Guinea* Corn, Rice, Pulse, Tobacco and Indigo. Wheat thrives well after the second Crop. Cotton-trees in plenty—Here are vast Meadows, which feed large Herds of great and small Cattle—Poultry are numerous, as well as wild Fowl." Yet it sometimes happens that there is a great scarcity in particular Places, arising from the unprovident Disposition of some of the *Negroes*, who have little thought of making any Provision but from one Harvest to another, so that they are liable to suffer when that fails, or when the Locusts devour the Produce; these Insects sometimes come in such Swarms as to darken the Air, and destroy every green Thing that lays in their Way.

Barbot says, "The Inland People employ themselves in Tillage and Trade, and supply the Markets with Corn, Fruit and Palm Wine; the Country producing such vast Plenty of *Indian* Wheat, that Abundance is daily exported, as well by *Europeans* as *Blacks*, resorting theither [towards there] from other Parts." He adds, "That the Country of *Delmina*, (which was formerly very powerful and populous, though not so much drained of its Inhabitants, by the intestine Wars fomented amongst the *Negroes* by the *Dutch*, that there does not remain enough Inhabitants to till the Country); abounded with fine well-built and populous Towns, enriched with vast Fields of Corn, Cattle, Palm Wine and Oil."

Peter Holben, who was sent from the Court of *Prussia* to make astronomical Observations at the *Cape Good-Hope*, which is situated on the southernmost Part of *Africa*, speaking of the Government and Disposition of the *Negro* Inhabitants of that Country, commonly called *Hottentots*, says "Every Village or Kraal has a Court of Justice, for civil and criminal Affairs, composed of the Captain and all the Men of Kraal, who meet for that Purpose in the open Field, sitting in a Circle. Justice among the *Hottentots* never suffers as in Europe, either by Corruption or which is as bad, Delay. They have no Lawyer, thank Heaven: The Plaintiff and Defendant plead their own Cause. The Court hears them, and by a Majority of Votes decrees Possession or Damage, in case of Assault or Battery, or other Trespass, without Appeal or Obstacle. . . . The *Europeans* may boast of their Learning, Arts and Politeness; but where among them can they show so wise, so happy a Government as that of the *Hottentots*; owing entirely to this, that it has for its Basis the most perfect Liberty of the People." They are the only *Negro* Nation that we know of, that are not engaged in making and selling *Slaves*; this wicked Practice appears to be unknown amongst these People.

John Barbot says, "The Slaves sold by the Negroes are for the most Part Prisoners of War, or taken in the Incursions they make into their Enemies Territories; others are stolen away by their own Countrymen. Abundance of little *Blacks*, of both Sexes, are stolen away by their Neighbors, when found abroad, on the Reads, or in the Woods, or else in the Corn Fields, at the Time of the Year when their Parents keep them there all Day, to scare away the devouring small Birds."

Bosman says . . . "When these Slaves come to *Fida*, they are put in Prison altogether; and when (says he) we treat concerning buying them, they are all brought out together in a large Plain, where, by our Surgeons, they are thoroughly examined, and that naked too, both Men and Women, without the least Distinction or Modesty. Those which are approved as good, are set on one Side; in the meanwhile a burning Iron, with the Arms or Name of the Companies, lies in the Fire, with which ours are marked on the Breast. When we have agreed with the Owners of the Slaves, they are returned to their Prisons, where, from that Time forward, they are kept at our Charge, cost us *Two-pence* a Day a Slave, which serves to subsist them like our Criminals on Bread and Water; so that, to save Charges, we send them on board our Ships the very first Opportunity; before which, their Masters strip them of all they have on their Backs, so that they come on board stark naked, as well Women as Men, in which Condition they are obliged to continue, if the Master of the Ship is not so charitable (which he commonly is) as to bestow something on them to cover their Nakedness—Six or Seven Hundred are sometimes put on board a Vessel, where they lie as close together as possible for them to be crowded—*I doubt not*, says the same Author, "*but this Trade seems very barbarous to you, but since it is followed by mere Necessity, it must go on.*"

Economic argument

"But it is false, that either we or our Colonies would be ruined by the Abolition of Slavery. It might occasion a Stagnation of Business for a short Time. Every great Alteration produces that Effect; because Mankind cannot, on a sudden, find Ways of disposing of themselves and of their Affairs: But it would produce many Effect. It is the Slavery which is permitted in America that has hindered it from becoming so soon populous, as it would otherwise have done. Let the Negroes free, and in a few Generations, this vast and fertile Continent would be crowded with Inhabitants."

Account of purchase in Africa

"That I may contribute all in my Power towards the Good of Mankind, by inspiring any of its Individuals with a suitable Abhorrence for that detestable Practice of trading in our Fellow-Creatures, and in some Measure atone for my Neglect of Duty as a Christian, in engaging in that wicked Traffic, I offer to their serious Consideration some few Occurrences of which I was Eyewitness. That being struck with the wretched and affecting Scene they may foster that humane Principle, which is the noble and distinguished Characteristic of Man, and improve it to the Benefit of their Children's Children.

About the Year 1749, I sailed from *Liverpool* to the Coast of *Guinea*: Some Time after our arrival I was ordered to go up the Country a considerable Distance; upon having Notice from one of the Negro Kings, that he had a Parcel of Slaves to dispose of; I received my Instructions, and went, carrying with me an Account of such Goods we had on board to exchange for the Slaves we intended to purchase. Upon being introduced, I presented him with a small Case of English Spirits, a Gun, and some Trifles, which having accepted, and understood by an Interpreter what Goods we had, the next Day was appointed for viewing the Slaves: we found about two Hundred confined in one Place. But here how shall I relate the affecting Sight I there beheld? How can I sufficiently describe the silent Sorrow which appeared in the Countenance of the afflicted Father, and the painful Anguish of the tender Mother, expecting to be forever separated from their tender Offspring; the distressed Maid wringing her Hands in Presage of her future Wretchedness, and the general Cry of the Innocent from a fearful Apprehension of the perpetual Slavery to which they were doomed. Under a Sense of my Offence to God, in the Person of his Creatures; I acknowledge I purchased eleven, who I conducted tied, two and two to the Ship. Being but a small Vessel (ninety Ton) we soon purchased our Cargo, consisting of one Hundred and seventy slaves. . . . We had not been a Fortnight at Sea, before the fatal Consequence of this Despair appeared: they formed a Design recovering their natural Right, Liberty, by raising and murdering every Man on board, but the Goodness of the Almighty rendered their Scheme abortive, and his Mercy spared us to have Time to repent. The Plot was discovered; the Ringleader tied by the two Thumbs over the Barricade Door, at Sun-rise received a Number of Lashes, in this Situation he remained till Sunset, exposed to the Insults and Barbarity of the brutal Crew of Sailors, with full Leave to exercise their Cruelty at Pleasure.

Disposition of the slaves

Truth, they want to recover their Liberty, and would attempt to do it, if they were not kept in Awe by hard Usage, and severe Discipline. In the Account of *Jamaica*, we are told that the *Negroes*, when first brought hither from *Guinea*, are very simple, innocent Creatures, but soon turn *roguish*, and when they come to be whipped, urge the Example of the Whites for their Excuse. Whereas, in that of *Barbados*, the same Author says, "That the Masters of the *Negroes* are obliged to treat them very severely, not only because of the stubborn, treacherous Temper, which is so peculiar to all of their Complexion and Country, but because they are three times the Number of the Whites in this Island, and have made frequent Attempts to get the Mastery."

Of capture

The Case of a poor *Negroe*, not long since brought from *Guinea*, is a recent Instance of this Kind. From his first Arrival he appeared thoughtful and dejected, the Cause of which was not known till he was able to speak *English*, when the Account he gave of himself was, that he had a Wife and Children in his own Country, that some of them being sick and thirsty, he went, in the Night-time, to fetch Water at a Spring, where he was violently seized, and carried away by some Persons who lay in Wait to catch Men, when he was transported to *America*.

The mistaken Opinion, which most People have entertained, that the Negroes in Africa, live in the same wild unsettled Manner as the *American Indians* do, has led many to think it impossible to bring them into that civilized Order which is requisite for their becoming good Members of Society, but, it is hoped, what has already been said on that Head, will convince the candid Reader, that this Opinion is founded on mistaken Apprehensions . . . amongst the many Nations living on that Part of *Africa*, inhabited by *Negroes*, which extend many Thousand Miles, there is doubtless some People of a more savage Disposition than others, yet certain it is, that the natural Disposition of the Generality of the *Negroes* is widely different from the roving Dispositions of our *Indians*; they generally settle together, and employ themselves in Agriculture and Commerce. Some large Nations are represented as industrious and careful in the Cultivation of their Lands; breeding Cattle, and carrying on a Trade to distant parts.

Discussion Points for *A Short Account of that Part of Africa*

1. Much of this account tried to show the unjust nature of slavery. Do you suppose the date of publication (1762) was significant for arguing against the slave trade? Moreover, what sort of language did the author use to convince the reader?
2. From the brief descriptions of Africa proper, what sense do you have as a reader about how Europeans experienced the continent, if at all?
3. How did Africans compare to other non-Europeans, specifically the Native Americans?
4. How did Christianity fit into this larger argument over slavery?
5. From this account, how much culpability did other Africans seem to have in the slave trade?

Selected Letters on Eurasia

Elizabeth Lady Craven, *A Journey through the Crimea to Constantinople in a Series of Letters* (Dublin: N.p., 1789).

A travel story told through letters serves a different function than the compilations that the authors probably intended to publish upon returning home. These letters served as part of Lady Craven's service to the Margrave of Brandenburg, Anspach, and Bareith in 1786. Such a diplomatic mission adds to the perceived authenticity but does little, of course, to verify her knowledge of the local customs, peoples, and ability to make judgments. Also, we should assume that this information was inoffensive, because censorship—on both ends and throughout the letters' journey—was commonplace.

Letter X – Voyaging to the South of France

Nothing can be more delightful than my last method of traveling by water. I have had high and contrary winds; but the Rhone's famed rapidity that I had heard so much of, was neither surprising nor terrifying—the shores on each side were rocks interspersed with vine-yards and castles—I landed the first day at Condrieux, where I bought some excellent wine for 25 sols a bottle, the growth of that place—About a league from thence is la Montagne Tupain, belonging to Mr. de la Condamine, where the best Cote-rotie wine is to be had; that word signifies really and truly roasted-coast, the grapes being almost broiled by the sun. The wine is of a red and strong kind—reckoned very fine; but like many other fine things, I did not relish it—A little farther on the left is l'Hermitage, a spot so called because formerly a hermit lived upon that hill, the wine of which is much known for me to say anything about it. I gave three livres a bottle for it, but found the white so much better than the red that I ordered some to be sent to Marseilles, from whence I shall have it shipped for England.

There is a small town called Vienne, that has a fine Gothic cathedral, which I went on shore to look at, together with a monument belonging to the Montmorin family, well executed.

I saw several people on the banks of the Rhone sifting gravel; they find among it little bits of solid gold, washed down from the mountains; a most horrid employment in this hot weather I should think; but what will not poor mortals do for gold, since the rich are often slaves to that which they ought to be masters of.

Montelimart is a castle from whence I am told three kingdoms are seen, and seven provinces. I did not stop to see this or any other of the many castles I passed by.

At the Point St. Esprit, which is a noble bridge indeed, I think the passage might be dangerous, if the boatmen were not very attentive—My coach is, so large, and has such excellent blinds, that I have not suffered from the heat at all—The shores lose all their beauty near Avignon, which I could not see, because it is surrounded by a high turreted wall.

Madame de Brancas, the Duc de Crillon's sister, was very civil to me, and we talk about—I dined with Lord—whose health is much impaired, and I hope this climate will do him good—Adieu, dear Sir, yours.

P.S. I am told by someone who knows Duc de Crillon very well, that his sister is exactly like him; which I can easily conceive, for she has as many projects about her gardens and houses as her brother had about the taking of Gibraltar: I hope they will succeed better than his have, for she is very good-humored.

Letter XXXII – St. Petersburg

The road between Warsaw and this place [Petersburg, Russia] is one insipid flat, except just in and about the town of Nerva, where I took a sledge and flew hither. When I wrote last, dear Sir, I think I was upon the point of doing to see the Princess C—, I passed two days with her at a country house of the Princess Lubomirska's, her sister-in-law; I was most sincerely glad to see her, and we parted with regret. I received a very civil message from the King, and M. de Stackelberg sent me six bottles of bishop, which I assure you was very serviceable to me; I did not stop at Warsaw on my return from the P—, and the messenger caught me just one post on this side of Warsaw; I can conceive nothing so *enuyant* as traveling in such a country as this, one flat plain; the view terminated by a forest, which you drive through, only to arrive at the same scene you have quitted, the frost was not hard enough to make the road good, till I came to Nerva. I am something like a country Miss, gaping at the window all day here, every creature that goes about the streets, seem as if they were in a violent hurry, they drove full gallop, traineaus with one horse ply at the corners of the streets as do your hackney-coaches and chairs. My S— informed me, it belonged to my dignity to have six horses on my coach, in order to pay my visits; and I beg you will imagine my surprise, when I found I had a coachman on the box, with three postillions, one to each pair of horses; and these sitting on the right hand, I go thus, full gallop, running races with every other *attelage* that falls in my way; the streets are luckily wide, and custom make the danger less than one should imagine.

I am interrupted, and therefore wish you a good night.

Letter XXXIII – from St. Petersburg

Petersburg is a cheerful and fine looking town; the streets are extremely wide and long, the houses stucco'd to imitate white stone; none above three stories high, which certainly adds to the lively and airy appearance of them. . . . The fashion of the day is most ridiculous and improper for this climate; French gauzes and flowers were not intended for Russian beauties, and they are sold at a price here which must ruin the buyers.

The Empress and the Princess d'Ashkow are the only ladies who wear the Russian dress; it is I think a very handsome one; and I am more surprised every day, that nations do not each preserve their own fashions, and not copy one country that is at present only the ape of every other—From Cherson, the new town on the Turkish frontiers, which is one thousand six hundred miles from hence, are brought many provisions; from Archangel likewise this town is provided, and from Astracan [Astrakhan] on the Caspian Sea, near two thousand miles, all the dainties, such as grapes, peas, beans, artichokes, are brought.

You may have heard much of Prince Potemkin; I see him everywhere, but he is reserved and converses very little with ladies. I was invited by him to dine in an immense palace he is building in the suburbs; the only room finished is too particular not to be described; it is three hundred feet in length, and on the side opposite the windows there are two rows of stone pillars, whose height and breadth are proportioned to the immense size of the room, which is an oblong square. . . . The music, the room, the cold, all was gigantic. I say by Prince Potemkin at dinner; but except asking me to eat and drink, I cannot say I heard the sound of his voice; so am unable to tell you what species of *espirit* has raised him to the fortunes and dignities he possesses, or what occasions Mr. S___ and others to call him a sensible man.

Letter XXXIV – from Moscow

I left my coach at Petersburg, and hired for myself and my small suite, the carriages of the country, called Kibitkas; they are exactly like cradles, the head having windows to the front which let down; I can sit or lie down, and feel in one like a great child, very comfortable defended from the cold by pillow and blankets. These carriages are upon sledges, and where the road is good, this conveyance is comfortable and not fatiguing. . . . Their method of driving is singular: they sit behind three horses that are harnessed abreast—a shrill whistling noise, or a savage kind of shriek is the signal for the horses to set off, which they do at full gallop. . . . I would never advise a traveler to set out from Petersburg as I have, just at the end of the carnival; he might with some reason suppose it is a religious duty for the Russian peasant to be drunk; in most villages I saw a sledge loaded with young men and women in such a manner, that four horses would have been more proper to draw it than one, which wretched beast was obliged to fly with this noisy company up and down the village, which is generally composed of houses in straight rows on each side of the public road.

The Russian peasant is a fine, stout, straight, well-looking man; some of the women, as I said before, are uncommonly pretty; but the general whiteness of their teeth is something that cannot be conceived; it frequently happened that all the men of the village were in a circle round my carriages—and rows of the most beautiful oriental pearl cannot be more regular and white than their teeth. . . . The children look all pale and sickly, till they are five or six years old. The houses and dresses of the peasants are by no means uncomfortably; the first is generally composed of wood, the latter of sheep-skins; but trees laid horizontally one upon another makes a very strong wall, and the climate requires a warm skin for clothing.

Letter XLI – Batcheserai, in the Crimea

In my way hither I dined at the Cossack Chief's post, and my entertainment was truly Cossack. A long table for thirty people; at one end a half-grown pig roasted whole; at the other a half-grown sheep, whole likewise, in the middle of the table an immense tureen of curdled milk; there were several side dishes made for me and the Russian, as well as the cook could imagine to our taste.

When a Cossack is sick he drinks sour milk for a few days, and that is the only remedy the Cossacks have for fevers—

At night I lodged at a house that had belonged to a noble Tartar, where there is a Russian post, with about twelve hundred of the finest men I ever saw, and uncommonly tall. A Tartarian house has always another building at a little distance from it for the convenience of travelers or strangers, whom the noble Tartar always treats with the greatest hospitality; here the General parted from us.

There are five thousand Tartar inhabitants here; I do not believe there was a man left in his house, the streets being lined with Tartarian men on each side; their countenances were very singular, most of them kept their eyes fixed on the ground, as we passed; but some just looked up, and, as it they were afraid of seeing a woman's face uncovered, hastily cast their eyes downward again; some diverted at the novelty, looked and laughed very much—There is a great trade here of blades for swords, hangers, and knives—I am assured many made here are not to be distinguished from those of Damascus.

The Khan's palace is an irregular building, the greatest part of it is one floor raised upon pillars of wood painted and gilt in a fanciful and lively manner, the arch, or last door-way, has fine proportions . . . [with a courtyard consisting of a variety of] apartments where the Khan walked from his own residence to the Harem, which is spacious and higher than the other buildings.

I never saw such a variety of colors—different colored gold and silver mixed together. The Kaima-Kan, and two other principal Tartars, supped with us, and I find nothing can exceed the ignorance and simplicity of these people. The Kaima-Kan is the Khan's first minister; he is totally ignorant of the geography of his own country; and says that England and Petersburg are the same thing; I am to dine with his sister to-morrow; she is married to a rich Tartar, who had given a certain yearly sum to possess, solely, the profits of the soap mines. For among the excellent productions of this peninsula, there is a mine of earth exactly like soap, and reckoned very good for the skin; the Turkish women consume a great quantity of it at Constantinople. . . . This Tartar Khan must have had a soul worthy of being loved by a Christian wife I think.

Discussion Points for *A Journey Through the Crimea*

1. How reliable do you think this account was? Do you have a sense of bias by the author?
2. What sorts of people did this lady come into contact with? Were they representative of the majority of the inhabitants?
3. How did she view the non-Russians she came across?
4. What about the inclusion of the part about France—what did she take note of and why would that be important?
5. What seemed to dominate village life in Russia?

ENDNOTES

1. See, for instance, the controversial book by Samuel P. Huntington, *Who are We? The Challenges to America's National Identity* (New York: Simon & Schuster, 2005).

2. See Carsten Niebuhr, *Travels through Arabia and other Countries in the East*, Robert Heron, trans. (Perth: R. Morison Junior, 1799), p. i.

3. Confucius, as cited in Lorraine Levathes, *When China Ruled the Seas: The Treasure Fleet of the Dragon Throne, 1405–1433* (Oxford: Oxford University Press, 1997), p. 33.

4. See Levathes, *When China Ruled the Seas.*

5. See Larry Wolff's two significant works on this topic: *Inventing Eastern Europe: The Map of Civilization on the Mind of the Enlightenment* (Stanford: Stanford University Press, 1994); and, *Venice and the Slavs: The Discovery of Dalmatia in the Age of Enlightenment* (Stanford, CA: Stanford University Press, 2001).

6. See "Europe's Mirror: The Enlightenment and the Exotic," in Dorinda Outram, *The Enlightenment* (Cambridge: Cambridge University Press, 1995).

7. See one of the many translated versions of Voltaire's famous *Candide, Or Optimism.* This author's favorite is the version translated by David Wootton, (New York: Hackett Publishing Company, 2000).

8. Immanuel Kant "Fundamental Principles of the Metaphysics of Morals," in *The Portable Enlightenment Reader*, Isaac Kramnick, ed. (New York: Penguin Books, 1995), p. 302.

9. A typical European response to the behavior of Native Americans, Asians, and Africans was that they were children who needed a correct upbringing in order to become proper men. For example, see the famous poem by Rudyard Kipling, "The White Man's Burden," available online at numerous sources, including the *Internet Modern History Sourcebook*, http://www.fordham.edu/halsall/mod/Kipling.html. "Take up the White Man's burden— / Send forth the best ye breed— / Go bind your sons to exile / To serve your captives' need; / To wait in heavy harness, / On fluttered folk and wild— / Your new-caught, sullen peoples, / Half-devil and half-child."

10. As Bishop-Prince of Montenegro from 1830 until 1851, Petar II Petrović-Njegoš was the "Vladika" as described by J. Gardner Wilkinson, *Dalmatia and Montenegro with A Journey to Mostar in Herzegovina* (London: John Murray, Albemarle Street, 1848), p. 465.

11. Seemingly countless media outlets from across the Balkans note the path to Europe as part of the reforms since the wars that ripped apart Yugoslavia during the 1990s. Joining Europe has also come to mean admission into the European Union. For one of the most recent, see "Ubire li Crna Gora plodove Beogradskog sporazuma?" Radio Slobodna Evropa [Radio Free Europe], 6 December 2009.

12. See Metternich in Larry Wolff, "'Kennst du das Land?'" the Uncertainty of Galicia in the Age of Metternich and Fredo," *Slavic Review*, 67:2 (Summer 2008), p. 287.

13. See Metternich in Larry Wolff, "'Kennst du das Land?'" p. 295.

14. See the propaganda pamphlet released by the Yugoslav government entitled, *Trieste*, (Belgrade: Federal People's Republic of Yugoslavia, 1946), p. 43.

15. See *Trieste*, p. 44. See also Maura Hametz, *Making Trieste Italian, 1918–1954* (Woodbridge: The Royal Historical Society, 2005), pp. 24–25. Hametz's argument examined how Trieste, as a border city of Italy, served as a locust of nationalist and irredentist fervor, but how unification with Italy after World War I only added to the woes of the city as prosperity disappeared to traditional Italian ports and political influence rang hollow in Rome. For more on Trieste as a "boundary" area, see Glenda Sluga, *The Problem of Trieste and the Italo-Yugoslav Border: Difference, Identity, and Sovereignty in Twentieth-Century Europe* (Albany: State University of New York Press, 2001).

16. See the foremost work on this topic, Bogdan Novak, *Trieste, 1941–1954: The Ethnic, Political, and Ideological Struggle* (Chicago, IL: University of Chicago Press, 1970), p. xvi. Novak claimed, "Yugoslavia effectively used both nationalism and ideology when entreating the support of the people of the Julian Region." With propaganda appealing to Croats and Slovenes coupled with a reaching out to Italian Marxists, Tito's case was indeed compelling, but nonetheless

fell short. For some information on the difficulties that the Italians had in Italianizing the area, see Hametz, *Making Trieste Italian, 1918–1954*, p. 3. See also, Sluga, *The Problem of Trieste*, p. 48. Sluga cited the transformation of these 500 schools in the short period from 1924 to 1927, which came in addition to the 1926 law that mandated Slav surnames altered to become more "aesthetically pleasing" to Italian ears.

17. See Michael E. Chapman, *Historian's Companion: Chronologies, Glossaries, Readings, Style Guide* (Reading, MA: Trebarwyth Press, 2008), p. 8.

18. See Chapman, *Historian's Companion*, p. 11.

19. Vladika was the reference to the ruler of Montenegro. Prior to 1910, the Bishop-Prince (Vladika) reigned but the title expired that same year when Prince-Bishop Nicholas won the right by the other European powers to call Montenegro a kingdom and reign as its king. This was a large increase in status and happened in part to offset the power of neighboring Serbia. For more see John D. Treadway, *The Falcon and the Eagle: Montenegro and Austria-Hungary, 1908–1914* (West Lafayette, IN: Purdue University Press, 1983).

20. There exists an ease among writers with which to note the high level of inter-regional conflict during the twentieth century as somehow representative of a "Balkan normalcy" or "Balkan mentality" that had even permeated the political leadership of the former Yugoslav state; after all, in comparison with the calm and peacefulness in Central and Western Europe, Yugoslav elites noted that the "situation in the Balkans" seemed "forever fluid." For a detailed argument on how Europeans depicted the Balkans as a powder keg, see Maria Todorova, *Imagining the Balkans* (New York: Oxford University Press, 1997). Even during the Cold War, members of the Yugoslav government expressed the view that nothing was stable in the Balkans. See Stane Dolanc in "Magnetofonske beleške i materijal sastanka Izvršnog bira," Arhiv Srbije i Crne Gore Savez Komunista IV K.7 7, 1971, p. 24. "Za razliku od popuštenja zategnutosti i smirivanja u centralnoj i severnoj Evropi, situacija na Balkanu još uvek je fluidna" [. . . the situation in the Balkans is always fluid].

21. T.E. Lawrence in Charles M. Doughty, *Travels in Arabia Deserta* (New York: Random House, 1921), pp. 17, 20.

22. John Windus, *A Journey to Mequinez; The Residence of the Present Emperor of Fez and Morocco* (Dublin: George Ewing, 1725), p. ix.

23. For instance, in his chapter entitled, "The old woman's story," Voltaire mocked how sailors conducted themselves: "We [the old woman and her mother] boarded a local galley, covered in gold like the altar of St. Peter's in Rome. Suddenly a pirate ship from Sale swooped on us and boarded us. Our soldiers defended us with all the courage you would expect of soldiers in the pope's service: they threw themselves on their knees, threw their weapons aside, and begged the pirates to absolve them of their sins as they were on the point of death. 'Immediately they were stripped as naked as monkeys; and my mother too; and our ladies-in-waiting; and myself. It was quite astonishing to see the speed with which these gentlemen got us all out of our clothes. . . . I will not try to tell you how painful it is for a young princess to be taken off to Morocco as a slave.'" From Voltaire, *Candide*, pp. 21–2.

24. See Kenneth Pomeranz and Steven Topik, *The World that Trade Created* (Armonk, NY: M.E. Sharpe, 1999), p. 85

25. See John Winter Jones, *The Travels of Ludovico di Varthema in Egypt, Syria, Arabia Deserta and Arabia Felix, in Persia, India, and Ethiopia* (New York: Burt Franklin 1965), p. 157.

26. George Makepeace Towle, *Marco Polo: His Travels and Adventures* (Boston, MA: Lee and Shepard, Publishers, 1880), p. iii.

27. Towle, *Marco Polo*, p. iv.

28. Towle, *Marco Polo*, p. iv.

29. Sir Thomas Henry Grattan Esmonde, *Round the World with the Irish Delegates* (Dublin: Sealy, Bryers and Walker, 1892), pp. 1–2.

30. See Thomas J. McCormick, *China Market: America's Quest for Informal Empire, 1893–1901* (Chicago, IL: Elephant Paperbacks, 1990).

31. See Jacques Gernet, *Daily Life in China: On the Eve of the Mongol Invasion, 1250–1276* (Stanford, CA: Stanford University Press, 1962), p. 135.

32. Carl Crow, *Four Hundred Million Customers: The Experiences—Some Happy, Some Sad of an American in China, and What they Taught Him* (New York: Harper & Brothers Publishers, 1937), p. 15.

33. Crow, *Four Hundred Million Customers*, pp. 43–4.

34. Crow, *Four Hundred Million Customers*, p. 302.

35. Thomas Paine's influential pamphlet, *Common Sense*, is widespread and easily obtainable. Reliable sources online also have the full text available for viewing. For example, see Early America.com at http://www.earlyamerica.com/earlyamerica/milestones/commonsense.html.

36. Despite his status as a noble, Alonzo de Guzman had sold his horse to survive and thus served as a common soldier. Typically, only commoners served in the infantry during the *Reconquista*—nobles and even wealthy merchants or artisans, if able to afford a horse, served in the cavalry.

37. John Pory, *The History and Description of Africa and of the Notable things Therein Contained, written by Leo Africanus*, Robert Brown, ed. (New York: Burt Franklin, 1963), pp. 13–4.

38. Pory, *The History and Description of Africa*, pp. 124–5.

APPENDIX: TEXTUAL ANALYSIS

As we have read each of these texts, we can no doubt point to similarities in the language of how these travelers communicated their thoughts and experiences to their audiences. A simple textual analysis of the words that they chose (whether originally in English or in translation) reveals much about their perceptions. I think we can safely assume that these adventurers were typically either some of the most prejudiced folks in their societies or the most open to understanding new cultures; with that in mind, how did their language match your expectations? What does it tell us about how these people understood their roles as storytellers, explorers, or civilizers? Finally, why do you think the language is so similar between the regions explored—or so different?

The main document contains 56,902 words, leaving out my introductions and discussion questions. I ran the text through a concordance program to determine the frequency of certain vocabulary words. Obviously, we must be careful when using data like this, but I chose words that I think can tell us something about the experience of travel, the perceptions of the authors, gender relations or interactions, and so on. There were 9,545 different words and naturally, the most common words were indefinite/definite articles and prepositions: "the" was the most used, with 9,076 occurrences, or about 7 percent of all words. "Of," "and," "to," "in," and "a" followed, with a dramatic drop to only 2,606 occurrences of "a," or a mere 2 percent. As might also be expected, the most common word lengths were three-letter words (21 percent), two-letter words (16.95 percent), and four-letter words (12.46 percent). Thereafer, five, six, and seven-letter words formed the bulk of the text with close to an additional 21 percent of the text (or about 26,000 occurrences). The listing of words at the end of this analysis shows my choices in descending order of frequency.

Using the whole text for analysis, we can observe some interesting things. First, if we think about "us" versus "them" and how otherness might have played a role in how these explorers thought, we can observe from the selections that "we" occurred 685 times, while "them" came in second at 544 uses. "Our" followed at 394 times, and "my" 225 times.

Looking at what the travelers looked at or for when they ventured forth, we can see a preoccupation with the mode of transport (instances of vessel, water, ships, etc), but also a detailed description of the people they encountered. Body parts like "hands," (29) "arms," (42) and "faces" (22) appeared often, as did words like "complexion" (12) and "eyes" (58). How the "natives" (53) dressed interested the travelers too—words like "covered," (48) "naked," (42) "half-naked," (4) appeared in most every case. In talking just of Eastern Europe, travelers used terms like “costumes” (12) to describe the dress and noted the coins or embroidery that detailed such articles of clothing.

It is fair to say, I think, that a gender bias dominated the thoughts of these adventurers against women. Variants of male-oriented words (man, men, husband, him, his, and so on) outnumbered the female equivalents. When mentioning women, though, it seemed as if the authors were interested in how so-called Orientals interacted—concepts like marriage and divorce, and naturally, concubine and harem figured prominently into the accounts.

Europeans tended to refer to more negative aspects of others than positive. The list below shows more of the negative words, as the frequency of positive attributes clearly waned in comparison, unless considering how the travelers described the land. In that latter case, “beautiful” (34) or “abundance” (71), in addition to things like “fish” (24) or “species” (4) clearly showed a bias towards Europeans’ use of the land.

In general, the Europeans spoke about the “poverty” (10) or “desolate” (4) “children” (49) who lived like “wild” (32) men. The “tribes” (39) that inhabited “villages” (30) or lived in “mud-huts” (2) instead of “proper” (9) cities like “civilized” (24) “Europeans” (39) no doubt showed prejudice. To emphasize the aspect of “trade” (86) across the globe, I also noted the words like “sugar,” (11) “opium,” (63) “silver,” (74) “tobacco,” (16) and “tea” (11). Of course, “gold” occurred 61 times, with reference to the quest that drove men like our Alonzo de Guzman, who sought riches in Peru.

Finally, I would highlight the importance of religion as a driving force in these accounts. While authors mentioned “Jews” (34) and “Hindus” (27) on occasion, the real dynamic was between Christians (164) and Muslims (Turks and Moors at 231 times). The variants on the last two words accounted for the majority of occurrences. If comparing economic reasons for exploration and travel with religious reasons, one might see a dominant interest in religious factors, though, these explorers were unique in that they were not policy-makers or part of entrenched business interests. They had a decided interest in making money and gaining glory, yet they were not captains of industry. Understanding the “superstitions” (8) of Asians, complete with the “wizards” (2) who performed “strange” (27) “ceremonies,” (12) the authors generally denied the existence of organized religion among Asians and Native Americans.

***The numbers in the following tables refer to the frequency throughout the text**

We 685
Them 544
People 343
No 304
Our 394
There 369
Great 266
Other 267
Him 247
My 231
Men 221
Most 226
Country 205
Us 214
Upon 201
Those 200
Any 181
Me 162
Little 151
Her 137
Chinese 136
Women 128
Man 126
Water 123
Good 119
Without 117
Land 114
Island 112
Every 112
Here 110
City 104
Same 103
Another 99
Own 96
White 88
East 87
Trade 86
See 86
Turks 85
Europe 85
Houses 84
Christians 83
Inhabitants 78
South 77
Life 76
Christian 75
Himself 74
Slaves 73
Indians 70
World 66
Far 66
Others 65
Old 65
Town 64
Language 64
Turkish 63
Generally 63
Seemed 63
Together 61
Gold 61
Ships 60
Opium 60
China 60
Eyes 58
Native 57
English 55
Always 54
Near 53
Hair 52
Hands 51
Power 50
Face 50
Church 50
Religion 48
Nothing 48
Covered 48
Children 48
Natives 53
Journey 47
Young 46
Taken 46
Ship 46
Known 46
Captain 46
Cairo 46
Black 46
Negroes 45
Moors 45
Islands 45
European 45
Different 45
Road 44
Nature 44
Heard 44
God 44
Chief 44
Asia 44
Streets 43
Red 43
King 43
Vessel 42
Morning 42
Indian 42
Eat 42
Arms 42
Public 41
Poor 44
North 41
Middle 41
House 41
Coast 40
Fine 39
Europeans 39
England 39
Emperor 39
End 38
Tribes 37
River 37
Voyage 36
Various 36
Kind 36
Egypt 36
Ancient 36
State 35
Persons 35
Person 35
India 35
Government 35
Empire 35
Dress 35
British 35
Africa 35
Towns 34
Rich 34
Received 34
Race 34
Natural 34
Nations 34

Merchants 34
Jews 34
Friends 36
Foreign 34
Force 34
Food 34
Sun 33
Bosnia 33
Arabs 33
Wine 32
Wild 32
Sometimes 32
Naked 32
Heads 32
Greatest 32
Customs 32
Blood 32
Beautiful 32
Villages 30
Obliged 30
Hot 30
Custom 40
Common 30
Arabia 30
Wore 29
Montenegro 29
Port 29
Hand 29
Goods 29
Civilized 29
Believe 29
Woman 28
Understand 28
Nation 28
Killed 28
Constantinople 28
Belonging 28
Army 28
American 28
Albanian 28
Village 27
Vessels 27
Something 27
Seems 27
Manners 27
Hindoos 27
Family 27
Turk 26
Spaniards 26
Dutch 26
Business 26
American 26
Aboriginal 26
Tartars 25
Money 25
Dead 25
Strangers 24
Savage 24
Silver 24
Religious 25
Reason 24
Mahometans 24
Lies 24
Inhabited 24
Fish 24
Father 24
Curious 24
Cold 24
Wealth 23
Taking 23
Peoples 23
None 23
Greeks 23
Features 23
Fear 23
Faith 23
Armed 23
Western 22
Spain 22
Province 22
Iron 22
Honor 22
Harbor 22
Free 22
Famous 22
Faces 22
Dark 22
Colored 22
Catholic 22
Canoes 22
Beasts 22
Beach 22
Strange 21
Salt 21
Sailors 21
Return 21
Human 21
Death 21
Tartar 20
Subjects 20
Shown 20
Served 20
Roman 20
Peasant 20
Myself 20
Mosques 20
Moslem 20
Liberty 20
Huge 20
Holy 20
Greek 20
Employed 20
Drunk 20
Canoe 20
Animals 20
Abundance 20
Your 19
Respect 19
Pirates 19
Oriental 19
German 19
Christ 19
Wounded 18
Wives 18
Wife 18
Stature 18
So-called 18
Rude 18
Receive 18
Picturesque 18
Orthodox 18
Ignorant 18
Lord 18
Married 18
Enemies 18
Evil 18
Discover 18
Curiosity 18

Company 18
Color 18
Civilization 18
Allowed 18
Travelers 17
Subject 17
Peace 17
Pacific 17
Opposite 17
Opinion 17
Neighbors 17
Lie 17
Eastern 17
Worthy 16
Wahaby 16
Tobacco 16
Soldiers 16
Silk 16
Slav 16
Prince 16
Peru 16
Persian 16
Ottoman 16
Masters 16
Law 16
Heaven 16
Harem 16
Governor 16
Danger 17
Coffee 16
Camels 16
Caliph 16
Blacks 16
Barbary 16
Arrows 16
According 16
Variety 15
Suffered 15
Stolen 15
Property 15
Pretty 15
Mecca 15
Leader 15
Islanders 15
Doubt 15
Died 15
Species 14
Seldom 14
Races 14
Populous 14
Peasants 14
Ordinary 14
National 14
Mystery 14
Mahomet 14
Jew 14
Indigenous 14
Ill 14
Fierce 14
Families 14
Duty 14
Difficult 14
Desire 14
Cotton 14
Churches 14
Bishop 14
Belonged 14
Beards 14
Barbarous 14
Anxious 14
Afraid 14
Abroad 14
Taught 13
Sought 13
Serve 13
Persians 13
Pepper 13
Noble 13
Nationality 13
Interpreter 13
Interesting 13
Interest 13
Honest 13
Extraordinary 13
Christianity 13
Brown 13
Wretched 12
Warlike 12
Turkey 12
Terrible 12
Tents 12
Suffering 12
Suffer 12
Success 12
Servant 12
School 12
Prayers 12
Perfect 12
Peculiar 12
Ourselves 12
Negro 12
Moslems 12
Milk 12
Love 12
Learn 12
Husband 12
Help 12
Guns 12
Girls 12
Fruit 12
Folk 12
Flies 12
Extreme 12
Equally 12
Enemy 12
Dangerous 12
Costumes 12
Complexion1 2
Ceremonies 12
Beads 12
Asses 12
Alone 12
Advanced 12
Aborigines 12
Tea 11
Sultan 11
Sugar 11
Stories 11
Probably 11
Pipe 11
Mean 11
Markets 11
Islam 11
Guilty 11
Fighting 11
Divided 11
Difficulties 11
Battle 11

Avoid 11
Yield 11
Worship 10
Unknown 10
Truth 10
Treaty 10
Terror 10
Sold 10
Slavery 10
Slave 10
Sick 10
Severely 10
Seized 10
Savages 10
Safe 10
Poverty 10
Poppy 10
Pleasure 10
Pearls 10
Mosque 10
Miserable 10
Mankind 10
Kindness 10
Inferior 10
Gorgeous 10
Fruits 10
Friend 10
Friendly 10
Fortune 10
Fearful 10
False 10
Cruel 10
Chinaman 10
Cannibals 10
Bible 10
Warfare 9
United 9
Superior 9
Simple 9
Sailor 9
Purchase 9
Proper 9
Plunder 9
Persia 9
Modern 9
Ignorance 9
Generous 9
Drug 9
Curiosities 9
Conquest 9
Believed 9
Apparently
African 9
Worst 9
Worse 9
Weapon 8
Virgin 8
Violence 8
Victims 8
Valuable 8
Understanding 8
Trouble 8
Turbans 8
Superstitious 8
Superstition 8
Seemingly 8
Rough 8
Remarkable 8
Precious 8
Possess 8
Plague 8
Outside 8
Ours 8
Occupied 8
Mutual 8
Moorish 8
Monkeys 8
Missionaries 8
Misery 8
Merchant 8
Manufacture 8
Mahometan 8
Laws 8
Infidels 8
Imitate 8
Humanity 8
Hopes 8
Hardy 8
Happy 8
Graves 8
Fruitful 8
Fortress 8
Foreigner 8
Eager 8
Dreadful 8
Dogs 8
Discipline 8
Difficulty 8
Crying 8
Cry 8
Converse 8
Conversation 8
Control 8
Command 8
Blubs 8
Ceremony 8
Capture 8
Bows 8
Bogomil 8
Baths 8
Arabic 8
Arabians 8
Annoyance 8
Amused 8
Amazed 8
Afflicted 8
Unfortunately 7
Uncivilized 7
Theirs 7
Spices 7
Settle 7
Missionary 7
Independence 7
Fortunes 7
Exchange 7
Eunuchs 7
Desperate 7
Arabian 7
Vulgar 6
Visitor 6
Visitors 6
Visits 6
Vain 6
Unpleasant 6
Universal 6
Understood 6
Tribe 6
Treasure 6

Spirits 6
Savior 6
Redemption 6
Reckoned 6
Quality 6
Purity 6
Pure 6
Punishment 6
Punished 6
Prosecution 6
Prisoners 6
Prisoner 6
Prison 6
Primitive 6
Police 6
Perished 6
Orientals 6
Oppressed 6
Nowhere 6
Nakedness 6
Muslims 6
Muslim 6
Morality 6
Mercy 6
Mistake 6
Justice 6
Jealous 6
Insult 6
Innocent 6
Humane 6
Healthy 6
Generosity 6
Fiercely 6
Ferocious 6
Exquisite 6
Cruelty 6
Courage 6
Conquerors 6
Conflict 6
Clean 6
Bathe 6
Bananas 6
Almighty 6
Soap 5
Sincere 5
Followers 5
Convert 5
Zealous 4
Well-looking 4
Untidy 4
Uninhabited 4
Uncanny 4
Peopled 4
Oppression 4
Odors 4
Mysterious 4
Mohammedans 4
Mohammed 4
Miserably 4
Magicians 4
Magician 4
Intermixture 4
Intermixed 4
Infidel 4
Hunters 4
Hideous 4
Half-naked 4
Half-grown 4
Good-natured 4
Good-looking 4
Forbidden 4
Ferocity 4
Feathers 4
Fanatical 4
Dignity 4
Devil 4
Despair 4
Despoiled 4
Desolate 4
Concubines 4
Colonists 4
Christendom 4
Chieftain 4
Chapel 4
Catholics 4
Abominable 4
Abandon 4
Veiled 3
Pilgrimage 3
Ostensibly 3
Oppressors 3
Offensive 3
Nomads 3
Humanitarian 3
Hostile 3
Cleanliness 3
Cleaner 3
Civilize 3
Civilizations 3
Barbarity 3
Wizards 2
Wife-man 2
Wife-beating 2
Whiteness 2
White-washed 2
Usurpers 2
Unhealthy 2
Unhappy 2
Unfriendly 2
Unfortunate 2
Unfathomably 2
Unfaithfully 2
Unexpert 2
Uncultivated 2
Uncomfortably 2
Uncleanly 2
Uncivil 2
Unbecoming 2
Unavoidably 2
Trustworthy 2
Treacherous 2
Treachery 2
Tolerantly 2
Thievish 2
Thief 2
Thieves 2
Ruthless 2
Ruthlessness 2
Rudeness 2
Rudest 2
Rudely 2
Ravenous 2
Pre-Christian 2
Mutiny 2
Mud-huts 2
Raped 1
Perceptions 1
Irresponsible 1

BIBLIOGRAPHY

Works used for the primary readings

Benezet, Anthony. *A Short Account of that Part of Africa, Inhabited By Negroes.* Philadelphia, PA: Dunlap, 1762.

Colquhon, Archibald R. *Across Chryse, Being the Narrative of a Journey of Exploration through the South China Border Lands from Canton to Mandalay.* New York: Scribner, Welford, & Co., 1883.

Craven, Elizabeth. *A Journey through the Crimea to Constantinople in a Series of Letters.* Dublin: N.p., 1789.

De Guzman, Alonzo. *Book of the Life and Acts of Don Alonzo Enrique de Guzman of Seville.* Clements R. Markham, ed. London: Hakluyt Society, 1862.

Doughty, Charles M. *Travels in Arabia Deserta.* New York: Random House, 1921.

Durham, M. Edith. *Twenty Years of Balkan Tangle.* London: G. Allen & Unwin Ltd., 1920.

Esmonde, Thomas Henry Grattan. *Round the World with the Irish Delegates.* Dublin: Sealy, Bryers and Walker, 1892.

Fortune, Robert. *Three Years Wanderings in the Northern Provinces of China.* London: John Murray, 1847.

Guillemard, F.H.H. *The Life of Ferdinand Magellan and the First Circumnavigation of the Globe, 1480–1521.* New York: Dodd, Mead & Company, 1890.

Hutchinson, F. Kinsley. *Motoring in the Balkans.* London: Hodder & Stoughton, 1910.

Kino, Eusebio Francisco S. J. *Kino's historical memoir of Pimería Alta, Pioneer Missionary Explorer, Cartographer, and Ranchman, 1683–1711.* Herbert E. Bolton, ed. Cleveland, OH: Arthur H. Clark Company, 1919.

Lithgow, William. *The Totall Discourse of The Raree Adventures & Painful Peregriniations of the long Nineteene Yeares Travayles from Scotland to the most famous Kingdomes in Europe, Asia and Affrica.* Glasgow: James MacLehose and Sons, 1906.

Macgowan, J. *Sidelights on Chinese Life.* London: Kegan Paul, Trench, Trübner & Co., Limited, 1907.

Niebuhr, Carsten. *Travels through Arabia and other Countries in the East.* Robert Heron, trans. Perth: R. Morison Junior, 1799.

Smith, Arthur D. Howden. *Fighting the Turk in the Balkans: An American's Adventures with the Macedonian Revolutionists.* New York: G.P. Putnam's Sons, 1908.

Sparks, Jared. *The Life of John Ledyard, the American Traveller; Comprising Selections from his Journals and Correspondence.* Cambridge: Hilliard and Brown, 1828.

Towle, George Makepeace. *Marco Polo: His Travels and Adventures*. Boston, MA: Lee and Shepard, Publishers, 1880.

Van Speilbergen, Joris. *The East and West Indian Mirror and The Australian Navigations of Jacob le Maire*. J.A.J. de Villiers, trans. London: Hakluyt Society, 1906.

Wilkinson, J. Gardner. *Dalmatia and Montenegro with a Journey to Mostar in Herzegovina, and the Remarks of the Slavonic Nations; The History of Dalmatia and Ragusa; the Uscocs*. London: John Murray, 1848.

Windus, John. *A Journey to Mequinez; The Residence of the Present Emperor of Fez and Morocco*. Dublin: George Ewing, 1725.

Works from the Footnotes

Chapman, Michael E. *Historian's Companion: Chronologies, Glossaries, Readings, Style Guide*. Reading, MA: Trebarwyth Press, 2008.

Crow, Carl. *Four Hundred Million Customers*. New York: Harper & Brothers Publishers, 1937.

Dolanc, Stane. "Magnetofonske beleške i materijal sastanka Izvršnog bira," Arhiv Srbije i Crne Gore Savez Komunista Jugoslavije IV K.7 7, 1971.

"Europe's Mirror: The Enlightenment and the Exotic," in Dorinda Outram, *The Enlightenment*. Cambridge: Cambridge University Press, 1995.

Gernet, Jacques Daily *Life in China: On the Eve of the Mongol Invasion, 1250–1276*. Stanford, CA: Stanford University Press, 1962.

Hametz, Maura. *Making Trieste Italian, 1918–1954*. Woodbridge: The Royal Historical Society, 2005.

Huntington, Samuel P. *Who are We? The Challenges to America's National Identity*. New York: Simon & Schuster, 2005.

Kant, Immanuel. "Fundamental Principles of the Metaphysics of Morals," in *The Portable Enlightenment Reader*. Isaac Kramnick, ed. New York: Penguin Books, 1995.

Levathes, Lorraine. *When China Ruled the Seas: The Treasure Fleet of the Dragon Throne, 1405–1433*. Oxford: Oxford University Press, 1997.

McCormick, Thomas J. *China Market: America's Quest for Informal Empire, 1893–1901*. Chicago, IL: Elephant Paperbacks, 1990.

Novak, Bogdan. *Trieste, 1941–1954: The Ethnic, Political, and Ideological Struggle*. Chicago, IL: University of Chicago Press, 1970.

Pomeranz, Kenneth and Steven Topik. *The World that Trade Created*. Armonk, NY: M.E. Sharpe, 1999.

Pory, John. *The History and Description of Africa and of the Notable things Therein Contained, written by Leo Africanus*. Robert Brown, ed. New York: Burt Franklin, 1963.

Sluga, Glenda. *The Problem of Trieste and the Italo-Yugoslav Border: Difference, Identity, and Sovereignty in Twentieth-Century Europe*. Albany: State University of New York Press, 2001.

Todorova, Maria. *Imagining the Balkans.* New York: Oxford University Press, 1997.

Treadway, John D. *The Falcon and the Eagle: Montenegro and Austria-Hungary, 1908–1914.* West Lafayette, IN: Purdue University Press, 1983.

Trieste. Belgrade: Federal People's Republic of Yugoslavia, 1946.

"Ubire li Crna Gora plodove Beogradskog sporazuma?" Radio Slobodna Evropa. 6 December 2009.

Voltaire. *Candide, Or Optimism.* David Wootton, trans. New York: Hackett Publishing Company, 2000.

Wolff, Larry. "Kennst du das Land?" the Uncertainty of Galicia in the Age of Metternich and Fredo." *Slavic Review*, 67:2 (Summer 2008), pp. 277–300.

——. *Inventing Eastern Europe: The Map of Civilization on the Mind of the Enlightenment.* Stanford, CA: Stanford University Press, 1994.

——. *Venice and the Slavs: The Discovery of Dalmatia in the Age of Enlightenment* Stanford, CA: Stanford University Press, 2001.